George Orwell Studies

Volume Nine

No. 1

George Orwell

Publishing Office
Abramis Academic
ASK House
Northgate Avenue
Bury St. Edmunds
Suffolk
IP32 6BB
UK

Tel: +44 (0)1284 717884
Fax: +44 (0)1284 717889
Email: info@abramis.co.uk
Web: www.abramis.co.uk

Copyright
All rights reserved. No part of this publication may be reproduced in any material form (including photocopying or storing it in any medium by electronic means, and whether or not transiently or incidentally to some other use of this publication) without the written permission of the copyright owner, except in accordance with the provisions of the Copyright, Designs and Patents Act 1988, or under terms of a licence issued by the Copyright Licensing Agency Ltd, 33-34, Alfred Place, London WC1E 7DP, UK. Applications for the copyright owner's permission to reproduce part of this publication should be addressed to the Publishers.

© 2024 George Orwell Studies & Abramis Academic

ISSN 2399-1267
ISBN 978-1-84549-839-9

Contents

George Orwell

Editorial
Finally: The rat has a voice – by Richard Lance Keeble — Page 1

Short Story
Nineteen Eighty-Four: The rat's tale – by D.J. Taylor — Page 2

Papers
Love, hate and freedom in *Nineteen Eighty-Four* – by Peter Brian Barry — Page 5
The picture of Winston Smith: George Orwell, Oscar Wilde and the *fin de siècle* legacy – by Henk Vynckier — Page 19
'A sinking sensation': George Orwell and the RMS *Titanic* – by Nathan Waddell — Page 33
Modernism, realism and 'natural narrative': Contrasting 'A hanging' and 'Shooting an elephant' – by Cris Yelland — Page 55
Samuel Butler: The Victorian Orwell – by Hassan Akram — Page 69
Reading Orwell from the Global South – by Débora Reis Tavares — Page 79
Orwell's middle age anxiety – by Carrie Kancilia — Page 96

Interview
L.J. Hurst in conversation with Masha Karp, author of the widely-acclaimed *George Orwell and Russia* — Page 111

Articles
Captain Robinson: 'The Most Disreputable Englishman in Mandalay' – by Phil Baker — Page 118
'A disillusioned little middle class boy': George Orwell, Harry Pollitt and *The Road to Wigan Pier* – by John Newsinger — Page 128
The two Arthurs – by Darcy Moore — Page 135
How I constructed the Newspeak language from Orwell's *Nineteen Eighty-Four* – by Brennan Conaway — Page 145

Poems
'That bloody book', by John Scarborough; 'Elephant', 'George ponders dictatorship' and 'Shot but full', by Steve Dalzell — Page 157

Book Reviews
Sarah E. Cornish on *Julia*, by Sandra Newman; Douglas Kerr on *Burma Sahib*, by Paul Theroux — Page 160

And Finally
A special diary column for Orwellians – by New Pitcher — Page 167

Editors
Richard Lance Keeble — University of Lincoln
Tim Crook — Goldsmiths, University of London

Reviews Editor
Megan Faragher — Wright State University

Production Editor
Paul Anderson — University of Essex

Editorial Board
Kristin Bluemel — Monmouth University, New Jersey
Dorian Lynskey — Author, journalist
Peter Marks — University of Sydney
John Newsinger — Bath Spa University
Marina Remy — Paris Sorbonne
John Rodden — University of Texas at Austin
Jean Seaton — University of Westminster
Peter Stansky — Stanford University, US
D. J. Taylor — Author, journalist, biographer of Orwell
Martin Tyrrell — Queen's University, Belfast
Nathan Waddell — University of Birmingham
Florian Zollmann — Newcastle University

With editorial assistance from Marja Giejgo

Cover image
The front cover image is by Ivy Hall, a 16-year-old queer artist based in the Lincolnshire Wolds. Their interests are painting portraits and sewing their own clothes.

EDITORIAL

Finally: The Rat Has a Voice

RICHARD LANCE KEEBLE

At a recent Zoom event organised by The Orwell Society to discuss some of the latest Orwellian publications, biographer D.J. Taylor bemoaned the fact that, given the seemingly endless spin-offs of *Nineteen Eighty-Four*, it would not be long before '*1984*: The rat's tale' appeared. I burst into laughter (fortunately my Zoom was on mute) and immediately dropped David a line suggesting he ponder writing a short story on that theme. Much to our delight, David agreed. And so here it is published for the first time in this edition of *George Orwell Studies*. It makes for a very, very funny and original twist to Orwell's (in many ways) deeply gloomy dystopian masterpiece. Perhaps 'The rat's tale' will now set a new trend and we'll shortly have '*1984*: By O'Brien's servant, Martin', or '*1984*: Winston Smith's wife, Katherine, finally has her say'. Or we could imagine an even more Kafka-esque off-shoot such as '*1984*: By Charrington's nose'.

David Taylor (getting into the spirit) comments: 'I am currently at work on "*Coming Up For Air*: Hilda responds" and "Life in Kyauktada: Some reminiscences by Dr Veraswami".'

And to accompany the short story we have a wonderful front cover illustration by 16-year-old Ivy Hall. What talent!

The rest of the current issue of *George Orwell Studies* (in its own way, I guess, yet another Orwellian spin-off) reflects the overall priorities of the journal. Along with the short story, there's a lively mix of genres: academic, theoretically underpinned papers, more discursive articles, an interview, poetry inspired by Orwell, book reviews and an anonymous diary column. Contributors include Orwellian experts, early career researchers, well-published poets and an extremely talented undergraduate student.

Indeed, the journal packs in so many original insights into Orwell, the man and his writings – all of the copy (even when tackling complex theoretical issues) written in accessible language aiming both to entertain, inform and inspire. In other words, following in a distinctly Orwellian tradition.

Richard Lance Keeble,
University of Lincoln

SHORT STORY

Nineteen Eighty-Four: The rat's tale

D.J. TAYLOR

To: The Chairman, Oceanian Society for the Prevention of Cruelty to Animals

From: Union of Oceanian Rodent Operatives (UORO), Airstrip One Central Collective, Ministry of Love Local

Dear Comrade,

We, the undersigned, should like to protest in the strongest possible terms about a series of gross libels to which certain of our members have recently been subjected. We refer to a publication entitled *Nineteen Eighty-Four*, by the malcontent Blair, which in the opinion of our legal department contains a variety of misrepresentations, exaggerations and outright calumnies that may be regarded as actionable.

We should particularly like to draw your attention to a passage on p. 298-9 in which a character named Winston Smith is threatened by torture at the hands – we should perhaps say paws – of a cage harbouring several of our members. A full investigation of this incident has been undertaken by the relevant personnel, and we are pleased to report that all those present in the container are entirely innocent of any wrongdoing. It appears that they had merely been placed there, without any explanation of what may or may not have been required of them, and were simply acting according to their natural instincts. These facts have been confirmed by Comrade O'Brien. No blame may be imputed, and indeed their very confinement may be regarded as an infringement of Ministry of Love regulation 13/4/b.

We should also like to refer you to a second passage [p. 150-1] in which the character Smith, having previously committed an immoral act with the woman Julia on premises owned by Comrade Charrington, offers the remark 'Of all the horrors in the world – a rat!' This follows an incident in which Julia hurls a shoe at a rat which has briefly emerged from the wainscoting. Again, we have conducted a full investigation of this deplorable episode and are happy to report that the rat involved was merely going about his lawful business – indeed proceeding to his family home in the outside drain-pipe bearing a quantity of cheese intended for his children – and had poked his snout through the wainscoting out of mere curiosity. The trauma inflicted on him by this savage assault may only be imagined, while the words spoken by the character Smith are surely libellous. In fact, the entire book may be regarded as speciesism of the worst kind.

Had this been a solitary example of the malcontent Blair's blatant prejudice against our members, we should have been prepared to let it pass in the interests of inter-species solidarity. Alas, then, that an examination of certain other texts to which this ingrate has put his name should reveal a catalogue of prejudicial remarks. From childhood on it appears that Blair has displayed a variety of unsavoury rattist attitudes. A letter from 1920 advises a friend that 'It is also rather sport to go at night to a corn-stack with an acetylene bicycle lamp, & you can dazzle the rats that are running along the side & whack at them – or shoot at them with a rifle.' We understand that, while living in Southwold as a boy, he was, additionally, responsible for sending a dead rat to a Mr Hurst, a borough official whose displeasure he had incurred (no doubt in the legitimate exercise of his authority.) Again, the feelings of this unfortunate individual, not to mention those of our members to whom it has been our regrettable duty to impart this information can only be imagined.

It is not our intention, comrade, to bore you with a full catalogue of Blair's depravity. Suffice it to say that, in the words of a recent biographer – whose casual attitude to our species may also be thought worthy of correction – 'the rodent cavalcade runs endlessly through his work, an unappeasable, yellow-fanged brood piped in and out of his consciousness.' Whether in Burma – where he pronounces a gross libel on several of our members who had quite innocently constructed their holes in the vicinity of a human burial ground, having no idea of the structure's purpose or nutritional value – Paris, Wigan or Spain, where he is thought *actually to have shot* a specimen who had wandered into his trench, his attitude to our rodent comrades displays a consistent malice and lack of regard for a race whose only desire has been to co-exist with him on friendly terms.

Even on the island of Jura, where we believe Blair to have until recently been living, we understand that these examples of prejudice have been allowed full rein. We refer you to a diary entry in which Blair recalls the sighting of a buzzard apparently carrying a rat in its claws and an incident from April 1947 in which a dog borrowed from his neighbour 'killed an enormous rat in the byre'. Elsewhere, Blair may be found gloating over the apparent ease with which

SHORT STORY

D.J. TAYLOR

our comrades allow themselves to be caught by their cruel human tormentors ('The traps are simply set in the runs, unbaited and unconcealed.') To callousness over the violent deaths of comrades who were merely going about their legitimate nocturnal activities may be added this final slur against their intelligence.

A full account of Blair's crimes against the rat may be found in the attached file. We are confident that the merest perusal of them will provide an unassailable case for the prolonged period of re-education which, we believe, is the only solution to this lifetime of calumny and contempt.

Long live Big Brother!

We remain yours faithfully,

S. Whiskers, A. Maria [50 other signatures and paw-marks].

D.J. Taylor's *George Orwell: The New Life* **(London: Constable) appeared last year.**

Love, Hate and Freedom in *Nineteen Eighty-Four*

PETER BRIAN BARRY

Nineteen Eighty-Four is just one of Orwell's works that reveals his continued interest in free will, and it may seem to epitomise an old thesis about how free will and our emotions are related: love makes us free, hate makes us unfree. However, his final novel suggests a much more complicated relationship and that sometimes hate can make us free and love can make us unfree. The philosophical question to be answered, then, is why should this be the case? Why does love make us free but only sometimes? If hate makes us unfree why not always? Some philosophy is needed to answer these questions, but Nineteen Eighty-Four *helps to illustrate why this should be so and reveals much that is important to Orwell's ethical philosophy generally. Properly understood,* Nineteen Eighty-Four *does not epitomise the old thesis, but suggests a much more nuanced conception of free will.*

Key words: love, hate, free will, loyalty, ethics, *Nineteen Eighty-Four*

Reflecting on the 21st century, the philosopher Martha Nussbaum identifies something 'Orwellian in the air', an attempt at 'extinguishing compassion and the complex forms of personal love and mourning that are its sources, and of replacing them with simple depersonalized forms of hatred, aggression, triumph, and fear' (Nussbaum 2005: 281). We are told early in *Nineteen Eighty-Four* that 'there were fear, hatred, and pain, but no dignity of emotion, or deep or complex sorrows' (*CWGO* IX: 32) and O'Brien, 'the Party's philosopher' (Rees 1961: 93), makes their goal clear:

> The old civilizations claimed that they were founded on love and justice. Ours is founded upon hatred. In our world there will be no emotions except fear, rage, triumph, and self-abasement. ... There will be no love, except the love of Big Brother (*CWGO* IX: 279).

The Party aims to 'make thoughtcrime literally impossible' by ensuring that 'there will be no words in which to express it' (ibid: 55), but it is not only nor even primarily via the manipulation of language that it aims to make persons unfree. By imposing a

PETER BRIAN BARRY

shattering moral psychology where love is all but dead and hate is routine, the Party aims for 'the end of human beings as we know them, the political overthrow of the human heart' (Nussbaum 2005: 282).

Nineteen Eighty-Four is a novel about many things. It is about human emotions, especially love and hate. It is also about free will, a subject of interest to Orwell (Barry 2023: 62-92). Really, it is about the 'lack of free will' (Bowen 2021: ix). Philosophers have had much to say about the relationship between love and free will (Pereboom 2017), but the Party's aims hint at an old thesis about their relationship, namely, that *love makes us free* and *hatred makes us unfree*. Erich Fromm has this old thesis in mind when he describes the 'Old Testament philosophy of history' according to which a human being 'develops his powers of reason and love fully, and thus is enabled to grasp the world' (Fromm 2003: 324) and worries that 'a society of automatons … will have lost every trace of individuality, of love, of critical thought' (Fromm 2003: 337). So does Iris Murdoch when she explains that 'Freedom … is brought about in all sorts of ways by impulses of love' (Murdoch 1993: 300). If the old thesis is correct, the dearth of love and prevalence of hate in Oceania ensures that free will is all but extinct. *Nineteen Eighty-Four* thus appears to epitomise the old thesis.

Yet *Nineteen Eighty-Four* is *not* the epitome of the old thesis. Instead, it illustrates that love sometimes yields unfreedom and hate can yield freedom. Section I examines the role that love plays in Orwell's ethics. Section II identifies instances in *Nineteen Eighty-Four* in which hate yields freedom and love yields unfreedom. The result is puzzling: why does love sometimes, but only sometimes, yield freedom? To explain, Section III explicates the work of the philosopher Harry Frankfurt concerning love and free agency. Section IV makes the case that hate, as much as love, enables freedom and for the same reasons that love does. Orwell, a 'good hater' (Rees 1936: 190) produced a text in which, *pace* the old thesis, hatred is sometimes expressive of freedom and love expressive of unfreedom.

LOVE AND LOYALTY IN OCEANIA

Talk of love and freedom is equivocal in Newspeak. The word *free* still existed in Newspeak, but it could only be used in such statements as 'This dog is free from lice' or 'This field is free from weeds'; 'political and intellectual freedom no longer existed even as concepts' (*CWGO* IX: 313). The final, Eleventh Edition of the Newspeak Dictionary does include the adjectives 'Minilovely' and 'Miniloveful' but not 'love' (ibid: 317). That the Party eschews talk of love and freedom might seem like evidence for the old thesis. Note, too, that in an early version of *Nineteen Eighty-Four*, the Party affirmed that 'love was evil' (ibid: 361). But why? Why should the Party tend to fear love? Recall that Winston wrote in his diary that the Party's 'real, undeclared purpose was to remove all pleasure from the sexual act' and that 'Not love so much as eroticism was the enemy', which suggests that love is *not* the Party's greatest perceived threat.

Winston also wrote: 'The aim of the Party was not merely to prevent men and women from forming loyalties which it might not be able to control' (ibid: 68). Further:

> What mattered were individual relationships, and a completely helpless gesture, an embrace, a tear, a word spoken to a dying man, could have value in itself. The proles, it suddenly occurred to him, had remained in this condition. They were not loyal to a party or a country or an idea, they were loyal to one another. For the first time in his life he did not despise the proles or think of them merely as an inert force which would one day spring to life and regenerate the world. The proles had stayed human. They had not become hardened inside. They had held on to the primitive emotions which he himself had to re-learn by conscious effort (ibid: 172).

Not love but loyalty demarcates the human proles from the inhuman Outer Party, a result that deserves comment. Elsewhere, Orwell objects to systems of ethics that call for us to ignore or minimise the moral value of individual relationships. In 'Reflections on Gandhi', which appeared in the American leftist journal, *Partisan Review*, in 1949, he endorsed as 'unquestionably true' Gandhi's thought that close friendships were 'dangerous' because 'friends react on one another' and 'through loyalty to a friend one can be led into wrong-doing'. But while Gandhi concluded that intimate relationships should be avoided for that reason, Orwell suggested that any 'ordinary human being' thinks that 'love means nothing if it does not mean loving some people more than others'. His reflection that 'The essence of being human is that one does not seek perfection, that one is sometimes willing to commit sins for the sake of loyalty' (*CWGO* XX: 7-8) is especially telling. Humanist ethics – Orwell's' ethics – understands right action as a function of what is demanded by loyalties endemic to individual relationships, and he rejects Gandhi's ethics as 'inhuman' (ibid: 8) just because it devalues those loyalties.

The pride of place that Orwell affords to familiar loyalties suggests that he emphasises *agent-relative* reasons for action, those reasons that make an essential reference to the person who has them. Agent-relative reasons are rivalled by *agent-neutral* reasons which do not make an essential reference to the person who has them (Parfit 1984: 27). Common-sense morality – Orwell's morality –

recognises fundamental agent-relative reasons to act on behalf of *our* friends, *our* family and so on, and affords them considerable moral weight. Orwell's complaint about Gandhi's ethics is that he wrongly diminishes the moral salience of familiar agent-relative reasons (Barry 2023: 52-53). The Party, too, denies their moral salience. Its ideal is illustrated by the fake Comrade Ogilvy who 'had taken a vow of celibacy, believing marriage and the care of a family to be incompatible with a twenty-four-hour-a-day devotion to duty' (*CWGO* IX: 50), individual relationships that risked generating agent-relative duties at odds with those to the Party. But Ogilvy did not only avoid loving relationships: he avoided all relationships that could ground agent-relative reasons. Friends have agent-relative reasons to act for the sake of their friends, comrades for their comrades, teachers for their students, and so forth. While these are all important relationships, they need not be based on love. Orwell's remembrance of the nameless Italian soldier with 'the face of a man who would commit murder and throw away his life for a friend' (*CWGO* VI: 1) described in his memoir of fighting during the Spanish Civil War in 1937, *Homage to Catalonia* (1938), suggests affection and loyalty, but no word of love. Yet his memory led Orwell to renew his support of 'the attempt of people like this to win the decent life which they knew to be their birthright' in 'Looking back on the Spanish War', published in the journal *New Road* in 1943 (*CWGO* XIII: 509) Overthrowing the human heart demands purgation of *all* such loyalties that give rise to agent-relative reasons in conflict with obligations to the Party, not merely those generated by loving relationships.

While love is not the only source of agent-relative reasons, the proponent of the old thesis ought to point out that in *Nineteen Eighty-Four* freedom is rebellion and rebellion is expressed by love: Julia's first observable rebellion is to slip Winston a note that reads simply 'I love you' (*CWGO* IX: 113). But love and hate are not simple matters in Oceania: sometimes love is expressive of unfreedom and hatred is expressive of free agency.

FREE HATE, UNFREE LOVE

At times, Winston and Julia seem to epitomise the old thesis. Winston expresses admiration for Julia when he explains that 'Her feelings were her own, and could not be altered from outside.' She understood that 'If you loved someone, you loved him, and when you had nothing else to give, you still gave him love' (ibid: 171-172). Of course, Julia's feelings are *not* unalterably her own and the hopeful suggestion 'They can't get inside you' (ibid: 173) is demonstrably false as she comes to acknowledge during their final meeting:

'Sometimes,' she said, 'they threaten you with something – something you can't stand up to, can't even think about. And then you say, "Don't do it to me, do it to somebody else, do it to so-and-so." And perhaps you might pretend, afterwards, that it was only a trick and that you just said it to make them stop and didn't really mean it. But that isn't true. At the time when it happens you do mean it. You think there's no other way of saving yourself, and you're quite ready to save yourself that way. You *want* it to happen to the other person. You don't give a damn what they suffer. All you care about is yourself' (ibid: 305, italics in the original).

'And after that,' she explains, 'you don't feel the same towards the other person any longer' (ibid: 305-306). She appears free when she loves Winston, unfree after their mutual betrayal. O'Brien's promise to Winston also seems to capture the old thesis:

We shall crush you down to the point from which there is no coming back. Things will happen to you from which you could not recover, if you lived a thousand years. Never again will you be capable of ordinary human feeling. Everything will be dead inside you. Never again will you be capable of love, or friendship, or joy of living, or laughter, or curiosity, or courage, or integrity. You will be hollow. We shall squeeze you empty, and then we shall fill you with ourselves (ibid: 268-269).

Winston also seems unfree when he is made incapable of love. But O'Brien's promise is puzzling, for Winston is *not* made incapable of love: arguably, *Nineteen Eighty-Four* is 'at heart a love story... between two, or possibly three, men' (Bowen 2021: xv). During his exchange with O'Brien, a needle slides into Winston's arm and he realises that he 'had never loved him so deeply as at this moment' (ibid: 264). And the final, terrible lines of *Nineteen Eighty-Four* affirm that 'He loved Big Brother' (ibid: 311). Winston becomes much like Jones, Aaronson and Rutherford who were emptied out with 'nothing left in them except sorrow for what they had done, and love of Big Brother' (ibid: 268). So, if love is sometimes expressive of freedom in *Nineteen Eighty-Four*, it is also sometimes expressive of unfreedom.

An obvious response is available: the proponent of the old thesis can deny that Winston's 'love' is the real thing. Winston only grows to love O'Brien and Big Brother after being tortured, and while the Party 'is able to manipulate not just behaviour, not just thoughts, but also emotions' (Phelan 1998: 111) it can do so only via manipulation. But, as the argument goes, we regard personal relationships as 'genuine' only given 'the assumption that the participants are free in adopting whatever emotional stances they take' (Ekstrom 2001: 12). Alternatively, 'love' that is 'ensured or made necessary ... is not true love' (Anglin 1990: 20). In any case, the response supposes that real love cannot be arrived at via manipulation; real and truly valuable love must be arrived at freely. If so, the 'ultimate horror' of *Nineteen Eighty-Four* is not when Winston 'crawls before his torturer' and 'grows to love him' (Rahv 1982: 314) since Winston never loved O'Brien nor Big Brother, not really.

A similar response helps disarm other ostensible counter-examples to the old thesis. Julia's rebellion is also expressed when she says that she 'hated the Party, and said so in the crudest words' (ibid: 138) and speaks of the Party 'with an open jeering hatred' (ibid: 128). And just before being taken to Room 101, Winston imagines that, prior to being executed, some shred of his hate 'would be unpunished, unrepented, out of their reach for ever'. 'To die hating them,' he says, 'that was freedom' (ibid: 294). Their hatred for the Party seems expressive of their freedom. But if 'love' that results only from processes inconsistent with free agency is unreal, then, by analogy, hate resulting only from such processes is equally unreal. And the hatred that infects them does, as the response goes, result from processes inconsistent with free agency, albeit more subtle processes than those utilised in Room 101.

The Two Minutes Hate is a powerful tool for manipulation. 'Before the Hate had proceeded for thirty seconds,' Winston explains, 'uncontrollable exclamations of rage were breaking out from half the people in the room' and 'the sight or even the thought of Goldstein produced fear and anger automatically' (ibid: 15). He 'could not help sharing in the general delirium' and 'chanted with the rest: it was impossible to do otherwise' (ibid: 19). In a lucid moment, Winston finds himself 'shouting with the others and kicking his heel violently against the rung of his chair' and discerns that:

> The horrible thing about the Two Minutes Hate was not that one was obliged to act a part, but, on the contrary, that it was impossible to avoid joining in. Within thirty seconds any pretence was always unnecessary. A hideous ecstasy of fear and vindictiveness, a desire to kill, to torture, to smash faces in with a sledge-hammer, seemed to flow through the whole group of people like an electric current, turning one even against one's will into a grimacing, screaming lunatic (ibid: 16).

The Two Minutes Hate operates via powerful social dynamics and environmental prompts, but other, less direct dynamics and prompts are equally operative in Oceania: people live under constant threat, their rights are consistently violated and their conformity is always demanded. After years of living in an oppressive dystopia, Winston and Julia understandably hate the Party: how couldn't they? But since their hatred is compelled, it is not arrived at freely, as the argument goes, and their 'hate', too, is unreal.

This defence of the old thesis assumes that real and valuable emotions only result from free agency, but that assumption is dubious. If the Party's influence is as pervasive as suggested, could there be *any* real emotions? Oceania's social environment more plausibly justifies deep scepticism about the existence of free agency, not confidence in its existence. Some philosophers sceptical of free will contend that our combined upbringing, environment and genetics deprives us of any serious control over being the sort of person we are and of anything akin to free agency (Pereboom 2014). Orwell sometimes sounds like a free will sceptic (Barry 2023: 87-90). In a talk for the BBC Home Service, in June 1945, on *The Way of All Flesh*, by Samuel Butler, he explained that:

> A human being is what he is largely because he comes from certain surroundings, and no one ever fully escapes from the things that have happened to him in early childhood. To some extent your character depends on the way your parents treated you, and their character depends on the way theirs have treated them, and so on. ... It is probably true that you can't give a really revealing history of a man's life without saying something about his parents and probably his grandparents (*CWGO* XVII: 181).

Oceanians, including Winston and Julia, are what they are because they come from certain surroundings, because they were treated by their parents in particular ways, in addition to their genetics, all of which were subject to the Party's influence to no small degree. But that pervasive influence arguably undermines what is supposedly necessary for real and valuable emotion. Worse, our emotions, also, are rarely if ever the product of voluntary choice or volition: it is hardly uncommon to be surprised that one has fallen for one's beloved or fallen in love at all, and love is often the result of chance encounters, unanticipated moments and seemingly irresistible attraction. None of this has led to widespread scepticism about the reality and value of love as we know it. The proponent of the old thesis needs another strategy to disarm apparent cases of free hate and unfree love in *Nineteen Eighty-Four*.

A different strategy makes the case that the nature of hate distinguishes it from love and makes it incompatible with freedom. Hatred is partly constituted by anger and an 'urge to attack' (Greenspan 1988: 50) the object of one's hatred, though not necessarily an overpowering urge. It also tends to involve 'an element of comfort at achieving an adequate distance from the object' (ibid: 135), though such comfort need not be irresistible. But consider how hatred is sometimes described in *Nineteen Eighty-Four*. Winston confesses to Julia that 'I hated the sight of you' and that he disliked her 'from the very first moment of seeing her'. As he explains, he 'disliked nearly all women, and especially the young and pretty ones', having assumed that they 'were the most bigoted adherents of the Party, the swallowers of slogans, the amateur spies and nosers-out of unorthodoxy' (*CWGO* IX: 12). Winston's misogyny could be as much the cause of his distorted judgements as the product of them. Hatred can distort value judgements, as Nietzsche recognised when he explains that the hatred of the weak and the plebeian, their *ressentiment*, led to the slave revolt in morality that generated the sickened morality of his day (Barry 2016: 49-50). A proclivity for distorted value judgements is evidence of a deficient capacity to deliberate and make conscientious decisions, a capacity surely necessary for free will. If hatred deprives us of that capacity, then hatred, unlike love, is incompatible with freedom.

Hatred also may be incompatible with freedom because it makes us singularly focused and obsessed. Consider Nussbaum's analysis here:

> *Hatred* is another negative emotion that focuses on the entirety of the person, rather than a single act. Although anger is directed at a person, its focus is an act, and when the act is disposed of somehow, anger could be expected to go away. Hatred, by contrast, is global, and if acts are involved it is simply because everything about the person is seen in a negative light. As Aristotle remarks, the only thing that will really satisfy hatred is that the person ceases to exist. If we think that hatred – an intensely negative attitude to the entire being of another person – is always a bad emotion to have, we are not required to think this about anger, which is fully compatible with liking or even loving the person (Nussbaum 2016: 50, italics in the original).

Hatred, so understood, swamps our motivational economy and ensures that nothing brings satisfaction but the elimination of what we hate. It tends to render our capacity to deliberate and make conscientious decisions ineffective, an incapacity that, again, is incompatible with freedom.

Neither attempt to show that hatred is uniquely incompatible with freedom is successful: neither properly conceives of hatred *per se*. Nietzsche is clear that *ressentiment* is a particular *kind* of hatred, one that arises only 'out of the cauldron of unsatisfied hatred' (Nietzsche 1989 [1887 and 1908]: 40), the impotence and frustration of the weak and the plebeian. Nussbaum, too, has identified a species of hatred, something akin to *blind rage*, but not hatred *per se*, as evidenced by the fact that we often talk about hating only an aspect of a person, not all of them: we sometimes say: 'I hate that about you' or 'I hate that part of you.' If there is something about hatred *per se* that makes it uniquely incompatible with freedom, it remains unidentified.

Nineteen Eighty-Four at least seems to describe cases in which hate makes us free and love makes us unfree, contra the old thesis, and thereby raises some puzzling questions. Why should love make us free but only sometimes? If hate can make us free, why not always? A bit of philosophy supplies an answer.

THE IMPORTANCE OF WHAT WE LOVE

That love and freedom should be linked at all is puzzling, partly because love is so rarely voluntary, but also because love often *restrains* us. Sometimes, as Simone Weil suggests: 'The attention turned with love towards God (or in a lesser degree, towards anything which is truly beautiful) makes certain things impossible for us' (2002 [1947]: 119). When Julia and Winston are sized up for membership in the Brotherhood, O'Brien, acting as an agent provocateur, queries: 'In general terms, what are you prepared to do?' Winston affirms they will give their lives, murder innocents, throw acid in the face of a child and 'do anything which is likely to cause demoralisation and weaken the power of the Party'. But the largely ignored Julia exclaims: 'No!' when O'Brien asks: 'You are prepared, the two of you, to separate and never see one another again?' (*CWGO* IX: 180). Her love ensures a limit to what she is willing to do. But if freedom is a function of what we are willing to do, her love makes her to that extent less free.

Or does it? Even if love invariably limits what we are willing to do, it does not follow that we are therefore less free. First, a will lacking any constraints is not free. If there is nothing a person is unwilling to do, then she is, to use a phrase popularised by Frankfurt, a *wanton*, someone lacking any preference as to which of her desires leads her to act (1988a: 20). A *wanton* person does not enjoy freedom of the will because there is no will that they want to have. Love ensures that there is some will we want to have, and that there are some wills we *don't* want to have. It supplies limits to what we are willing to do insofar as it strongly disposes us to perform some actions and forbear others: it greatly disposes us to protect and promote the well-being of our beloved and to refrain from harming or neglecting them. By supplying our will with limits, love ensures that, like Julia, there is some will that we want and some that we do not want.

Second, love enables us to engage in deliberation and conscientious decision-making, capacities necessary for free will.

PAPER

Loving, Frankfurt thinks, 'is a mode of caring' (1999b: 165) and caring is important because 'it is the indispensably foundational activity through which we provide continuity and coherence to our volitional lives' (ibid: 163). Love supplies us with final ends, those 'goals that we consider to be worth attaining for their own sake' (Frankfurt 2004: 52). Someone who has no final ends, who finds nothing intrinsically valuable, will have a difficult time getting started when considering what to do: why prefer one course of action rather than another? If nothing is intrinsically valuable, why do anything at all? Lovers, who have final ends – say, the protection of their beloved or the promotion of their well-being – are not paralysed as concerns practical reasoning just because there is at least one thing they find intrinsically valuable. Love is not the only source of final ends; someone who loves nothing may think that beauty or knowledge are intrinsically valuable. But love does supply the material we need to engage in deliberation and conscientious decision-making, capacities necessary to orientate our practical reasoning and to have free will.

Love can make us free even as it limits us for another reason. Julia wants to stay with Winston, but if she came to feel that her will was changing, say, if she found herself tempted to leave Winston to serve the Brotherhood, she would be aggrieved and greatly motivated to restore her will to its preferred condition. If she has no interest in revising her overall psychological economy, no feelings of unrest or discontent, then she enjoys the happy condition of *wholeheartedly identifying* with her will (1999a: 101-105). While her will is constrained, someone who wholeheartedly identifies with their will has the will that she wants, and she would have it no other way. Love 'characteristically affects a person less by impelling him into a certain course of action than by somehow making it apparent to him that every apparent alternative to that course is unthinkable' (Frankfurt 1988b: 85-86). But being unable to bring oneself to perform an action is not the same thing as 'being overwhelmingly averse to performing it' (Frankfurt 1988c: 182). Julia's hostile reaction to the prospect of separating from Winston shows that she finds their separation unthinkable, but her love is not thereby regarded as an obstacle to overcome. Instead, it is a welcome source of liberation.

Love cannot guarantee that we are free, and it is not immutable. Faced with the prospect of the rat mask, love and self-interest will surely conflict, and what was once unthinkable – say, sacrificing one's beloved – can seem like a real option. We can also love unhappily: if we wish we did not love our beloved, then we are unsatisfied with the condition of the will and do not have the will we want to have. That is why there can be unfree love. Still, love tends to ensure that we have what is needed for free agency in the first place and explains why unthinkability is not necessarily inconsistent with freedom. When loves makes us free, it makes us free for these reasons.

THE IMPORTANCE OF WHAT WE HATE

For better or worse, love is not the only emotion that can make us free. Hate can, too, and for the same reasons that love does. *Nineteen Eighty-Four* illustrates as much.

First, someone possessed of hate is not a wanton: there is a will she wants to have, and wills that she does *not* want to have. Someone who finds herself motivated to promote the well-being of the object of her hate will likely be confused, distressed and will not wholeheartedly identify with her will. Hate, as much as love, tends to ensure that we are not indifferent to the condition of our will, a necessary condition for having a free will at all.

Second, hate can supply final ends necessary for deliberation and conscientious decision-making, although the mechanism by which hate supplies them is somewhat different. We tend to regard the object of our love as intrinsically valuable, and we may regard the object of our hate as intrinsically *dis*valuable. But we may hate something because it stands in the way of something else we think is intrinsically valuable: I don't regard thunderstorms as intrinsically disvaluable, but I hate the ones that frighten my beloved and keep me from her. In such cases, we think that elimination of the object of our hate is instrumentally valuable, as useful for getting something else we think is intrinsically valuable. (There is no analogue with love: to think of something as merely intrinsically valuable, as merely useful, is not to love it.) Having come to hate the thing in question, we will have ends that we previously lacked. This just is the sort of deliberation and decision-making necessary for free will in action.

Third, hate, as much as love, explains why finding some course of action unthinkable is not incompatible with freedom. Someone who hates an adversary may find themselves unwilling to lay down their sword, make concessions, or bite their tongue; their hatred rules out some options from the start. But we can wholeheartedly identify with our hatred as much as our love: someone who hates a rival football club or the political opposition may have no qualms about the condition of their will and wouldn't change it if they could. True, we do not always identify with our hate – we can be puzzled by it, wish we could eliminate it and so forth – but when we do wholeheartedly identify with our hatred, we have the will we want to have absent any unrest or discontent. Winston, for example, retains his hatred for Big Brother before being taken to Room 101 and loses it only after being subject to the most extreme of manipulations: his hatred was so central to his identity that losing it destroyed him as a person.

Hate can enable freedom for another reason. Winston, lying next to a sleeping Julia, reflects:

> The young, strong body, now helpless in sleep, awoke in him a pitying, protecting feeling. But the mindless tenderness that he had felt under the hazel tree, while the thrush was singing, had not quite come back. He pulled the overalls aside and studied her smooth white flank. In the old days, he thought, a man looked at a girl's body and saw that it was desirable, and that was the end of the story. But you could not have pure love or pure lust nowadays. No emotion was pure, because everything was mixed up with fear and hatred (*CWGO* IX: 132-133).

Oceanian emotions are impure given the Party's influence, but they are mixed for another familiar reason: love can generate extraordinary pressure to hate something else. This is not only a feature of degenerate cases of love bordering on mania. Love, insofar as it tends to greatly dispose us to protect the object of our love, can motivate us to oppose the enemies and oppressors of our beloved, to want to attack them and to find comfort in securing distance from them. Our beloved may, not always manipulatively, encourage us to hate what they hate: if divided loyalties or muted animus are evidence that our love is shallow or insincere, our beloved may understandably react in ways that encourage us to replace tepid dislike with full-blown hate. For all these reasons, it can be extraordinarily difficult to avoid hating that which opposes what we love. But if there is no clean division between love and hate, then hate will sometimes be expressive of freedom if love is.

There are ways of conceiving of love that sanitise it from these unfortunate tendencies, but Orwell understood that such conceptions are unduly rosy. Just after O'Brien reveals that the Party longs for power for its own sake, Winston objects that a civilisation founded on fear and hatred and cruelty 'would never endure', that 'It would disintegrate'. O'Brien replies curtly: 'You are under the impression that hatred is more exhausting than love. Why should it be?' (ibid: 281). O'Brien's question deserves an answer and Orwell may be on O'Brien's side. In his critique of Gandhi, Orwell speculated that the primary motive for Gandhian non-attachment was 'a desire to escape from the pain of living, and above all from love, which, sexual or non-sexual, is hard work' (*CWGO* XX: 8). Love *is* sometimes hard work and can be just as exhausting as hate. But they can also be liberating and work in harmony. Love can make us unfree just as hate sometimes does, but hate can also make us as free as love.

CONCLUSION

Nussbaum is correct when she says that '*Nineteen Eighty-Four* is a novel, not a philosophical argument' (Nussbaum 2005: 283), but she knows better than most how useful literature can be in evaluating philosophical theses. *Nineteen Eighty-Four* is especially problematic for the old thesis insofar as it illustrates that love need not make us free and hate need not make us unfree. Love and hatred enable free agency when they ensure that we have a will, enable our capacities for deliberation and decision-making, and when we wholeheartedly identify with them such that we welcome finding some courses of action unthinkable. All of this is on display in *Nineteen Eighty-Four*, evidence that it does not epitomise the old thesis. Hatred is a morally problematic emotion: too many of us feel it too much and too often, and it is probably incompatible with important moral and civic virtues. Still, nothing about hatred makes it incompatible with freedom as Orwell, a good hater, seems to have recognised.

REFERENCES

Anglin, W.S. (1990) *Free Will and the Christian Faith*, Oxford: Oxford University Press

Barry, Peter Brian (2016) *The Fiction of Evil*, New York: Routledge

Barry, Peter Brian (2023) *George Orwell: The Ethics of Equality*, Oxford: Oxford University Press

Bowen, John (2021) Introduction, *Nineteen Eighty-Four*, Oxford: Oxford University Press

Ekstrom, Laura (2001) *Free Will: A Philosophical Study*, Boulder: Westview

Frankfurt, Harry (1988a) Freedom of the will and the concept of a person, Frankfurt, Harry, *The Importance of What We Care About: Philosophical Essays*, Cambridge: Cambridge University Press pp 11-25 (originally published in *The Journal of Philosophy*, Vol. 68, No. 1 January 1971 pp 5-20)

Frankfurt, Harry (1988b) The importance of what we care about, Frankfurt, Harry, *The Importance of What We Care About*, Cambridge: Cambridge University Press pp 80-94 (originally published in *Synthese*, Vol. 53, 1982 pp 257-272)

Frankfurt, Harry (1988c) Rationality and the unthinkable, Frankfurt, Harry, *The Importance of What We Care About*, Cambridge: Cambridge University Press pp 177-190

Frankfurt, Harry (1999a) The faintest passion, Frankfurt, Harry, *Necessity, Volition, and Love*, Cambridge: Cambridge University Press pp 95-107 (originally published in *Proceedings and Addresses of the American Philosophical Association*, Vol. 66, No. 3, November 1992 pp 5-16)

Frankfurt, Harry (1999b) On caring, Frankfurt, Harry, *Necessity, Volition, and Love*, Cambridge: Cambridge University Press pp 155-180

Frankfurt, Harry (2004) *The Reasons of Love*, Princeton: Princeton University Press

Fromm, Erich (2003) Afterword, *Nineteen Eighty-Four*, New York: Penguin, Centennial Edition

Greenspan, Patricia S. (1988) *Emotions and Reasons: An Inquiry into Emotional Justification*, New York: Routledge

Murdoch, Iris (1993) *Metaphysics as a Guide to Morals*, New York: Allen Lane

Nietzsche, Friedrich (1989 [1887 and 1908]) *The Genealogy of Morals and Ecce Homo*, Kaufmann, Walter (ed.) New York: Vintage Books

Nussbaum, Martha C. (2005) The death of pity: Orwell and American political life, Gleason, Abbott, Goldsmith, Jack and Nussbaum, Martha C. (eds) *On Nineteen Eighty-Four: Orwell and Our Future*, Princeton: Princeton University Press pp 279-299

Nussbaum, Martha C. (2016) *Anger and Forgiveness: Resentment, Generosity, Justice*, Oxford: Oxford University Press

Parfit, Derek (1984) *Reasons and Persons*, Oxford: Oxford University Press

Pereboom, Derk (2014) *Free Will, Agency, and Meaning in Life*, Oxford: Oxford University Press

Pereboom, Derk (2017) Love and freedom, Grau, Christopher and Smuts, Aaron (eds) *The Oxford Handbook of Philosophy of Love*, Oxford: Oxford University Press pp 575-593

Phelan, James (1998) Character, progression, and thematism in *1984*, Holderness, Graham, Loughrey, Bryan and Yousaf, Nahem (eds) *George Orwell: Contemporary Critical Essays*, London: Macmillan Press pp 97-115

Rahv, Philip (1982) The unfuture of utopia, Howe, Irving (ed.) *Orwell's* Nineteen Eighty-Four: *Text, Sources, Criticism*, New York: Harcourt Brace Jovanovich, Inc., second edition pp 310-315

Rees, Richard (1936) Review of *Keep the Aspidistra Flying*, *Adelphi*, June

Rees, Richard (1961) *George Orwell: Fugitive from the Camp of Victory*, Carbondale, Illinois: Southern Illinois University Press

Weil, Simone (2002 [1947]) *Gravity and Grace*, New York: Routledge

NOTE ON THE CONTRIBUTOR

Peter Brian Barry is the Professor of Philosophy and the Finkbeiner Endowed Professor in Ethics at Saginaw Valley State University. He is the author of three books, most recently of *George Orwell: The Ethics of Equality*, and dozens of papers on ethics, legal philosophy and the philosophy of literature.

PAPER

The Picture of Winston Smith: George Orwell, Oscar Wilde and the *Fin de Siècle* Legacy

HENK VYNCKIER

This paper examines the work of George Orwell in light of the fin de siècle *legacy and proposes that he presents an intriguing example of the afterlife of this legacy in the age of modernism. At first sight, any endeavour to read Orwell in this manner seems to go against his nature since devoting himself to 'make political writing into an art' and championing 'prose like a window pane', he developed a political and artistic ethos which diverged radically from that of the aesthetes and decadents of the turn of the century. Yet, his early fiction centred on themes such as bohemianism and hatred of the bourgeoisie and was, as he admitted, full of 'purple passages', whereas several of his novels, culminating in his great last novel* Nineteen Eighty-Four, *originally titled* The Last Man in Europe, *settled on a familiar turn of the century pattern involving* dernier homme *heroes who are fixated on their family lineages and exist in a mental climate of failure and lassitude. The latter novel, moreover, reveals considerable similarities with Oscar Wilde's* The Picture of Dorian Gray *and suggests that Orwell, in spite of his denunciation of aestheticist and decadent doctrines, was indebted to core* fin de siècle *ideas and forms.*

Key words: Orwell, *fin de siècle*, aestheticism, decadence, Oscar Wilde, literary influence

ORWELL *A REBOURS*?

In addressing George Orwell in the context of aestheticism and decadence, a subject which he is generally not associated with, it may be useful to begin with the following eulogy.[1] His greatness as a writer is partly the result of the sympathy he demanded for society's victims. He championed socialism but feared socialist governments. Dying at the age of forty-six, he left behind a substantial literary legacy and, while he was proficient in a variety of fiction and non-fiction genres, his language is often considered his finest achievement. Many of his contemporaries opposed him when he was alive, but also remembered him fondly

HENK VYNCKIER

in their memoirs. As for the reading public, it has not failed in its devotion to him, within the English-speaking countries or abroad, where his genius shines through in translation. He is not one of those writers who as the centuries change lose their relevance. His wit is an agent of renewal, as pertinent now as it was in his time.

Readers familiar with Orwell's life and writings will no doubt agree that the above paragraph is a valid assessment of the literary legacy of the author of *Animal Farm* (1945) and *Nineteen Eighty-Four* (1949). But much of this eulogy is largely pieced together with phrases from Richard Ellmann's two-page Introduction to his 1984 *Oscar Wilde* biography with many of the 134 words in the passage being copied literally from Ellmann (xv-xvii). I merely selected and threaded together sentences and added two interspersed statements about socialism and the age at which the author died, which was, indeed, 46 for both Orwell (25 June 1903 to 21 January 1950) and Wilde (16 October 1854 to 13 November 1900). The fact that the description applies equally well to two seemingly unrelated and perhaps even contrary figures such as Orwell and Wilde, however, sets the stage for a consideration of the literary lineages that connect Orwell with Wilde and through him the aesthetes and decadents of the turn of the century.

I must acknowledge that the above opening gambit of presenting a descriptive paragraph that fits two outwardly unconnected figures is inspired by a similar opening in Douglas Kerr's article on 'Orwell and Kipling: Global Visions' (2013). All three authors – Orwell, Kipling and Wilde – pursued active public lives as writers, book reviewers and public speakers, and addressed a wide range of literary, political and cultural subjects. They also spoke through masks and crafted public personas that differed greatly from their private selves. Similarities are likely to develop under those circumstances, and conversations among the authors become possible. Notwithstanding this caveat, I am intrigued by the opportunity to encourage this conversation and engage Orwell in a dialogue with Wilde and the *fin de siècle* generation. Dickens, Kipling, Joseph Conrad, George Gissing, H.G. Wells and other Victorians and Edwardians have long been rightfully understood as being part of, to borrow Henry James's phrase, Orwell's 'visitable past' (James 1908 [1888]: xxiv).[2] The question, then, is whether Wilde, Baudelaire, Anatole France, J.K. Huysmans, M.P. Shiel and others associated with the various decadent, symbolist, aestheticist and other movements that coalesced around the turn of the century should be considered as well? If yes, then Orwell's work presents an intriguing example of the afterlife of the *fin de siècle* in the age of modernism. It may be noted in this respect that on 17-18 April 2015 a conference took place at the University of London on the theme of 'Aestheticism and Decadence in the Age of Modernism: 1895-1945'. The conference CFP included a long list of 'notable cases' for consideration, from W. B. Yeats and T. S. Eliot to James Joyce and D. H. Lawrence, as well as Cyril Connolly, Orwell's good friend and classmate at St Cyprian's Preparatory School and Eton, but not Orwell. At first sight, the suggestion that Orwell, the most important political writer of the twentieth century, deserves to be placed alongside the above and examined in light of the *fin de siècle* legacy may seem puzzling. Hence, the suggestion that this undertaking is *à rebours*, that is, it goes against his nature, with the notion *à rebours* here echoing the title of Joris-Karl Huysmans's notorious 1884 novel *A Rebours* (*Against Nature*), which became known as the 'bible of decadence'.³

Any number of aspects of Orwell's biography and literary production may be mentioned, from his early days as an imperial policeman in Burma to his service as an anarchist militiaman in Spain, to affirm that this was, indeed, not someone who, to quote the title of a famous painting by the Belgian symbolist painter Fernand Khnopff (1858-1921), 'locked his door upon himself'.⁴ In 'Inside the whale' (1940), moreover, he explicitly criticised what he called the essential Jonah act of escaping into amoral quietism and beauty worship, and in his essay 'Why I write' (1946) rejected art for art's sake in favour of a project 'to turn political writing into an art' (*CWGO* XVIII: 319). Most of his best-known writings, such as *Animal Farm* (1945), *Nineteen Eighty-Four* (1949) and 'Politics and the English language' (1946), as well as early work such as 'A hanging' (1931), 'Shooting an elephant' (1936), and *The Road to Wigan Pier* (1937), are overtly political and address the themes of empire, class and ideology – the themes which have become known as Orwellian. Another meaning of the adjective Orwellian refers to his theory of style, the idea that 'good prose is like a window pane', and that 'purple passages, sentences without meaning, decorative adjectives, and humbug generally' are to be avoided (*CWGO* XVIII: 320). Other aspects of his legacy also clash with decadent and aestheticist themes, as, though coming from what he called the 'lower-upper-middle class' (*CWGO* V: 113), he strove to project a common man image and wore working class jackets, rolled his own cigarettes and slurped his tea from his saucer, not exactly the sort of lifestyle that is associated with those who, as Huysmans's hero Des Esseintes, wished to live in a 'refined Thebaid' (1969 [1884]: 6).

'I HAVE ALWAYS BEEN VERY PRO-WILDE'
Yet, in spite of the above caveat, traces of Orwell's engagement with the turn of the century legacy can be discovered in many places in his writings and biography. George Woodcock, a friend of Orwell's

HENK VYNCKIER

and later lecturer in English literature at the University of British Columbia, already pointed out the connection more than half a century ago in his pioneering *The Crystal Spirit: A Study of George Orwell* (1980 [1966]) when he commented on Orwell's interest in Wilde in a discussion of his friend's tramping expeditions following his return from the East. Woodcock, it must be noted, in addition to his pioneering study *Crystal Spirit*, wrote two books on Wilde, namely *The Paradox of Oscar Wilde* (1949) and *Oscar Wilde: The Double Image* (1989). He also prepared a new edition of Wilde's *The Soul of Man under Socialism* in 1948, which was reviewed sympathetically by Orwell in the *Observer* of 9 May 1948. Woodcock begins his analysis of Orwell's tramping adventures with the observation that 'the whole idea of going into the slums has a peculiar *fin-de-siècle* literary flavor reminiscent of Sherlock Holmes setting off in disguise from his flat in Baker Street to seek in some criminal slum the lost fact that will complete the case that he is about to solve'. But he also sees in it 'the fascination of disguise, of putting on a new self' and a 'kind of *nostalgie de la boue*, a fastidious man's urge to submerge himself in a hideous and malodorous setting, rather as the decadent poets did in an earlier generation' (Woodcock 1948: 93). He also comments on Orwell's interest in Wilde and especially in *The Picture of Dorian Gray*, which, he says, 'lodged in his mind when he was a youth at Eton and which he was still defending in the late 1940s' (ibid). The latter statement may refer to a letter from Orwell to Woodcock dated 18 June 1947, which is not quoted by Woodcock in his study, but can be found in Vol. XIX of the *Complete Works*. Orwell there observes: 'I'm glad … that you contemplate writing something on Wilde. I have always been very pro-Wilde. I particularly like "Dorian Gray," absurd as it is in a way. I just recently read Hesketh Pearson's life of him – only the ordinary hack biography, but I found bits of it quite interesting, especially the part about Wilde's time in prison' (*CWGO* XIX: 157). Other evidence regarding Orwell's abiding interest in Wilde and *The Picture of Dorian Gray* can be found in a 'Talk on *Lady Windermere's Fan* by Oscar Wilde' which Orwell produced for the BBC's Eastern Service on 21 November 1943. In this talk, he praises *Lady Windermere's Fan* as a skilful attack on 'British hypocrisy', and commented on *Dorian Gray* as 'a deeply moral book' which, though 'denounced as cynical, frivolous and so forth at the time when it was published', is 'in essence a religious parable' (*CWGO* XV: 334-337).

Wilde, however, was not the only late 19th century author whose work he enjoyed as a youth and returned to in later years. As Orwell biographers have noted, while enrolled at St Cyprian's, the young Eric was captivated by Bram Stoker's *Dracula*, first published in 1897 with a garish yellow cloth cover, as well as Compton Mackenzie's

Sinister Street, which, though dating to 1913, exudes a belated *fin de siècle* atmosphere with its florid language and scandalous content.[5] Some of these literary interests, moreover, outlasted his teenage years. In a letter dated 26 April 1932, for example, he wrote to his agent Leonard Moore about his disappointment that the publisher Chatto & Windus had not taken up his offer of translating French writers, including Zola and Huysmans, the latter, of course, being the author of *À Rebours* (*CWGO* X: 243). He also enjoyed the work of M.P. Shiel (1865-1947) who contributed a strain of adventure and science fiction writing to the *fin de siècle*, including *The Yellow Danger* (1898) and *The Purple Cloud* (1901). Shiel, moreover, is listed in a letter from Orwell to Max Plowman dated 12 January 1931 as one of the authors whose work he would enjoy reviewing (*CWGO* X: 195) and, as Shiel editor John Sutherland notes, the copyright of *The Purple Cloud* and a number of other Shiel titles was purchased in the late 1920s by Victor Gollancz, Orwell's first publisher, who was pioneering a line of science fiction (2012 [1901]: xliv).

Fin de siècle modes, to be sure, died slowly and languorously in the opening decades of the 20th century as authors such as Shiel, Frederick Rolfe (1860-1913) and Ronald Firbank (1886-1926) continued publishing into the 1910s and 20s and a similar persistence of this legacy was visible in French, German, Russian, Dutch and other continental literatures. Examples abound even in American literature as Ezra Pound, among others, recognised for his significant contribution to the development of imagism, vorticism and literary modernism generally, started as a turn-of-the-century aesthete and included a poem entitled 'The decadence' in his first collection *A Lume Spento* (1908).[6] Even movements which may be considered far beyond the reach of the *fin de siècle* were affected. Jean Pierrot, for example, concludes *The Decadent Imagination, 1880-1900* (1981) with a demonstration of the profound influence of the French decadents on the surrealists André Breton, Michel Leiris and others. The inter-war period, finally, was also when serious literary scholarship began mapping the *fin de siècle* legacy: Edmund Wilson, in his celebrated *Axel's Castle: A Study in the Imaginative Literature of 1870-1930* (1931), traced the lineages that connect modernists such as Eliot, Joyce, Proust and others to the French symbolists, while Mario Praz emphasised the continuities that linked what he called 'the Romantic-Decadents' from the Marquis de Sade to Villiers de L'Isle Adam, Gabriele D'Annunzio and Oscar Wilde in his 1933 study *The Romantic Agony*. In sum, this was a literary and cultural legacy which hardly any serious intellectual growing up in the opening decades of the 20th century could be unaware of.

HENK VYNCKIER

EARLY WRITINGS: *PARIS SPLEEN* AND PURPLE PASSAGES

Returning to the Orwell corpus, as noted by Woodcock, the first text which may be examined for traces of *fin de siècle* literary modes is his first book, *Down and Out in Paris and London* (1933). In this memoir of his life in Paris and London, Orwell organises his narrative around the themes of bohemianism and descent and, while there are vivid sections which prefigure his later crystalline prose, there are also purple passages of the kind he would come to loathe. As Woodcock notes: 'There are still passages mingled with the generally spare and colloquial prose of *Down and Out in Paris and London* which might have fitted very well into one of the decadent magazines of the 1890s' and he cites 'the interpolated tale of Charlie and his sadistic adventure in the red-tapestried cellar' (1984 [1966]: 94) as an example.

The story of the young Parisian by the name of Charlie in Chapter Two, indeed, appears as a rewrite of a familiar 19th-century scenario. Charlie, 'a youth of family and education' and 'one of the local curiosities' (*CWGO* I: 6) in the bistro which Orwell frequented, narrates a late-night adventure which ends with a sadistic assault on a sex slave, a heavily made-up 20-year old peasant girl, somewhere in a garish red bedroom in a cellar under the streets of Paris. Charlie chides his audience for not having cultivated 'the finer sensibilities of love' (ibid: 10), philosophises about the beauty and joy he experienced that day and mourns the 'dust, ashes, and nothingness' which followed this moment of supreme ecstasy following his return to his 'cold, solitary room' (ibid: 11). Orwell biographer Gordon Bowker identifies this sort of 'interlude' as a 'Maupassant-style' short story probably first written as a discrete piece (2003: 144). While this reference is certainly valid, one can also trace this scene back to an even earlier literary ancestor, namely, Baudelaire and his collection of 50 prose poems *Paris Spleen* (1869), which contains numerous stories about prostitutes, drunkenness and sadomasochistic sexuality. In poem 47, 'Mademoiselle Bistouri' ('Miss Scalpel'), for example, the poet encounters a young woman who has a morbid fetishistic attraction to doctors in medical gowns with a little blood on it, thus causing the poet to exclaim: 'What oddities one finds in big cities when one knows how to roam and how to look!' (1970 [1869]: 98). Jean Lorrain's decadent novel *Monsieur de Bougrelon* (1897), the story of an aged trickster who pretends to be the last descendant of an ancient aristocratic family, features a wide variety of such scenes, and reveals to what an extent such Baudelairean sentiments and phraseology had become standard fare in depictions of modern city life.

Another early passage which reveals a very different stylistic approach from the window pane style that would become Orwell's hallmark is found in Chapter Eight of *Burmese Days* (1934) when the protagonist, Flory, and his guest, Elizabeth, attend a *pwe*, a classic Burmese dance performance. Woodcock quotes this passage as the first in a sequence of three, with the second one coming from Orwell's comic novel *Coming Up For Air* (1939) and the third from *Animal Farm,* to illustrate Orwell's development from a rather decorative and ornate style to one which, as Woodcock observes, 'grows so near to the subject that one no longer thinks of it as a style' (op cit: 278). The dancer in *Burmese Days* was 'very young, slim-shouldered, breastless, dressed in a pale blue satin *longyi* that hid her feet. The skirts of her *ingyi* curved outwards above her hips in little panniers, according to the ancient Burmese fashion. They were like the petals of a downward-pointing flower' (*CWGO* II: 106). Woodcock notes that several more similes follow in one short paragraph, including one which compares the movements of the dancer to 'those of jointed wooden figures on a roundabout', another which describes her hands 'twisting like snakeheads with the fingers close together' and finally the phrase 'the panniers of her *ingyi* flying out about her like the petals of a snowdrop' (ibid: 106-107). These are, as Woodcock concludes correctly, signs of the sort of precious, *recherché* style which Orwell would turn away from in later years. Furthermore, in terms of subject matter, much of this description of a female dancer echoes images of female figures and dancers in symbolist and decadent literature, from Baudelaire's poetry to Wilde's one-act tragedy *Salomé* (1891), and also in the visual style of turn of the century painting, sculpture, architecture and decorative arts.

However, while Woodcock correctly ascertains the presence of what he calls 'a Wildean influence at this early stage' (op cit: 94), it can be claimed that this influence continues in Orwell's writings at a later stage as well. It is noteworthy, for example, that several of his novels develop a familiar pattern involving 'last man' or, what is called in French, *dernier homme* heroes: women and men who are haunted by their family lineages and exist in a mental climate of failure, boredom and lassitude. This is clearly the case for *A Clergyman's Daughter* (1935) and *Keep the Aspidistra Flying* (1936), in which both protagonists come from formerly well-established families now in serious decline, but it can be argued that this pattern resurfaces in *Nineteen Eighty-Four*, which was originally titled *The Last Man in Europe.*

The significance of this theme, then, is that the decadent concept involving the last descendants of ancient families, found in examples ranging from *À Rebours* to Rainer M. Rilke's *The Notebooks of Malte Laurids Brigge* (1910), intersects with the apocalyptic and dystopian 'last man' theme initiated by Mary Shelley in her *The Last Man* of

PAPER

HENK VYNCKIER

1826. The latter's protagonist, Lionel Verney, to be sure, is a last man in both senses of the word in that he is both the orphaned descendant of a nobleman and the last survivor of a global pandemic which wipes out human civilisation. As Stephen Arata demonstrates in his study *Fictions of Loss in the Victorian* Fin de Siècle*: Identity and Empire* (1996), such narratives of loss and decline became particularly important in the closing decades of the 19th century. As for the childless Winston Smith, in *Nineteen Eighty-Four*, it may be surmised that he, too, is a last man in the decadent sense of the word as there are hints that suggest a potentially substantial family lineage. He remembers his mother, namely, as a 'tall, statuesque, rather silent woman with slow movements and magnificent fair hair' and his father as a man who was 'dressed always in neat dark clothes … and wearing spectacles' (*CWGO* IX: 31). He later also reflects that his mother 'had possessed a kind of nobility, a kind of purity, simply because the standards that she obeyed were private ones' (ibid: 171). Characteristics such as these – a statuesque appearance, magnificent hair and nobility – are, of course, the sort of qualities typically featured in the ancestral portrait galleries of England's noble families. Orwell, himself, descended from such a lineage and, being 'keenly aware of his Blair ancestry' (Bowker 2004 [2003]: 4), owned an oil portrait of his 18th century ancestor Lady Mary Blair. His pride in this family heirloom is evident from the numerous photographs which show him seated in front of this ancestral portrait in his flat in Islington.[7] Smith, therefore, may be understood on the basis of these various textual as well as contextual clues as not only a dystopian seeker after truth but also as a last man adrift from his family heritage.

NINETEEN EIGHTY-FOUR AND *THE PICTURE OF DORIAN GRAY*

Nineteen Eighty-Four, furthermore, constitutes an interesting site for a discussion of Orwell's interest in *The Picture of Dorian Gray*, which is another important example of a *fin de siècle* 'last man' narrative. As stated above, Woodcock was one of the first critics to call attention to Orwell's appreciation of this novel, but he focused Orwell's interest narrowly on Dorian Gray's descents into the lower depths in search of opium and other forbidden pleasures as he believed that those specific passages in Wilde's novel 'may well have helped to determine Orwell on his course of self-submersion in the slums' (op cit: 94). I would argue, however, that *The Picture of Dorian Gray* not only influenced *Down and Out in Paris and London* but was also important to other aspects of Orwell's literary agenda including, in particular, *Nineteen Eighty-Four*, which reveals a number of remarkable correspondences with Wilde's novel.

Orwell's restless protagonist Winston Smith, namely, is completely submerged in Party culture and craves what his totalitarian masters call 'ownlife', that is, the freedom to pursue private pleasures and interests, whereas Dorian Gray's story is that of a man whose 'ownlife' is without limits. As Dorian reflects, his aim is to achieve a 'new Hedonism that was to recreate life and to save it from that harsh, uncomely puritanism that is having, in our own day, its curious revival' (2007 [1891]: 108). Such an existence, to be sure, is denied to Ministry of Truth employee Smith, but not unlike Dorian Gray, he attempts to escape the relentlessly 'harsh' and 'uncomely' age of Big Brother by turning to urban *flânerie*, descents into proletarian neighbourhoods, intoxication, sexual adventures, reverie and the cultural practice of collecting, all this set against a background atmosphere of dreamy nostalgia and crepuscular decline. Smith, at the beginning of the novel, gives up his lunch in the Ministry canteen and escapes to his flat in order to, in the words of Khnopff's painting, lock his door upon himself. There, indeed, taking advantage of 'the unusual geography' of his room (*CWGO* IX: 7), he sits down in an alcove out of view of his telescreen and for the first time in his life begins writing his diary. Edmund Wilson characterises the essential *fin de siècle* programme as an attempt to move 'the arena of life, from an objective to a subjective world, from an experience shared with society to an experience savoured in solitude' (op cit: 211). Smith's gesture of withdrawal and inwardness in the opening chapter of *Nineteen Eighty-Four* fundamentally coheres with this agenda.

Firstly, however, it is useful to examine the novel at a basic level of plot and character as there, too, a number of interesting similarities between the two novels can be delineated. For example, whereas Dorian Gray's turn towards hedonism would not have been possible without the encouragement and guidance of Lord Henry Wotton, Smith finds comfort and strength in his relationship with Inner Party member O'Brien. The latter, it could be said, comes as close to a Lord Henry-type dandy or aesthete as is possible in Oceania and, like Lord Henry, appears to be on the side of the sinner Smith in his rebellion against the Party faithful. He does so, of course, in order to betray Smith all the more fatally in the long run, but this is not apparent to Smith at first. O'Brien, in spite of his 'thick neck, and … coarse, humorous, and brutal, face' (*CWGO* IX: 12), always appears to be calm, suave and urbane and has a way of re-settling his glasses on his nose which 'recalled an eighteenth-century nobleman offering his snuff-box' (ibid). He is, furthermore, a literate connoisseur of the delights of Newspeak and admires Smith's facility with words. He also promises Smith an advance copy of the latest edition of the Dictionary of Newspeak and, inviting

HENK VYNCKIER

him to his residence, offers him for the first time in his life a glass of red wine. All these are the amenities of a pleasurable and cultured existence craved by Smith. Another character, meanwhile, namely Julia, the girl from the Fiction Department, may also be quoted in this constellation of characters and can be placed alongside Sybil Vane, the actress in a third-rate theatrical venue who is betrayed by her Prince Charming, as she calls Dorian, as soon as she attempts to escape from her Fiction Department, that is, the fantasy world of the theatre and become a real person. In *Nineteen Eighty-Four*, Julia is feared, even hated, by Smith as long as she is nothing but 'the girl from the Fiction Department', that is, a party fanatic who appears to be ready to denounce him at the first opportunity (*CWGO* IX: 11). Yet, unlike Sybil, it is only when she discards this put-on persona of the bigoted Party adherent that she becomes Julia, a real person and his lover. This relationship, too, however, ends in betrayal, under torture in Room 101, and a gloomy last encounter in the Chestnut Tree Café.

One other aspect which deserves special attention is that both novels feature books to illustrate crucial turning points in the development of the respective protagonists. In *The Picture of Dorian Gray*, Gray's journey into hedonism, triggered by his first encounter with Lord Henry Wotton, is confirmed following the suicide of Sybil Vane by his reading of a 'yellow book' (op cit: 103) sent to him by Lord Henry. It is, as he reflects, not only 'the strangest book he had ever read', but even 'a poisonous book' (ibid: 104) and he summarises its fascination and power as follows: 'The whole book seemed to him to contain the story of his own life, written before he had lived it' (ibid: 105). As for Smith, while exploring some streets in the proletarian part of town, he sees a book in the window of a little junk shop and is 'stricken immediately by an overwhelming desire to possess it' (*CWGO* IX: 8). He buys the book and begins the journey home knowing that what he carries is 'a compromising possession' (ibid). During a later inspection in his apartment, he notices how special this book is: 'It was a particularly beautiful book. Its smooth creamy paper, a little yellowed by age, was of a kind that had not been manufactured for at least forty years past. He could guess, however, that the book was much older than that' (ibid). Thus, Smith's yellowed book, though a blank, unused keepsake diary, rather than a novel, echoes the yellow book which Dorian receives from Lord Henry and, as the latter, this book will contain the story of his life as he will record in its pages his memories of his childhood, his visits to prostitutes in proletarian neighbourhoods and his rebellion against Big Brother.

As I discussed in my 'A portrait of the artist as a collector: Tracing Orwell's collecting project from Burma to Big Brother' (2015), even though in Big Brother's Oceania such efforts to indulge in subjectivity and treasure 'ownlife' are forbidden, this purchase of the beautiful keepsake is the start of an open-ended collecting project by Smith in support of his ongoing personal and political awakening. He pays further visits to the junk shop and buys an antique glass paperweight with a bit of red coral embedded in its core, charmed by 'the air it seemed to possess of belonging to an age quite different from the present one' (ibid: 99). He also listens to the proprietor's reminiscences and inspects an upstairs bedroom with an old engraving of St Clement Dane's Church which he will soon rent for his encounters with Julia. Moreover, Orwell himself was an eclectic collector of pamphlets, comic postcards, candleholders, Victorian commemorative mugs and other objects which he kept for their 'curiosity value … rather than for their convenience or beauty' (Crick 1980: 346). It is reasonable to surmise, therefore, that Chapter 11 of *The Picture of Dorian Gray*, which contains one of the most astonishing descriptions of a collector in literature, would have interested Orwell and that he may also have been familiar with Huysmans's *À Rebours* (1884) and the extraordinary collections of its protagonist des Esseintes.[8] The relevance of the collecting theme in *Nineteen Eighty-Four* in comparison with *The Picture of Dorian Gray*, therefore, is that Smith turns to collectible objects in order to, as Dorian states, 'create worlds' and engage in a 'search for sensations that would be at once new and delightful' (*CWGO* IX: 102). However, unlike Dorian, the wealthy descendant of an ancient aristocratic lineage who is able to collect the rarest books, jewels, musical instruments, textiles, furniture and works of art, Smith, living in an age in which the past has been relentlessly suppressed and altered, is limited to 'scraps of beautiful rubbish' (ibid: 104). These scraps, moreover, are merely made available to him by the Thought Police in order to entrap him.

One final intriguing aspect of this engagement with *The Picture of Dorian Gray* is that throughout their adventures both Smith and Gray are locked into fateful struggles with portraits. Wilde's protagonist, encountering his own beauty in Basil Hallward's masterful portrait, makes a Faustian bargain whereby he shall forever be young while his portrait grows old. Being granted his wish and seeing his portrait sullied by his evil life, he then hides this mirror of his corrupt soul in his boyhood room where it remains unseen by anyone but Dorian himself until after his death. As for Smith, he is confronted by portraits of Big Brother from the first page of the novel when he returns home and sees the coloured wall poster in the hallway of the Victory Mansions to the very last when he sits in the Chestnut Tree Café opposite a vast portrait. His efforts along the way to live his life away from the influence of this portrait – for

HENK VYNCKIER

example, when he squeezes into the alcove next to the telescreen in his flat or hides in the junk shop bedroom with Julia – are futile as the surveillance mechanisms and communal vision of the state cannot be evaded. Quite remarkably, both novels end with affirmations of the portraits to symbolise the defeat of the protagonists. In Wilde, the dead Dorian is found, withered and loathsome, on the floor in his boyhood room with his portrait restored to its former splendour triumphantly presiding over him, whereas Smith, in an interesting inversion, still alive, but tears trickling down his nose, looks up at the image of a man with piercing eyes and ruggedly handsome features in the Chestnut Tree Café and finally realises that he loves Big Brother. It is, to recall the title of Stanley Kubrick's film *Dr Strangelove: Or How I Learned to Stop Worrying and Love the Bomb* (1964), the moment when Smith learns to stop worrying and love Big Brother, but it is also the moment when his death may be anticipated – even though this final act is not described in the novel.

This reading of the last scene in *Nineteen Eighty-Four* adds another interesting dimension to the *à rebours* analysis of Orwell's last novel and its intriguing linkages with Wilde's 'deeply moral book'. Yet, no claim is made here that a direct, exclusive relationship exists between these two novels. Many heterogeneous influences are at work in *Nineteen Eighty-Four*, including the Victorian and Georgian authors listed above, but also Jack London, Yevgeny Zamyatin, Arthur Koestler and others. Nevertheless, it is stimulating to see how Orwell appropriated specific themes and narrative devices from turn of the century fiction, such as his *dernier homme* protagonist, urban *flânerie* in the stone labyrinths of the city, interest in street scenes and popular culture, sexual transgression, the collecting theme, escapism, reverie and lassitude, and brilliantly overhauled these to address the political agendas of his time. This achievement by Orwell, therefore, not only demonstrates the consistency of his development as an author from his earliest writings to his final masterpiece, but also presents an intriguing and unexpected case study of the afterlife of the *fin de siècle* literary heritage in the 20th century.

NOTES

[1] See later for an acknowledgement of indebtedness regarding this opening

[2] Loraine Saunders, in *The Unsung Artistry of George Orwell: The Novels from Burmese Days to Nineteen Eighty-Four* (2008), pays particular attention to George Gissing, but also mentions Dickens, G.B. Shaw and H.G. Wells as important influences

[3] See Julia Przyboś (1988) De la poétique décadente: La bibliothèque de des Esseintes, *L'Esprit Créateur* Vol. 28, No 1 pp 67-74

[4] The painting 'I locked my door upon myself' dates from 1891 and shows a mysterious, otherworldly figure enclosed in a private space with wilting irises, a bust of Hypnos, the Greek god of sleep, a red poppy, mirrors, and various other, difficult to identify objects

[5] Jeffrey Meyers quotes Orwell at St Cyprian's 'expressing interest in *Dracula* and vampires' (2000: 24) and D.J. Taylor states that still later at Eton, he gave Jacintha Buddicom a copy of *Dracula* (2004 [2003]: 49). As for *Sinister Street*, Bowker, in his chapter on St Cyprian's, devotes a paragraph to the reasons why this novel 'should so rivet young Eric' (2003: 46)

[6] The poem begins as follows: 'Tarnished we! Tarnished! Wastrels all! / And yet the art goes on, goes on' (44)

[7] See the photographs by Vernon Richards in *George Orwell At Home (and Among the Anarchists)*

[8] This novel was first published in English translation in 1931 around the time when Orwell expressed interest in translating other works by Huysmans

REFERENCES

Arata, Stephen (1996) *Fictions of Loss in the Victorian* Fin de Siècle: *Identity and Empire*, Cambridge: Cambridge University Press

Baudelaire, Charles (1970 [1869]) *Paris Spleen*, trans by Varèse, Louise, New York: New Directions

Bowker, Gordon (2003) *George Orwell*, London: Little, Brown

Crick, Bernard (1980) *George Orwell: A Life*, London: Secker & Warburg

Ellmann, Richard ((1988 [1984]) *Oscar Wilde*, NY: Alfred A. Knopf

Huysmans, Joris-Karl (1969 [1884]) *Against the Grain (À Rebours)*, NY: Dover Publications

James, Henry (1908 [1888]) Preface, *The Aspern Papers*, London : Macmillan and Co.

Kerr, Douglas (2014) Orwell and Kipling: Global Visions, *Concentric: Literary and Cultural Studies* Vol 40, No 1 pp 35-50

Lorrain, Jean (2016 [1897]) *Monsieur de Bougrelon*, trans by Richter, Eva, Las Vegas, NV: Spurl Editions

Meyers, Jeffrey (2001 [2000]) *Orwell: Wintry Conscience of a Generation*, New York: Norton

Orwell, George (1996-1998) *The Complete Works*, (*CWGO*), Davison, Peter (ed.) London: Secker & Warburg

Pierrot, Jean (1981) *The Decadent Imagination, 1880-1900*, trans by Coltman, Derek, Chicago: University of Chicago Press

Pound, Ezra (1976) *Collected Early Poems of Ezra Pound*, New York: New Directions

Praz, Mario (1970 [1933]) *The Romantic Agony*, Oxford: Oxford University Press, second edition

Richards, Vernon (1998) *George Orwell At Home (and Among the Anarchists)*, London: Freedom Press

Saunders, Loraine (2008) *The Unsung Artistry of George Orwell: The Novels from Burmese Days to Nineteen Eighty-Four*, Aldershot, Hampshire: Ashgate

Shiel, M.P. (2012 [1901]) *The Purple Cloud*, Sutherland, John (ed.) London: Penguin

Taylor, D.J. (2004 [2003]) *Orwell: The Life*, London: Vintage

Vynckier, Henk (2015) A portrait of the artist as a collector: Tracing Orwell's collecting project from Burma to Big Brother, *George Orwell Now!* Keeble, Richard Lance (ed.) New York: Peter Lang pp 47-62

HENK VYNCKIER

Wilde, Oscar (2007 [1891]) *The Picture of Dorian Gray*, Gillespie, Michael Patrick (ed.) New York: Norton and Company

Wilson, Edmund (1984 [1931]) *Axel's Castle: A Study in the Imaginative Literature of 1870 to 1930*, London: Fontana Paperbacks

Woodcock, George (1984 [1966]) *The Crystal Spirit: A Study of George Orwell*, London: Fourth Estate

NOTE ON THE CONTRIBUTOR

Henk Vynckier is Professor in the Department of Foreign Languages and Literatures at Tunghai University and Dean of the College of Tourism and Hospitality Management at Overseas Chinese University, Taichung, Taiwan. His interests in research include George Orwell and dystopian literature and collecting as a literary theme and cultural practice. Co-edited, with John Rodden, 'Orienting Orwell: Asian and Global Perspectives on George Orwell' (special issue of *Concentric: Literary and Cultural Studies*, March 2014); published 'Big Brother is coming to an iPad near you: Teaching Orwell in Taiwan' (*George Orwell Studies*, special issue on 'Teaching Orwell', December 2017) and 'Orwell's vision of China: From beastly tea to sickly rice-spirit' (*The Wenshan Review of Literature and Culture*, December 2018).

PAPER

'A Sinking Sensation': George Orwell and the RMS *Titanic*

NATHAN WADDELL

This paper speculatively traces the allusive and evocative presence of the sinking of the RMS Titanic *in Orwell's fiction. Its cultural-historical point of departure is Orwell's memory of his response to the sinking, as outlined in his essay 'My country right or left' (1940), and its focus is the many instances of sinking-ship imagery in Orwell's essays and novels. Situating Orwell's work in relation to contemporary accounts of the disaster from 1912 and alongside more recent academic studies of the sinking, the paper suggests alternative ways of interpreting the imagery of scuppered vessels and drowning people that appear so often in his writing. Its key claim is that the loss of the* Titanic *may well have been an originating, vicarious catastrophe that made Orwell into the water-fixated, sinking-ship-concerned writer he increasingly became.*

Key words: Orwell, the *Titanic*, sinking-ship imagery, drowning people, water-fixation, maritime images, metaphors and similes, Titanica

Four days into its maiden voyage, on 14 April 1912, at 11.40 pm (ship's time), the RMS *Titanic* hit an iceberg in the mid-Atlantic Ocean. Significant damage to the hull of the ship, leading to an unstoppable inflow of sea water, caused it to go down bow-first. Two hours and forty minutes later it sank. Although the *Titanic* had been designed to withstand the flooding of several of the semi-watertight bulkheads that transected its lowest decks, the ship could not stay afloat with its first five compartments filled. Films such as Roy Ward Baker's *A Night to Remember* (1958) and James Cameron's *Titanic* (1997) have helped to give this fact, and its terrifying realisation on the night in question, a mythic resonance. As Walter Lord put it:

> The bulkhead between the fifth and sixth compartments went only as high as E deck. If the first five compartments were flooded, the bow would sink so low that water in the fifth compartment must overflow into the sixth. When this was full, it would overflow into the seventh, and so on. It was a

NATHAN WADDELL

mathematical certainty, pure and simple. There was no way out (2012 [1956]: 26).

It took just under three hours for the jewel in the crown of the White Star Line shipping company to disappear into the sea. Before it did so, the colossal strains put on its hull as the ship's stern lifted out of the water cracked it in half. Some 712 people out of 2,208 on board survived (Fitch, Layton and Wormstedt 2015: 272). Death came for the rest: those who fell or jumped, or who were taken by the disintegrating ship into the ocean – among them the captain, E. J. Smith, the American financier, John Jacob Astor, the journalist W.T. Stead and the mystery writer Jacques Futrelle – where they drowned or were killed by the ship's crumbling superstructure, or perished in the cold.

Few disasters have had such an immediate, lasting impact on the world, and arguably no ship has become more meaningful in culture than the *Titanic*, which has steadily passed from history into legend.[1] 'Her name,' writes Gareth Russell, 'has become a synonym for catastrophe', just as the ship itself 'has become both cultural touchstone and looking glass' ever since it foundered (2019: xvii, xxii). From the outset the sinking generated widespread expressions of disbelief and sorrow. Reflecting on the ship's loss a month after the tragedy, a correspondent wrote as follows to the editor of the *Freewoman*:

> [it] may almost be said to have caused the senses of civilised humanity to suspend their normal functions temporarily, whilst our hearts are strained indeed to the verge of breaking point with inexpressible sympathy, not only for family bereavements, but for the loss the world has sustained by the removal from our midst of the many heroic victims of this all too sad disaster (A.I.B. 1912: 477).

Simultaneously, the sinking was interpreted as a decisive counteraction to human overconfidence. It was a 'forcible reminder', in the words of a report published in *The Times*, 'of the existence of natural forces which from time to time upset all our calculations and baffle all our precautions' (Anon. 1912a: 9). The *Manchester Guardian* ran a piece that claimed the sinking as 'more than a great shipping disaster; it is one of the most terrible sea tragedies of all time – tragedy not merely in the magnitude of the losses, but in the cruel overthrow by Fate of human pride and achievement' (Anon. 1912b: 8). The Bishop of Winchester captured the wider mood in describing the ship's loss as 'a monument to human presumption' (quoted in Davie 2012: 250).

William Alden Smith, the senator who led the American inquiry into the disaster, indicted the ship's captain with exactly this charge.

He accused him of being a modern-day Icarus who inexplicably neglected his duty to safeguard the *Titanic* and everyone aboard. Senator Smith emphasised that 'some traces' of Captain E. J. Smith's 'lofty spirit' persisted in 'his manly bearing' and in 'his tender solicitude for the safety of women and little children … when dark clouds lowered all about him and angry elements stripped him of his command' (Foster 2000: 183). Yet the senator was astonished by the captain's baffling 'indifference to danger', given that he and his second officer, Charles Lightoller, had learned during the voyage itself that they might cross the path of an iceberg.[2] Senator Smith stated: 'Science in shipbuilding was supposed to have attained perfection and to have spoken her last word; mastery of the ocean had at last been achieved; but over-confidence seems to have dulled the faculties usually so alert' (ibid). In response to the New York inquiry's focus on 'the luckless "Yamsi"' – i.e. J. Bruce Ismay, chairman of the White Star Line and one of the most controversial survivors of the sinking – Joseph Conrad lamented the 'real tragedy of the fatuous drowning of all these people who to the last moment put their trust in mere bigness, in the reckless affirmations of commercial men and mere technicians and in the irresponsible paragraphs of the newspapers booming these ships' (ibid: 194). Disbelief at the hubris involved ran throughout the innumerable newspaper reports, interviews and poems that emerged in response to the disaster, which also prompted widespread articulations of grief at 'the site of panic' (Foster 2002: 114) the ship became in its final moments and at the awful loss of life it occasioned.

A 'COMPARATIVELY PETTY DISASTER'

George Orwell was a nine-year-old boy when the *Titanic* sank, and news of the disaster – which he, along with so many others, experienced vicariously through newspaper reports – made a decades-long impression on him. Writing nearly thirty years after the event in his essay 'My country right or left' (1940), he contrasted the effect of hearing about the sinking with the impact of 'the big events' that occurred just a few years later during World War One:

> I must admit that nothing in the whole war moved me so deeply as the loss of the *Titanic* had done a few years earlier. This comparatively petty disaster shocked the whole world, and the shock has not quite died away even yet. I remember the terrible, detailed accounts read out at the breakfast table (in those days it was a common habit to read the newspaper aloud), and I remember that in all the long list of horrors the one that most impressed me was that at the last the *Titanic* suddenly up-ended and sank bow-foremost, so that the people clinging to the stern were lifted no less than three hundred

feet into the air before they plunged into the abyss. It gave me a sinking sensation in the belly which I can still all but feel. Nothing in the war ever gave me quite that sensation (Orwell 2002a: 269).[3]

Orwell took the loss of the ship as a 'comparatively petty disaster' only in relation to the devastations of 1914-1918, the millions of casualties suffered during those years in his view overshadowing the fifteen hundred people who died in April 1912.[4] Orwell was too young to fight in World War One which, for him as for many other boys his age, happened elsewhere and far away. The loss of the *Titanic*, by contrast, was a more intimate concern, albeit one distanced by his lack of direct involvement in it. The *idea* of the sinking, though, affected Orwell deep in his body, prompting him in retrospect to use what would become a favoured expression: 'a sinking sensation in the belly'. A real sinking, heard about at the breakfast table, generated a sinking feeling, even as the sinking feeling paled in comparison to the real experience of sinking that so many poor souls went through on that awful night three decades earlier.

The feeling mattered, nevertheless, and it was widely shared. Orwell's horror at the up-ending of the ship was suffered by victims, survivors and the public alike. One memorable evocation of it came from Filson Young, a journalist who published the first book on the disaster a little over a month after it occurred:

> The slope of the deck increased, and the sea came washing up against it as waves wash against a steep shore. And then that helpless mass of humanity was stricken at last with the fear of death, and began to scramble madly aft, away from the chasm of water that kept creeping up and up the decks. Then a strange thing happened. They who had been waiting to sink into the sea found themselves rising into the air as the slope of the decks grew steeper. Up and up, dizzily high out of reach of the dark waters into which they had dreaded to be plunged, higher and higher into the air, towards the stars, the stern of the ship rose slowly right out of the water, and hung there for a time that is estimated variously between two and five minutes; a terrible eternity to those who were still clinging (Foster 2000: 77-78).[5]

The spectacle gave Young pause: 'We dare not linger here, even in imagination; dare not speculate; dare not look closely, even with the mind's eye, at this poor human agony, this last pitiful scramble for dear life that the serene stars shone down upon' (ibid: 78). The final moments of the ship's above-water existence was an event that, in being represented, raised the larger ethical question of whether it should be represented at all.

It's not clear whether anxieties over the ethical implications of representation itself lay behind the fact that very few of the period's leading authors wrote about the sinking of the *Titanic*. What is obvious, however, is that only some of the writers one may expect to have written publicly about the disaster actually wrote about it. Thomas Hardy's poem 'The convergence of the twain' (1912) remains probably the most well-known literary response, with its image of the 'intimate welding' of ship and ice that took the *Titanic* into 'a solitude of the sea' (see Biel 1998: 26, 25). An intriguing side-note to the period's literary history can be glimpsed in the possibility that T.S. Eliot alluded to the disaster in an early draft of the 'Death by water' section of *The Waste Land* (1922), which mentions 'a long white line, / A wall, a barrier' ahead of a schooner travelling in the Atlantic (see Nelson 1997: 356). Virginia Woolf – who, in John Wilson Foster's words, 'had a pathologically developed fear of and fascination with the subaqueous, the fitting element of the self in crisis' (2002: 57) – wrote in private about the sinking but not elsewhere, as did Henry James and John Galsworthy. Frances Wilson points out that the ocean-minded Joseph Conrad 'produced more words on the *Titanic* than any of his literary contemporaries' (2012: 285), even though his published output in this context was only two fairly short articles: 'Some reflections, seamanlike and otherwise, on the loss of the *Titanic*' and 'Certain aspects of the admirable inquiry into the loss of the *Titanic*', both 1912. Wilson adds that G.K. Chesterton, H.G. Wells, George Bernard Shaw and Arthur Conan Doyle 'produced newspaper copy when they were asked to do so, but there is no mention of the subject in their private correspondence'; it bled neither 'into their subsequent work' nor into the work of contemporaries such as W.B. Yeats, D.H. Lawrence and E.M. Forster. It was the general public, Wilson emphasises, not these literary celebrities and their ilk, 'who discovered a bottomless capacity for reading and writing about the *Titanic*' (ibid: 286).

Orwell appears not to have been among those gripped by this 'bottomless capacity' for so-called 'Titanica'. A superficial search of his output suggests that he had only a glancing concern with the *Titanic*, in an oblique way in the context of the French translation of *Down and Out in Paris and London* (1933) and then most noticeably in 'My country right or left'.[6] Yet Orwell did appear to be 'moved … deeply' by the loss of *Titanic* long after the event itself was over, and this stimulus, I claim, is evident in his writings of the 1930s and 1940s. Many of Orwell's works from this period suggest that he responded by means of recurrent maritime images, metaphors and similes, if not directly to the ship's loss, then certainly to the 'horror' it produced. In 1941, a year after he published 'My country right or left', Orwell stated that a 'morbid appeal' attaches to 'a sinking

PAPER

NATHAN WADDELL

ship' (2002a: 447), and on the evidence of texts such as *Keep the Aspidistra Flying* (1936), *The Road to Wigan Pier* (1937), *Coming Up For Air* (1939) and *Nineteen Eighty-Four* (1949), it seems that he was gripped by a macabre fascination with sinking ships right to the end of his life. This fascination is not finally reducible to a concern with the *Titanic* alone; the evidence, as we will see, is overdetermined. However, the apparent allusions to the sinking of the *Titanic* in Orwell's work make it likely that the 'shock' it gave him in 1912 never quite faded away.

To suggest this reading of Orwell's output is to invoke a place for it in the constantly evolving cultural history of the *Titanic*. The scale of this subject area reflects the fact that very soon after the sinking the ship and its fate 'had infiltrated almost every aspect of popular cultural expression, from music to film, and from painting and sculpture to a wide range of literary formats and genres' (Womack and Bergfelder 2003: 1). Within weeks the ship's 'disaster narrative' was turned into an 'enduring literary subject' and ever since it has given storytellers 'a dramatic backdrop for spinning their tales of adventure, courage, and romance' (Womack 2004: 85). Yet scholars working in this field have had very little concern with Orwell. His remark about the sinking's relative 'pettiness' has been quoted by Richard Howells and by Sarah Gregson, but otherwise Orwell barely registers in cultural- or literary-historical accounts of the disaster.[7] Orwell scholars, likewise, have not been tempted to do much more than mention the *Titanic* in connection with 'My country right or left'; Orwell's insistence in this essay on the disaster's importance to him, both as a nine-year-old and by implication as a man in his late thirties remembering the boy he was, does not seem to have held their attention for long.[8] But Orwell's place in the cultural history of the *Titanic* is deserved: not because of the scarce references to the disaster in his writing but due to the range of sinking feelings discoverable in his prose, which leads us covertly back to the shocked nine-year-old boy hearing newspaper reports discussed and worried about over breakfast.

DEATH BY WATER

Orwell stated in his essay 'Writers and Leviathan' (1948) that when 'you are on a sinking ship, your thoughts will be about sinking ships' (2002b: 288). He thought about sinking ships a good deal more often than the point implies. The sinking of the *Titanic* 'impressed' itself on him as a young boy who became a writer obsessed with the imagery of scuppered vessels and sinking or drowning people. One reason for this is because the idea of sinking itself could give metaphorical shape to wider sentiments of political decay; as Jed Esty remarks, in a book named in homage to Hugh Kenner's *A*

Sinking Island (1988), Orwell was one of several mid-century writers – some of the others being Graham Greene, Evelyn Waugh, W.H. Auden and Philip Larkin – who had a 'historical sense of pervasive national decline' (Esty 2004: 9). Another reason, as we will see, is that in 1948 Orwell himself came very close to drowning at sea in the Gulf of Corryvreckan, just off the island of Jura in Scotland (also the place where so much of *Nineteen Eighty-Four* was written). The fact that the *Titanic* sinking enters the reminiscences of 'My country right or left', a key political essay, suggests that Orwell carried on remembering the traumatised boy he once was, just as the remembered trauma, in being remembered, shaped the later statement of political principles. To quote Lisa Mullen, in a discussion of Orwell's late work: 'Personal feelings', for him, 'are not just permissible but essential to political understanding' (Orwell 2021: xxv). The loss of the *Titanic* may well have been an originating, vicarious catastrophe that made Orwell into the water-fixated, sinking-ship-concerned writer he increasingly became.

The 'personal feeling' of fear of death by water haunted Orwell's imagination as a kind of political imaginary. Sinking metaphors variously appear in Orwell's essays and reviews to describe getting bogged down in statistics, to signal hypocrisy, to evoke anonymity and to announce the insidiousness of capitalism, among many other emphases, and several characters in his novels experience sinking feelings of one kind or another.

An early instance is in his novel *Burmese Days* (1934), in which the young socialite Elizabeth Lackersteen recoils in horror at the sight and thought of her mother's studio in Paris, which fills her 'with the sense of sinking into some horrible lower world' (Orwell 2009: 94). A 'sinking feeling' goes through the entrails of Dorothy Hare, the heroine of Orwell's next novel, *A Clergyman's Daughter* (1935), when she discovers an unpaid bill (Orwell 1990a: 13). In a different way, the titular metaphor of *Coming Up For Air* (1939) contrasts with the experience of descending into murky depths: 'You know the feeling I had. Coming up for air! Like the big sea-turtles when they come paddling up to the surface, stick their noses out and fill their lungs with a great gulp before they sink down again among the seaweed and the octopuses' (Orwell 1990b: 177). The emphasis changes in *Homage to Catalonia* (1938), Orwell's account of his time fighting in the Spanish Civil War, to a concern with the 'sea[s] of mud' that sucked combatants on all sides down into their 'filthy, slimy' morasses (Orwell 2003: 15, 68). Like Elizabeth Lackersteen flinching at the 'cold, dusty pigsty' (Orwell 2009: 94) of her mother's studio, liquid earth made Orwell flinch at the adhesive gloopiness of the war machine: 'I remember feeling a deep horror at everything,' he recalled, 'the chaos, the darkness, the frightful din, the slithering to and fro in the mud' (2003: 76-77). This is different again from the 'sinking ship of individualism' invoked in Orwell's review of *The Unquiet Grave* (1945), pseudonymously written by Cyril Connolly, in which Orwell looks wryly at the idea that 'so-called collectivist systems' are really 'a sham covering a new form of class privilege' (2001: 21, 22).

These examples articulate the general structure of sinking moods and manners that shape the imaginative techniques of Orwell's writing. Although it bears on the issue at hand in some obvious ways, that structure is not itself a response to the loss of the *Titanic* as such. Sinking feelings, after all, do not have to be about water's horrifying dangers. They can also be about hatred and resistance or disgust. Gordon Comstock, the morose protagonist of *Keep the Aspidistra Flying* (1936), offers a case in point. Dissatisfied with his job in the New Albion Publicity Company, Comstock's intense, alienating hunger for abjection makes him seek experiences that will take him underground, down into 'the safe soft womb of earth, where there is no getting of jobs or losing of jobs, no relatives or friends to plague you, no hope, fear, ambition, honour, [nor] duty' (Orwell 1989a: 227) – into abjection, in other words. He has the chance to make money, but decides instead to sink 'into the same rut of poverty' (ibid: 63) that trapped his ancestors. This brings upon him the scorn of Rosemary, his girlfriend, who bitterly accuses him of wanting to let himself go to pieces: 'free to sink … down, down into quiet worlds where money and effort and moral obligation did not exist' (ibid: 218). Comstock wants to be a down and out in London, a goal that proves very difficult to realise. 'Better to sink than rise,' he reflects. 'Down, down into the ghost-kingdom, the shadowy world where shame, effort, [and] decency do not exist!' (ibid: 233). Sinking, for Comstock, means rebellion, but it also means becoming part of the so-called 'submerged tenth' – those forgotten individuals who constitute the urban underclass.

Comstock's hopes of sinking 'into grey, deadly failure' (ibid: 240) connects him with the monochrome inhabitants of Knype Hill, the fictional setting of the beginning and the end of Orwell's preceding novel, *A Clergyman's Daughter*. They also belong to the same conceptual emphasis that generates one of the most memorable images in *Keep the Aspidistra Flying*, which appears after Comstock's drunken assault on Rosemary as he stands gazing at the lights at Piccadilly Circus:

> He stood on the kerb gazing out into the hideous midnight-noon. For a moment he felt quite deathly. His face was burning. His whole body had a dreadful, swollen, fiery feeling. His head in particular seemed on the point of bursting. Somehow the baleful light was bound up with his sensations.

He watched the sky-signs flicking on and off, glaring red and blue, arrowing up and down – the awful, sinister glitter of a doomed civilisation, like the still blazing lights of a sinking ship (ibid: 187).

We are not quite in *Titanic* territory, although we are touching on trauma – 'glitter' being a loaded term in Orwell for anything that is deceptively appealing or attractive. Here, Comstock's sinking feelings, or yearnings, are given an objective counterpart in the guise of the 'ship of state' metaphor (later used by Orwell in 'Burnham's view of the contemporary world struggle', 1947), which, in turn, evokes the imagery used by survivors of the *Titanic* as they watched the vessel disappearing into the Atlantic. Lawrence Beesley, writing in his book *The Loss of the RMS* Titanic*: Its Story and Its Lessons* (1912), was one such witness:

> I had often wanted to see [the *Titanic*] from some distance away, and only a few hours before, in conversation at lunch with a fellow passenger, had registered a vow to get a proper view of her lines and dimensions when we landed at New York: to stand some distance away to take in a full view of her beautiful proportions, which the narrow approach to the dock at Southampton made impossible. Little did I think that the opportunity was to be found so quickly and so dramatically. The background, too, was a different one from what I had planned for her: the black outline of her profile against the sky was bordered all round by stars studded in the sky, and all her funnels and masts were picked out in the same way: her bulk was seen where the stars were blotted out. And one other thing was different from expectation: the thing that ripped away from us instantly, as we saw it, all sense of the beauty of the night, the beauty of the ship's lines, and the beauty of her lights – and all these taken in themselves were intensely beautiful – that thing was the awful angle made by the level of the sea with the rows of porthole lights along her side in dotted lines, row above row. The sea level and the rows of lights should have been parallel – should never have met – and now they met at an angle inside the black hull of the ship (2013: 65-66).

Eva Hart, the seven-year-old survivor who saw the sinking from one of the lifeboats, painted a similar picture in a reminiscence first published in 1994:

> Slowly, very slowly, we could see the *Titanic* getting lower in the water. As the slope of the decks became even greater there was an increasing amount of noise, from the people still on board, from loose articles sliding along the decks and from

the boilers as they eventually tore loose from the ship's body and fell through the length of the hull. Then, for a short time, she seemed to hang almost vertically as if suspended from the sky with her stern clearly above the water. We all seemed to hold our breaths for what we knew would be the end of that fabulous liner that had been our home for just a few days. … The horror of seeing that incredible ship sink was unbelievable. One minute the ship was there with its lights still ablaze and illuminating the sea all around, and the next minute it was gone and the only light was from the stars. At the same time there was a great noise from the screams and cries of hundreds of people plunged into the penetratingly cold, icy, Atlantic with little hope of being saved (2014: 38-39).

Orwell does not mention the *Titanic* by name in *Keep the Aspidistra Flying*, but the language of a plummeting ship with its lights ablaze is so comparable to accounts like Beesley's and Hart's that the impression of a *Titanic* 'presence' in the novel, given Orwell's emphasis on a sinking ship as the sign of civilisation's hubris, is hard to resist.

Two other 1930s texts by Orwell, *The Road to Wigan Pier* and *Coming Up For Air*, contain passages seemingly written within the affective scope of a pair of other widely reported features of the disaster: the view that the ship was an 'unsinkable' testament not only to scientific progress but also to the upper-class passengers – and by extension the upper classes more generally – who supposedly deserved more than anyone else to survive its destruction; and the fact that surviving the sinking was, for some on board, a matter of taking from others the opportunity to live. Both emphases come together in the testimony of First-Class passenger Ella White, who insisted in response to Senator Smith's questioning that two of the men who came with her on lifeboat 8, the second to leave the ship, gained entry to it under false pretences. Posing as able seamen, so she recalled, they were, in fact, 'dining-room stewards' with little rowing experience who came aboard at the expense of the 'magnificent fellows' left on *Titanic* who would have been 'such a protection' to her and everyone else in the lifeboat (see Davie 2012: 233).

I never saw a finer body of men in my life than the men passengers on this trip – athletes and men of sense – and if they had been permitted to enter these lifeboats with their families the boats would have been appropriately manned and many more lives saved, instead of allowing the stewards to get into the boats and save their lives, under the pretense that they could row, when they knew nothing about it (ibid: 239).[9]

The 'manning' of the lifeboats comes down to a question of 'appropriateness', and with it some very hard judgements about who does and who does not deserve to survive.

Orwell's most explicitly class-focused book, *The Road to Wigan Pier*, ends with a series of reflections on the thin 'line of cleavage' in capitalism between 'exploiter and exploited'. For Orwell, the 'essential point' was that 'all people with small, insecure incomes are *in the same boat* and ought to be fighting on the same side', a group in which he put not only 'manual labourers' and 'the navvy and the factory-hand', but also 'the clerk, the engineer, the commercial traveller, the middle-class man who has "come down in the world", the village grocer, the lower-grade civil servant and all other doubtful cases' who seemed to be 'the robbed' rather than 'the robbers' (Orwell 1989b: 211, emphasis added). Orwell was addressing himself to those socialists who engaged in what he called 'rather meaningless and mechanical bourgeois-baiting' (ibid: 212), by which he meant forms of criticism and ridicule that allowed 'minor issue[s]', such as the question of differences in manners between bank clerks and dock labourers, to block 'a major one' (ibid: 212-13) – namely, the risk of 'large sections of the middle class' making 'a sudden and violent swing to the Right' (ibid: 214) and into the waiting arms of fascism. Orwell argued the point as follows:

> Economically, I am in the same boat with the miner, the navvy and the farmhand; remind me of that and I will fight at their side. But culturally I am different from the miner, the navvy and the farmhand; lay the emphasis on that and you may arm me against them. If I were a solitary anomaly I should not matter, but what is true of myself is true of countless others. Every bank clerk dreaming of the sack, every shopkeeper teetering on the brink of bankruptcy, is in essentially the same position. These are the sinking middle class, and most of them are clinging to their gentility under the impression that it keeps them afloat. It is not good policy to *start* by telling them to throw away the life-belt (ibid: 213, italics in the original).

Orwell's account of class injustice differs from Ella White's even as it describes a similarly thin 'line of cleavage' between the exploiters and the exploited. On the one hand, the line between the impoverished proletariat and the penniless bourgeoisie – those who work with 'a pick-axe' and those who work with 'a fountain pen' (ibid: 213) – even though 'the interests of all exploited people are the same' (ibid: 214). On the other, the line between a first-class passenger who saw 'athletes and men of sense' as more fit to survive a human tragedy than the 'uncivilised' crewmen who in her view should have drowned.

NATHAN WADDELL

Orwell reconsiders the zero-sum aspect of sinking ship scenarios in *Coming Up For Air*, which deploys similar imagery to address the different but related question of a nation turning itself into a fascist state in the very attempt to resist the fascist menace. In Part III of the novel, the protagonist, George Bowling, attends a lecture on 'The menace of fascism' delivered by a speaker whose oratory seems made up of precisely the shop-worn phrases that Orwell bemoaned in 'Politics and the English language' (1946): the sort of talk that's 'just like a gramophone. Turn the handle, press the button and it starts' (Orwell 1990b: 153). The people who will 'turn out on a winter night to listen to a lecture of this kind' are, Bowling asserts, 'the outposts of an enormous army': 'the long-sighted ones, the first rats to spot that the ship is sinking'; those who are ready to smash others to avoid being smashed themselves; those who are so 'terrified of the future' that they will jump 'straight into it like a rabbit diving down a boa-constrictor's throat' (ibid: 157-158).[10] The idea has already been signalled in *Coming Up For Air* in Bowling's reflections on 'the realities of modern life', whose chief characteristic, he insists, is 'an everlasting, frantic struggle to sell things'. Bowling contends that, in most instances, this market impulse takes the form of people selling themselves in ways that deny others the opportunity to do so (such as successfully competing for a job). 'It's brought a peculiar, ghastly feeling into life,' he insists. 'It's like on a sinking ship when there are nineteen survivors and fourteen lifebelts' (ibid: 132). Both instances – the anti-fascists whose activities turn them into what they affect to despise; the capitalist subjects who spend their lives competing for ever-dwindling prospects – highlight the logics that keep people opposed to each other in situations where co-operation would serve them better than rivalry.[11]

PLUMMETING VESSELS

We should not discount the possibility that the maritime emphases of Orwell's inter-war texts derive from other, more contemporaneous sources. Bernard Crick points out that 'there is no way of knowing what frame of mind [Orwell] was in or quite what burden, if any, he thought he was carrying' (1992: 141) when, in 1922, he went on the month-long voyage from England to Burma aboard the *SS Herefordshire*, which took him to his five-year career as an imperial policeman. Nevertheless, it is not unreasonable to assume that Orwell had at least some opportunity to think about sinking ships on the way over. A literary source may have been Conrad, whose novels Orwell knew intimately. He particularly admired *Lord Jim* (1900), a novel that has found its own *Titanic*-related afterlife in Wilson's *How to Survive the Titanic: Or: the Sinking of J. Bruce Ismay* (2011), which traces connections between Ismay's life and Jim's.

In his 1945 review of Conrad's *The Nigger of the Narcissus* (1897), *Typhoon* (1902) and *The Shadow Line* (1917), Orwell deemed the passages in *Lord Jim* dealing with Jim's abandoning of the *Patna*, a passenger ship which *doesn't* sink, particularly 'brilliant' (Orwell 2001: 191).[12] Given the Conradian flavour of much of Orwell's early fiction, it's likely that his precarious boats and sinking ships derive at least in part from the Polish-born novelist's work. There are, nevertheless, some uncanny connections between *Keep the Aspidistra Flying*, *The Road to Wigan Pier*, and *Coming Up For Air* and the 1912 *Titanic* sinking, an event which, according to the perspective of 'My country right or left', had such a lasting impact on him.

Nineteen Eighty-Four contains the clearest evidence of this stimulus. Filled with references to water and liquidity, the novel is in any case one of the most 'aqueous' that Orwell produced. Hearts turn to 'ice' and bellies to 'water' on more than one occasion and small details like the fact that the novel begins in the same month as the sinking, April – 'a cruel month for some', Graham Nelson quips in his discussion of *Titanic* and T.S. Eliot (1997: 356) – make the connection seem tantalisingly palpable even though the details themselves can be shown to have other explanations (see Orwell 1992: 104, 115, 118).[13] It's tempting to speculate that Orwell may have had in mind the wartime sinking of the *Titanic*'s sister-ship, the HMHS *Britannic*, when he incorporated into Goldstein's Book the claim that war 'is a way of shattering to pieces, or pouring into the stratosphere, or *sinking into the depths of the sea*, materials which might otherwise be used to make the masses too comfortable, and hence, in the long run, too intelligent' (ibid: 198-9, emphasis added). But then again this passage could just as easily have been about the *Titanic* itself, or about any of the many wartime 'sinkings at sea' (Orwell 2002c: 112) that occurred during World War Two.[14] Moreover, by the time he finished *Nineteen Eighty-Four*, Orwell had also come to know what it means to lose control of a seacraft and nearly to drown. On 19 August 1947, while entertaining visitors on Jura, he lost control of a small boat in the Corryvreckan whirlpool and put all aboard in life-threatening danger. No one died, even though the turbulent water capsized the boat. He thought everyone was doomed (see Meyers 2000: 271-273).

Orwell's near-death experience surely determined at least some of *Nineteen Eighty-Four*'s fixation on watery death: the dreamy image of Winston Smith's mother 'drowning' in a 'sunken ship' (Orwell 1992: 171), for example, or the occurrence of 'drowning' in the list of 'worst thing[s] in the world' (ibid: 296) that O'Brien announces to Winston before his torture in Room 101. As a metaphor, drowning structures many other dynamics in the novel, too, among them the roar of crowds, the overwhelming of consciousness by rhythmic noise and the destruction of memory. Drowning becomes political in the war film that Winston watches at 'the flicks' on the evening before the novel begins: a 'very good one of a ship full of refugees being bombed somewhere in the Mediterranean'. One of the refugees, 'a great huge fat man', sinks after being shot to pieces by a military helicopter. Seconds later, a child's arm goes 'up up up right up into the air' having been explosively detached from its torso by the bomb dropped on it by the helicopter, or maybe in a gesture of panicked appeal as the child slips under the waves (ibid: 10). In this sequence, drowning marks the link between the human victims of Oceania's xenophobic intolerance and the voyeuristic protocols that sustain its operations, in which the spectacle of violent death is little more than light entertainment for the masses.

Lyndsey Stonebridge has pointed out that the 'vulnerability of the drowning refugees opens up a narrative path to Winston's own vulnerability and so, many have argued, to his nascent humanity' (2018: 75). She continues in her analysis by insisting that the Jewishness of the refugees is 'central to the novel's political moralism', because it bears out how carefully Orwell understood totalitarianism to draw on nationalism and colonialism (ibid). This seems absolutely right to me, yet the scene, nevertheless, draws much of its impact from a wider pattern of imagery in *Nineteen Eighty-Four* concerning the desperation of people drowning at sea and facing imminent death aboard sinking seacraft. Bombed and shot at, the refugees will do anything to survive. The desperation of the refugees – a boy and a woman 'screaming' and 'blue' with fright – simultaneously evokes Winston's opinions and the distress of the 'mob' of several hundred proletarian women he remembers 'crowding round the stalls of a street market, with faces as tragic as though they had been the doomed passengers on a sinking ship' (Orwell 1992: 73). These women belong to a 'submerged and despised class' (ibid: 68) of humanity, the submerged tenth, with only one way to go. Unlike the thought that bursts into Winston's mind 'like a lump of submerged wreckage breaking the surface of water' (ibid: 291), the proles are destined to stay 'in the forests of the sea bottom' (ibid: 28) without escape.

So too, it seems, are Winston's mother and sister, who haunt his imagination as an interruptive symptom of an originating trauma. The burden Winston must bear is an intense guilt that comes from betrayal. He remembers a time long ago when he was given chocolate by his mother, who also gave some to his sister. In a moment of greed, Winston snatched the chocolate from his sister's hand and ran away. When he returned, satiated, his mother and his sister had disappeared, never to be seen again. The likelihood is that they were sent to a labour camp, or killed. Re-animated in Winston's dreams, they come back to him in later life as otherworldly figures 'sitting in some place deep down beneath him', the denizens of a 'subterranean' world; at 'the bottom of a well, for instance, or a very deep grave', or perhaps in 'the saloon of a sinking ship, looking up at him through the darkening water' (ibid: 31).[15] At one point, Winston associates the dream with the same 'enveloping, protecting gesture of the arm' (ibid: 171) he sees made by the Jewish refugee woman who tries to protect the screaming little boy on the Mediterranean boat by 'putting her arms round him and comforting him' (ibid: 10).

Discussing this association, Douglas Kerr carefully positions the image of Winston's mother embracing his sister and the Jewish refugee embracing the little boy as shared components of a 'Madonna-and-child' motif, one that functions throughout *Nineteen Eighty-Four* as the focus for an 'extraordinarily rich and suggestive cluster of feelings':

> … the mother's self-sacrifice and her brave if useless attempt to shield her child, the child's cruelty and betrayal in one instance, and helplessness in another, and always looming over the group the menacing presence of authority and violence bent on the destruction of human feeling and natural relations (2022: 109).

But if we focus on Winston's memory of his mother and sister looking up at him from 'the *saloon* of a sinking ship', another 'menacing presence' from *Titanic* lore comes into view – namely, the horrifying thought that those inside the ship as it sank into the Atlantic may have had a brief, terrifying experience of the sinking from within trapped interior pockets of air. The depths and pressures involved made this impossible. Anyone carried down with the sinking *Titanic* would have died soon into its journey to its resting place on the seafloor (nearly two and a half miles below the water line), not only due to the rapid escape of air from within the ship as it filled with seawater but also because of uncontrolled decompression during its descent.[16] Yet the dreadful thought of trapped survivors persists in *Nineteen Eighty-Four*, perhaps, in Winston's traumatised impression of his mother and sister, who – within the logic of a dream – are still alive and breathing inside a sinking ship's saloon (Orwell 1992: 31-32).[17]

Orwell did not itemise the 'long list of horrors' that are mentioned in 'My country right or left'. However, among them may well have been the fact that as the evacuation of the *Titanic* gathered pace, it increasingly became what Thomas Mann, in *The Magic Mountain*, called a situation in which people were flung 'back upon primitive conditions and fears' (1960 [1927]: 690). It transformed the *Titanic* into a zone of terrified self-preservation and alarm. And just as the passengers on the ship in its last moments afloat found themselves doing whatever they could to survive, so too does Winston find himself in a similar predicament under conditions of unparalleled duress in Room 101 – an instinct to survival described by O'Brien as a desire no more cowardly than coming up from 'deep water' (Orwell 1992: 297) and filling your lungs with air. We are in the realm of Winston's suspicion that 'on the battlefield, in the torture chamber, *on a sinking ship*, the issues that you are fighting for are always forgotten, because the body swells up until it fills the universe' (ibid: 106, emphasis added). But coming up for air, in Winston's case, means pushing someone else underwater – namely Julia, the woman he loves and must betray if he is to endure.

Peter Conrad has glossed Mann's insight into the final moments of the *Titanic* as a testament to the ease with which 'people who are buoyed up by their mechanical comforts and their confidence in a mechanistic world' can degenerate 'into a scrambling mob. Respect for the rights of others is a luxury which the drowning man cannot afford. Fear simplifies his ideas: the need to save your own life makes life itself the supreme imperative' (1998: 373). This describes Winston's experience in Room 101 almost exactly. As O'Brien moves the cage filled with rats closer to Winston's face, terror sets in:

> Winston heard a succession of shrill cries which appeared to be occurring in the air above his head. But he thought furiously against his panic. To think, to think, even with a split second left – to think was the only hope. Suddenly the foul musty odour of the brutes struck his nostrils. There was a violent convulsion of nausea inside him, and he almost lost consciousness. Everything had gone black. For an instant he was insane, a screaming animal. Yet he came out of the blackness clutching an idea. There was one and only one way to save himself. He must interpose another human being, the *body* of another human being, between himself and the rats (Orwell 1992: 299).

And so it proves. Winston gives up Julia, thereby saving himself. But saving himself means transferring the threat of his punishment to the person he loves, which in turn annihilates the saving principle of love on which his rebellion has been based. As he shouts: 'Do it to Julia!' the world collapses. Echoing the fate of a passenger going down with a ship, Winston falls backwards 'into enormous depths, … through the floor, through the walls of the building, through the earth, through the oceans' (ibid: 300).

THE *TITANIC* 'PRESENCE'

Such details indicate how *Nineteen Eighty-Four* can be constructed as an illustrative case of what seems like a traumatic fixation on the *Titanic* disaster. Like his writings of the inter-war period, it is possible to find in *Nineteen Eighty-Four* a response to the sinking not through direct reference but by means of the arms-length strategies of resonant allusions, images and similes. We may also say that in that very distance, counter-intuitively, is a kind of intimacy: the exceptional event, vicariously experienced yet intimately felt, has become a form of shorthand, thereby bringing its trauma under narrative control even as it signals the lingering psychological effects on the disturbed mind. Orwell seems never to have quite recovered from hearing about the loss of the *Titanic*, a 'petty' disaster that shocked a young boy, just as it shocked the whole world, into never quite letting go of its horrors. While my claim in this paper has been that the force of that shock persisted into Orwell's fiction of the 1930s and 1940s, there is a chance, too, that it was present in much more that he wrote, contributing in its buried terror to the very terms of his textual engagement (literary, essayistic, journalistic) with his times. It would make perfect sense for the loss of the *Titanic*, constructed in the aftermath of the sinking as a terrible point scored against a naïve trust in mechanical perfectibility, to have struck a chord with the Orwell who wrote so widely and sceptically about 'the man of the machine' – a figure who travesties the ideals of a figure such as Matthew Arnold by offering 'sweetness and light' in the glitter of polished, promising steel (see Orwell 2002a: 191).

Orwell can in this sense be considered part of a much broader tradition of *Titanic* reimagining. 'It has been the fate of those who perished,' writes Foster, 'to have become members of a cast of legend, to have died and then in the imagination of following generations to have died and died again' (1997: 12). There is evidence to suggest that Orwell restaged in his fiction the death of those who died in the *Titanic* disaster as a personal working-through of trauma and as a kind of narrative monumentalisation. As someone not directly or even marginally involved in the sinking, Orwell was not working with or against the strategy of 'forced forgetting', 'the conscious or unconscious suppression of memories', identified by Andrew Wilson as one of the coping mechanisms many of the *Titanic*'s survivors had to employ in order to survive their pain (2011: 5). Instead, the *Titanic* dead die again in Orwell's writing: for his sake as a distant observer and for a world that had paid inadequate heed to the ideological and scientific origins of their deaths – one that hadn't learned not to worship the machine and which was heading, through a different but related process of mechanisation, into totalitarianism. Orwell made the victims of the *Titanic* along with the victims of many other sinkings – think about those refugees on their boat in *Nineteen Eighty-Four* – resonate with a world that was quickly forgetting the progress-obsessed ideology that killed them, just as the leviathanic industry of *Titanic*-related memoirs, historical studies and conspiracy theories – which took off in the 1950s and has hardly paused ever since – was starting to gather pace.

In *Down with the Old Canoe* (2012), Steven Biel writes that the *Titanic* disaster 'has stimulated imaginative forms of engagement with present and past and performed significant … cultural work. For many people and for many reasons, the memory of the disaster has seemed worth possessing' (2012: 234). I have suggested here that Orwell possessed a memory of the *Titanic* as technique (the older writer turning mass death, its hubristic causes and its devastating repercussions into literary form) having first experienced it as trauma (the nine-year-old boy shocked by foreseeable and avoidable yet unavoided mass suffering). This accords with established strategies for identifying the *Titanic*'s presence in twentieth-century literary history. Foster, writing about similar uncertainties in Woolf's apparently allusive response to the sinking, insists that her 'concern with submergence and the subaqueous seems to have been reinforced if not inspired by *Titanic*'s fate' (2002: 112). Orwell's concern with sinking ships and drowning people could in principle be reduced to the same kind of reinforcement. The dull, sinking pain that troubles Winston's stomach in *Nineteen Eighty-Four* may well have its roots here. It seems that putting the *Titanic* down on paper in some measure helped Orwell to work through the disquieting 'sensation' in the belly which never quite left him. To the extent that literary critics and cultural historians still pore over seemingly encoded responses to the *Titanic*, it appears that this sinking feeling hasn't quite left us, either.

- The author wishes to thank Douglas Kerr, Darcy Moore and Richard Lance Keeble for their very helpful comments on earlier versions of this essay. He remains entirely responsible for the final version.

NOTES

[1] See Paul Heyer's claim: 'Assessing the mythic connotations of the *Titanic* disaster requires that we go beyond any attempt to objectively ascertain what exactly happened (that would be history)' (2012: 183). John Welshman offers a corrective: '… in the recent emphasis on myth,' in accounts of the *Titanic* disaster, 'the focus on individual passengers and crew members, and their stories, [has] been lost' (2012: 6).

[2] Cf. Davie: 'Lightoller had ordered the [ship's] lookouts to keep a special eye out for ice; Captain Smith had ordered an alteration of course to the south of the regular shipping lane; both actions showed that danger was foreseen. If danger was foreseen, it was not unforeseeable' (2012: 270).

[3] Later research into the sinking has generated a more precise understanding of the ship's final moments. As the ship started to separate, 'the bow took a sudden cant forward. This then pulled the stern higher out of the water to an angle of perhaps 30° before it started to settle back. This occurred about 2.17a.m. ATS [apparent time on ship], when all the electric lights suddenly went out as the ship

was seen to break in two. After first returning to a near horizontal position, the forward part of the remaining stern section started to flood very rapidly causing the poop to rise up to a relatively steep angle before it started to slip forward' (Halpern et al. 2011: 281; a more detailed description of the ship's break-up can be found at pp 118-122). See also Fitch, Layton and Wormstedt (2015: 232-235)

[4] Later historians have conveyed similar sentiments. Fran Brearton writes that the sinking 'has acquired a significance out of all proportion either to the scale of the disaster, or to its economic and political effect on the British Empire' (2003: 174). See also Russell (2019: xviii)

[5] Contemporary accounts differ as to the exact sequence and nature of events with the sinking of the stern, but Young's version is indicative (cf. Fitch, Layton and Wormstedt 2015: 235). Of the ship's final moments, when the stern appeared 'upright like a column', the survivor Lawrence Beesley wrote: 'We could see her now only as the stern and some 150 feet of her stood outlined against the star-specked sky, looming black in the darkness, and in this position she continued for some minutes – I think as much as five minutes, but it may have been less. Then, first sinking back a little at the stern, I thought, she slid slowly forwards through the water and dived slantingly down; the sea closed over her and we had seen the last of the beautiful ship on which we had embarked four days before at Southampton' (2013: 71)

[6] Réné-Noël Raimbault, writing in January 1934 to Orwell about his French translation of *Down and Out*, remarked that a footnote to 'Nearer, my God, to Thee' (mentioned in chapter XXXI of the book) was 'unnecessary', because the 'French, since the shipwreck of the *Titanic*, know what it means' (Orwell 2006: 41). Infamously, 'Nearer, my God, to Thee' was one of the hymns played by the *Titanic*'s band during the sinking (see Fitch, Layton and Wormstedt 2015: 302-305)

[7] See Howells (2012 [1999]: 2) and Gregson (2008). Orwell does not make the cut in Steven Biel's admittedly America-focused *Down with the Old Canoe: A Cultural History of the* Titanic (2012), nor does he appear in Foster (2002); Bergfelder and Street (eds) (2004) nor Heyer (2012). There is a glancing reference to Orwell in Anderson (2005: 402), which concerns Orwell's views on a novel by Ernest Raymond – who also wrote a play about the sinking called *The Berg* (1929)

[8] Two references to the *Titanic* in Orwell scholarship can be found in Crick (1992: 88) and in Bowker (2003: 39), though there may be others. See also Bracco (1993: 172)

[9] See also Fitch, Layton and Wormstedt (2015: 240)

[10] See also Orwell's review of *Union Now* (1939) by Clarence K. Streit, in which he raises the possibility that extended preparations for war might cause England to 'sink almost unresisting into some local variant of austro-fascism' (Orwell 2000: 361). Orwell recycles the image of the rabbit and the boa-constrictor in 'Second thoughts on James Burnham' (1946)

[11] There is a hint, too, in Bowling's simile of a sinking ship without an adequate quantity of safety provisions of the scandalous fact that the *Titanic* carried too few lifeboats. Cf. Davie: 'although there had been a shortage of lifeboats, there had been no shortage of lifebelts; the overwhelming majority of passengers and crew had been wearing them' (2012: 306-307). It simply was not possible, in a sinking with no large ships nearby to which evacuated passengers could be ferried, for all aboard the *Titanic* to leave it without getting into seawater. Due to the freezing cold, this proved fatal to almost everyone who did so. The survival time for those who remained in the -2.2°C water was forty-five minutes at most, with unconsciousness occurring in as little as fifteen minutes (Fitch, Layton and Wormstedt 2015: 238)

¹² Orwell wrote in this review that the *Patna* had been 'scuttled' (deliberately sunk) rather than abandoned, but corrected this in a subsequent letter to C.E. de Salis (29 June 1945)

¹³ In discussing Eliot's oft-quoted 'I had not thought death had undone so many', Foster suggests that it's 'easy to imagine an allusion also to the *Titanic* dead in that line' (2002: 234)

¹⁴ In his journalism, Orwell refers to the sinking of ships throughout World War Two

¹⁵ Patricia Rae, of Queen's University, Kingston, Ontario, Canada, has pointed out to me in private correspondence that this image evokes the imagery of Fred Spear's 'Enlist' poster, which shows a mother cradling a child as they drown. The poster appeared after the sinking of the RMS *Lusitania* in 1915 when it was torpedoed by a German U-Boat

¹⁶ See Foster (2002: 56-57), Fitch, Layton and Wormstedt (2015: 358) and Russell (2019: 254)

¹⁷ Orwell may also have emphasised the detail of the saloon because the spectacular luxury of the saloons on board the *Titanic* was one of the ship's most widely trumpeted features (see Davenport-Hines 2012: 24)

REFERENCES

A.I.B. (1912) Titanic Morality, *The Freewoman*, Vol. 24, No. 1, 2 May p. 477

Anderson, D. Brian (2005) *The Titanic in Print and on Screen: An Annotated Guide to Books, Films, Television Shows, and Other Media*, Jefferson, NC: McFarland

Anon. (1912a) The *Titanic* disaster, *The Times*, 16 April p. 9

Anon. (1912b) The *Titanic* disaster, *Manchester Guardian*, 16 April p. 8

Beesley, Lawrence (2013 [1912]) *The Loss of the* Titanic, Stroud: Amberley

Bergfelder, Tim and Street, Sarah (eds) (2004) *The Titanic in Myth and Memory: Representations in Visual and Literary Culture*, London: I.B. Tauris

Biel, Steven (2012 [1996]) *Down with the Old Canoe: A Cultural History of the* Titanic, New York: W.W. Norton

Biel, Steven (ed.) (1998) *Titanica: The Disaster of the Century in Poetry, Song, and Prose*, New York: W.W. Norton

Bowker, Gordon (2003) *George Orwell*, London: Little, Brown

Bracco, Rosa Maria (1993) *Merchants of Hope: British Middlebrow Writers and the First World War, 1919-1939*, Providence, RI: Berg

Brearton, Fran (2003) *The Great War in Irish Poetry: W.B. Yeats to Michael Longley*, Oxford: Oxford University Press

Conrad, Peter (1998) *Modern Times, Modern Places: Life and Art in the Twentieth Century*, London: Thames & Hudson

Crick, Bernard (1992) *George Orwell: A Life*, London: Penguin

Davenport-Hines, Richard (2012) Titanic *Lives: Migrants, Millionaires, Conmen, and Crew*, London: HarperCollins

Davie, Michael (2012) Titanic: *The Death and Life of a Legend*, New York: Vintage, updated edition

Esty, Jed (2004) *A Shrinking Island: Modernism and National Culture in England*, Princeton, NJ: Princeton University Press

Fitch, Tad, Layton, J. Kent and Wormstedt, Bill (2015) *On a Sea of Glass: The Life and Loss of the RMS* Titanic, Stroud: Amberley, third edition

Foster, John Wilson (1997) *The* Titanic *Complex*, Vancouver, BC: Belcouver

Foster, John Wilson (2002) *The Age of* Titanic: *Cross-Currents of Anglo-American Culture*, Dublin: Merlin

Foster, John Wilson (ed.) (2000) *The* Titanic *Reader*, New York: Penguin

Gregson, Sarah (2008) *Titanic* 'down under': Ideology, myth, and memorialization, *Social History*, Vol. 33, No. 3 pp 268-283

Halpern, Samuel et al. (2011) *Report into the Loss of the SS* Titanic: *A Centennial Reappraisal*, Stroud: History Press

Hart, Eva (2014 [1994]) *A Girl Aboard the* Titanic, as told to Ron Denney, Stroud: Amberley

Heyer, Paul (2012) Titanic *Century: Media, Myth, and the Making of a Cultural Icon*, Santa Barbara, CA: Praeger

Howells, Richard (2012 [1999]) *The Myth of the* Titanic, Basingstoke: Palgrave Macmillan

Kerr, Douglas (2022) *Orwell & Empire*, Oxford: Oxford University Press

Lord, Walter (2012 [1956]) *A Night to Remember*, introd. Brian Lavery, London: Penguin

Mann, Thomas (1960 [1924]) *The Magic Mountain*, trans. by Lowe-Porter, H. T., London: Everyman

Meyers, Jeffrey (2000) *Orwell: Wintry Conscience of a Generation*, New York: W.W. Norton

Nelson, Graham (1997) *The Waste Land* drafts, 'The engine', and the sinking of the *Titanic*, *Notes and Queries*, Vol. 44, No. 3 pp 356-358

Orwell, George (1989a [1936]) *Keep the Aspidistra Flying*, Davison, Peter (ed.) London: Secker & Warburg

Orwell, George (1989b [1937]) *The Road to Wigan Pier*, Davison, Peter (ed.) London: Secker & Warburg

Orwell, George (1990a [1935]) *A Clergyman's Daughter*, Davison, Peter (ed.) London: Secker & Warburg

Orwell, George (1990b [1939]) *Coming Up For Air*, Davison, Peter (ed.) London: Secker & Warburg

Orwell, George (1992 [1949]) *Nineteen Eighty-Four*, Davison, Peter (ed.) London: Secker & Warburg

Orwell, George (2000) *The Complete Works of George Orwell: Facing Unpleasant Facts, 1937-1939, Vol. XI*, Davison, Peter with Angus, Ian and Davison, Sheila (eds) London: Secker & Warburg, revised edition

Orwell, George (2001) *The Complete Works of George Orwell: I Belong to the Left, 1945, Vol. XVII,* Davison, Peter with Angus, Ian and Davison, Sheila (eds) London: Secker & Warburg, revised edition

Orwell, George (2002a) *The Complete Works of George Orwell: A Patriot After All, 1940-1941, Vol. XII*, Davison Peter with Angus, Ian and Davison, Sheila (eds) London: Secker & Warburg, revised edition

Orwell, George (2002b) *The Complete Works of George Orwell: It is What I Think, 1947-1948, Vol. XIX*, Davison, Peter with Angus, Ian and Davison, Sheila (eds) London: Secker & Warburg, revised edition

Orwell, George (2002c) *The Complete Works of George Orwell: Our Job is to Make Life Worth Living, 1949-1950, Vol. XX*, Davison, Peter with Angus, Ian and Davison, Sheila (eds) London: Secker & Warburg, revised edition

Orwell, George (2003 [1938]) *Homage to Catalonia*, Davison, Peter (ed.) London: Penguin

Orwell, George (2006) *The Lost Orwell*, Davison, Peter (ed.) London: Timewell Press

Orwell, George (2009 [1934]) *Burmese Days*, Davison, Peter (ed.) London: Penguin

Orwell, George (2021 [1938]) *Homage to Catalonia*, Mullen, Lisa (ed.) Oxford: Oxford University Press

Russell, Gareth (2019) *The Ship of Dreams: The Sinking of the* Titanic *and the End of the Edwardian Era*, New York: Atria

Stonebridge, Lyndsey (2018) *Placeless People: Writing, Rights, and Refugees*, Oxford: Oxford University Press

Welshman, John (2012) Titanic*: The Last Night of a Small Town*, Oxford: Oxford University Press

Wilson, Andrew (2011) *Shadow of the* Titanic*: The Extraordinary Stories of Those Who Survived*, London: Simon & Schuster

Wilson, Frances (2012) *How to Survive the* Titanic*: or, the Sinking of J. Bruce Ismay*, New York: Bloomsbury

Womack, Kenneth (2004) Reading the *Titanic*: Contemporary literary representations of the ship of dreams, Bergfelder, Tim and Street, Sarah (eds) *The* Titanic *in Myth and Memory: Representations in Visual and Literary Culture*, London: I.B. Tauris pp 85-93

Womack, Kenneth and Bergfelder, Tim (2003) Titanica: An introduction, *Interdisciplinary Literary Studies*, Vol. 5, No. 1 pp 1-3

NOTE ON THE CONTRIBUTOR

Nathan Waddell is a Professor of Twentieth-Century Literature at the University of Birmingham, UK, where he works in the Department of English Literature. He is the editor of *The Cambridge Companion to Nineteen Eighty-Four* (Cambridge University Press, 2020) and the Oxford World's Classics edition of Orwell's *A Clergyman's Daughter* (Oxford University Press, 2021). His creative counter- or quasi-biography of Orwell, *A Bright Cold Day*, is due out from Oneworld in 2025, as is his edited collection, *The Oxford Handbook of George Orwell* (Oxford University Press).

Modernism, Realism and 'Natural Narrative': Contrasting 'A Hanging' and 'Shooting an Elephant'

CRIS YELLAND

This paper argues that Orwell's essays 'A hanging' (1931) and 'Shooting an elephant' (1936), though usually treated as similar, are very differently written. The paper makes a close analysis of the language of both essays, in terms of their pronominal use, their syntax and their structure. It argues that the structure of 'Shooting an elephant' is a clear example of a recounting of personal experience, what William Labov later analysed as 'natural narrative', whereas 'A hanging' shares some of the same structural features, but is a dysfunctional natural narrative, with a traumatised 'unreliable' narrator. The earlier essay is a modernist piece of writing, the later one not so. The differences between the two make them important stages in Orwell's complicated journey away from experimental modernism towards the documentary realism which is typical of 1930s writing.

Key words: Orwell, 'natural narrative', modernism, 'A hanging', 'Shooting an elephant'

ORWELL AND THE NEW WRITING OF THE 1930S

Orwell's 'Inside the whale' (1970 [1940]) is a wide-ranging essay; one of the topics it deals with is literary history and a change from experimental writing to realism: 'But quite suddenly, in the years 1930-1935, something happens. The literary climate changes. A new group of writers, Auden and Spender and the rest of them, has made its appearance ... Still, it is broadly true that in the twenties the literary emphasis was more on technique and less on subject matter than it is now' (ibid: 559-560). Orwell was not alone in pointing out this contrast; he cites Louis MacNeice's *Modern Poetry* (1938) as a source and also Cyril Connolly's *Enemies of Promise* of the same year. Connolly classified Orwell as a writer of the 'New Vernacular' school, along with Hemingway and Isherwood, and even carried out the odd experiment of knitting a paragraph together out of *The Road to Wigan Pier*, *To Have and Have Not* and *Goodbye to Berlin* to try to show that the three writers were so alike that you could not see where one ended and another began (Connolly 1988 [1938]: 70-82).

There is a more recent development of the same historical taxonomy in David Lodge's model of modernism (which he associates with the period 1910-1930) and 'anti-modernism' (which might also be called 'realism' and is associated with the 1930s). Lodge had an early version of this model in *Language of Fiction* (2002 [1966]), developed it in *The Modes of Modern Writing* (2015 [1977]) and again in *Working with Structuralism* (1981). In Lodge's account, modernist writing is concerned with questions of how things are represented and tends towards formal experimentation and difficulty. Classic modernist texts include T.S. Eliot's 'The waste land' (1922), James Joyce's *Ulysses* (1922) and Virginia Woolf's *Mrs Dalloway* (1925). 'Antimodernist' writing, on the other hand, characteristic of the 1930s, regards formal experiment as frivolous or elitist and holds that writing can and should describe the real as directly as possible. Like Connolly, Lodge has no doubt about where Orwell belongs in this taxonomy. He cites *The Road to Wigan Pier* as an example of typical 1930s writing, and also quotes from 'Politics and the English language' of 1946: 'Let the meaning choose the word, rather than the other way round' (Orwell 1970 4 [1946]: 30) and from his essay, 'Why I write': 'Good prose is like a window pane' (Orwell 1970 I [1946] Both are strongly, even naively, 'realist' things to say. It is not so much a theory of language and representation as an antitheory. So there is Orwell, captaining Lodge's team of antimodernists. But that is not in fact what Orwell does in 'Inside the whale'. Much of the essay is taken up with enthusiasm for the bible of modernist fiction, Joyce's *Ulysses*, and it is notably unconvinced by the new realist school, in part because the new writers were so connected to Soviet communism. Orwell's position in the shift from modernism to realism was more complicated than Lodge (or Connolly) would allow, and his writing is harder to categorise. Vincent Sherry (1987) and more recently Douglas Kerr (Kerr 2022b) argue for the importance of Orwell's admiration of T.S. Eliot as a poet though not as a political thinker. Kristin Bluemel argues that Orwell's closeness to Stevie Smith, Inez Holden and Mulk Raj Anand in wartime London constitutes a kind of 'intermodernism', or modernism by association (Bluemel 2004). Patricia Rae argues that Orwell's confused and disillusioned narrator in *Homage to Catalonia* (1937) is a modernist device (Rae 2009). Keith Alldritt, in *The Making of George Orwell*, argues that although his reputation is based on realism he went through a development period of modernist influence, and that 'A hanging' is an example of Orwell's early manner (Alldritt 1969: 97-102).

In a more recent study, *Or Orwell*, which contains the longest discussion of 'A hanging' yet published, Alex Woloch suggests the essay is 'an assertion of mediating form … a text that calls attention to its own elusiveness and unreliability … [and] foregrounds the contingent nature of the narrator's observation …' He adds: This is another trick, then, that the text plays on the reader' (Woloch 2016: 71-79). Woloch does not use the term 'modernism' about 'A hanging' – but he clearly places the essay a long way from straightforward documentary realism. Douglas Kerr (Kerr 2022a:159) argues that Orwell's reputation as a straightforwardly realist writer is overstated. Roger Fowler places Orwell in the shadow of modernist writers of the 1920s, arguing: 'In the 1930s, Orwell made his experiments with *avant-garde* techniques, and was not comfortable with them' (Fowler 1995: 7). Orwell's journey away from modernism was not a road-to-Damascus moment, rather an uneven process over time. That is what I want to explore in 'A hanging' and 'Shooting an elephant'.

ARE 'A HANGING' AND 'SHOOTING AN ELEPHANT' TWO OF A KIND?

Both essays are examples of what Lodge calls 'historical' writing: 'Thirties writing tended to model itself on historical kinds of discourse – the autobiography, the eye-witness account, the travel log' (Lodge 1981: 8). Both pieces offer themselves as eye-witness accounts, and both pieces are almost invariably treated together, as essentially similar. When they were first published in book form, in *Shooting an Elephant and Other Essays* (1950), Christopher Sykes and Edmund Wilson treated them together (Meyers 1975: 9-10). Seventy-four years later, they are still together in the *Guardian*, as 'two peerless eyewitness essays' (Adams 2024). Even when a writer is sceptical about Orwell's credentials as an anti-imperialist, the two essays make their joint appearance: 'two of Orwell's best essays, "A hanging" and "Shooting an elephant" draw directly on his time in Burma' (Kumar 2022). Orwell's biographers also tend to put the two essays together. Peter Stansky and William Abrahams have them as 'the two essays drawn from his police experience' and 'the two Burmese pieces mixing reportage and reflection' (Stansky and Abrahams 1974: 157 and 177); Bernard Crick describes both pieces as 'documentary short story' (Crick 1982: 186); Jeffrey Meyers has 'these autobiographical, confessional pieces' (Meyers 2000: 69); D.J. Taylor treats the two together as 'two of his finest sketches' (Taylor 2023: 99); John Sutherland describes 'A hanging' as 'one of the two very fine articles to come out of his Burmese service' (Sutherland 2017: 100) while Douglas Kerr connects the two pieces at least eight times (Kerr 2022a).

CRIS YELLAND

In literary-critical writing as well as in biography, the same approach appears. Chapters in *The Cambridge Companion to George Orwell* see the two essays as so similar they can be treated together. John Rossi and John Rodden have 'his essays about his job as a policeman … his best writing about Burma' (Rossi and Rodden 2007: 2); William Cain talks of 'such classics' as 'A hanging' and 'Shooting an elephant' (Cain 2007: 77) while John Rossi highlights 'some of his best writing' such as the essays 'A hanging' and 'Shooting an elephant' (Rossi and Rodden 2007: 88). Where there has been disagreement it has focused less on how the essays are written than on questions of 'authenticity', about whether Orwell actually did shoot an elephant or witness a hanging, or about which details belonged to Orwell's experience, and which he found in other writing (Biederstadt 2022). Recent research has established that Orwell did shoot an elephant (Meyers 2022) and that, although his job did not involve being present at hangings, being sent to watch one was an initiation trial for young policemen, to see whether they were tough enough (Taylor 2023: 99).

The critical consensus that the two essays are similar seems overwhelming, and it may seem perverse to argue against it. But that is what I want to argue here: that "A hanging" and "Shooting an elephant" are very differently written because they belong to different stages in Orwell's development as a writer.

Let me begin with a simple, but I think startling, observation about the way the two essays are written; it is about the pronoun 'I'. This is, of course, the basic pronoun for authentic writing based on personal experience and one would expect to see it used frequently in both essays. 'Shooting an elephant' is an authentic, vivid narrative of personal experience, and its narrator uses 'I' 111 times. There are 29 uses of 'me' and 16 uses of 'my' as well. 'A hanging' is also an authentic, vivid narrative of personal experience, but its counts are startlingly different: the narrator uses 'I' only seven times, with only one 'me' and one 'my'. These two essays, then, have different approaches to narrating personal experience and very different narrators. The narrator of 'Shooting an elephant' is an informative, occasionally humorous persona who can describe things vividly and explain what they mean; hence the insistent presence of that confident and confiding 'I'. The narrator of 'A hanging' has a much more problematic relationship with his own experience, even such a guilty one that he seems to want to efface his presence at the event which he is compelled to narrate.

'SHOOTING AN ELEPHANT' AS A NATURAL NARRATIVE

Of the two essays, it is 'Shooting an elephant' which has achieved a special status as standard reading for courses about how to write essays of personal experience, as John Rodden has made clear

(Rodden 1989: 390-393; Rodden 1991: 503-530). The essay is so much a model of good practice that by 1999 it had been anthologised 565 times (Bloom 1999: 401-430) and a quarter of a century on, that count will probably need to be increased. One reason for the popularity and canonical status of 'Shooting an elephant', why it seems to be such a good rendition of experience, is that it corresponds completely with our intuitive sense of how a story of personal experience will be structured, what William Labov called a 'natural narrative'. The term comes from Labov's study of spoken language, especially of 'Black English vernacular', the sociolect spoken by young African-Americans in Harlem. In the course of his research, Labov recorded and collected stories from a wider range of respondents too: 'The narratives that we have obtained … form a large body of data on comparative verbal skills, ranging across age levels, classes, and ethnic groups' (Labov 1972: 355). Labov noticed that these stories, which he called 'natural narratives', tended to resemble each other in structure; he described the structure like this:

(i) Abstract. This is a short statement which gives the overall theme of the story.

(ii) Orientation. This is scene-setting, about people, places or situations which form the background to the story.

(iii) Complicating Action. What happened? This often begins with a phrase like 'One day …' or 'This one time …'. It leads into an account of sequences of actions, usually in the past simple tense.

(iv) Evaluation. At a crisis-point in the action, the sequence of events is paused and the narrator talks about what the events meant and thus why the story is being told. Labov also discusses 'evaluation' as a function of narrative as well as a component of it. Evaluation can occur in a story immediately before the concluding action, but can also be expressed throughout it.

(v) Concluding Action. What happened next? This brings the events to a resolution.

(vi) Coda. This marks the end of the story, often with a shift to the present time of the narration rather than the past time of the events narrated.

It may seem anti-historical to consider Orwell's writing in the 1930s in terms of Labov's model from the 1970s. But the model is relevant because many readers (and hearers) of stories have an intuitive idea of the form which a story of personal experience is likely to take (Graddol, Cheshire and Swann 1996: 231). Labov's list of functions, scene-setting, saying what happened, saying why

CRIS YELLAND

it is important, saying what happened next and signalling that the story is finished, all sound familiar and common-sensical elements of stories. As Rob Pope puts it, 'natural narrative' is 'a schema that has been widely observed in many kinds of narrative, oral and otherwise' (Pope 1998: 211). Labov's model is still widely used for analysing stories of personal experience in therapeutic settings (Li et.al. 2020: 15-17; Kurtz 2014: 35-44). It has also been applied to literary texts, including those from well before 1972 (Pratt 1977: 38-78; Simpson 2004: 114-118, 200). Certainly, the different elements of 'natural narrative' are very clearly observable in 'Shooting an elephant'. We can analyse the piece in Labov's terms like this:

Abstract. The title.

Orientation. This is very clearly marked. The first two long opening paragraphs tell us a great deal about the narrator, his job, and the conflicting feelings he has about it. Note that the length and the relaxed, discursive quality of the orientation are two of the things which differentiate 'Shooting an elephant' from a newspaper report. Journalists are trained to 'front-load' stories, to give information about the what/who/where/when/why of an event in the first sentence or two. One example would be this, from the *Rangoon Gazette*, of 22 March 1926:

> Major E.C. Kenny, subdivisional officer, Yamethin, when on tour in the Tatkon township on 16 March 1926, came across a rogue elephant feeding in a plantation grove at Dayouk-ku village 5 miles east of Tatkon and brought it down to the delight of the villagers. The elephant had killed a villager and caused great havoc in the plantations. It is not known whether this is the elephant proclaimed by the Bombay Burma Trading Corporation (Davison 2017: 506).

As Peter Davison points out (ibid), there are similarities in detail here to 'Shooting an elephant'; but structurally the two pieces of writing are utterly different. Note, too, that although the orientation of 'Shooting an elephant' contains a lot of detail, it is clearly a preliminary to the story proper. This is because the narrator is narrating iteratively and illustratively, describing things which are commonplace. The European woman in the bazaar, the somebody who spits, the nimble Burman on the football field, the referee, the jeering Buddhist priests, the any Anglo-Indian official, they are all generic and representative figures, not individual ones. No doubt they could all have central roles in stories of their own, but they are part of the background for this one.

Complicating Action. The third paragraph announces a shift from orientation into complicating action. The shift could hardly be clearer – it begins with 'One day something happened …' (Orwell 1970 I [1936]: 266) and then the next four paragraphs narrate a sequence of events about looking for and finding the elephant. At the end of these paragraphs the action is paused: 'I decided that I would watch him for a little while to make sure that he did not turn savage again, and then go home' (ibid: 269).

Evaluation. The next paragraph immediately contradicts the end of the previous one, and once again the shift from one phase of the narrative to the next is very clearly marked: 'But at that moment … And suddenly I realised … And it was at this moment …I perceived in this moment' and the narrator realises that he is not in control of events (ibid). This realisation takes up the next three paragraphs, ending with a return to action: 'I shoved the cartridges into the magazine and lay down on the road to get a better aim' (ibid: 270).

Concluding Action. The next three paragraphs take us through the very moving description of the elephant's death. The action part of the story ends when the narrator leaves the scene, in the paragraph beginning: 'In the end I could not stand it any longer and went away' (ibid: 272).

Coda. The last paragraph begins: 'Afterwards, of course …', which announces its 'coda' function. The 'of course' also reduces the emotional tension from the main part of the story. We end with an iterative expression which takes us a long way in time from the events of the story, 'I often wondered …' (ibid).

So 'Shooting an elephant' is structured in a way that corresponds to our intuitive expectations of a personal, individual story about a real experience. The linguistic devices which move it through its different stages are clearly marked. It is also very memorably written. As well as its engaging ordinariness of tone at the beginning, there are some passages of intense descriptive writing. When the first bullet hits the elephant he 'looked suddenly stricken, shrunken, immensely old'; when he falls after the third shot 'he seemed to tower upwards like a huge rock toppling, his trunk reaching skyward like a tree'. When the next shots hit him 'The thick blood welled out of him like red velvet' (ibid: 271-272). Best of all are the two wonderful adjectives which describe his peaceful demeanour before he is killed: he is cleaning a bunch of grass against his knees 'with that preoccupied grandmotherly air that elephants have' (ibid: 270). 'Shooting an elephant' combines a confessional, ordinary-man tone and an intuitively familiar structure with some very powerful writing. It is authentic-sounding natural narrative, but turbo-charged with talent.

'A HANGING' AS A DYSFUNCTIONAL NATURAL NARRATIVE

What about 'A hanging'? Applying Labov's model to 'A hanging' produces fascinating results. The piece has a complicated relationship with natural narrative, as if it sets out to be a straightforward story,

CRIS YELLAND

but fails. It 'fails' in ways which are very artful, and which give the story its distinctive power. The structure is like this:

Abstract. As with 'Shooting an elephant' there is a short literal title, 'A hanging'.

Orientation. The first paragraph of the story reads something like an orientation, but a deficient one. Whereas in 'Shooting an elephant' we are told all about the narrator, his job and his feelings about it, here this contextual material is missing. We do not learn who the narrator is, nor why he is present at the hanging at all. Nor do we learn why the prisoner is being hanged. Emma Larkin describes a crime wave in Burma during Orwell's time there: 'Violent crime in Burma had risen at an alarming rate. Dacoity – defined as crime committed by roving gangs of more than five hooligans – had doubled in the last ten years, as had murder rates, giving Burma the dubious distinction of being the most violent corner of the Indian Empire' (Larkin 2011 [2005]: 71); Jeffrey Meyers notes that 'there were hundreds of hangings every year in Burma' (Meyers 2000: 69), and Bernard Crick gives precise numbers: 'It could have been any one of the 116 hangings in 1923, the 145 in 1924, the 162 in 1925, or the 191 in 1927' (Crick 1982: 151). If the opening of 'A hanging' included any of this material it would locate the story in the world of the comprehensible and explicable. It would function as an orientation. But it doesn't. Instead, we have what looks like an orientation, but a bizarre one, which goes into detail about things like the 'sickly light, like yellow tinfoil' but says nothing about why the event is happening. The oddity of the 'orientation', the way it fails to do what is ostensibly its job, is apparent in the first sentence, even its first word: 'It was in Burma, a sodden morning of the rains' (Orwell 1970 [1931]: 66). Ten words, and you could say that the sentence 'sets the scene'. There's the 'Burma', and what the weather was like. So far, so familiar perhaps – but the effect isn't to make Burma familiar to UK readers, or to introduce what is going to happen. Instead, the sentence, short as it is, is dysfunctional. It is built on two references which are actually discomforting. The first is 'It' – what is 'It'? The narration addresses us as if we already know. The same device is used with 'the corpse' in Orwell's essay 'Marrakech' (1939) and at the opening of his novel *Coming Up For Air* (1939): 'The idea really came to me the day I got my new false teeth' (CWGO VII: 3). What idea? As ordinarily efficient communication this is defective; as a literary device it is powerful, and quite common. There is a more subtle instance of the same literary device in 'the rains', which is how you would refer to them if you were familiar with the Burmese climate, but not otherwise. There is no explanatory sentence, no 'In Burma the months from June until September are the rainy months' nor anything like it.

Instead of explaining, the narrative moves on to a startling simile: 'A sickly light, like yellow tinfoil, was slanting over the high walls into the jail yard' (ibid). The comparison is unexpected, and it is made uncanny by the repeated 'the' attached to the walls and the yard. Once again, these are context-dependent, presented as if we already know them, as if we are actually there. In 'Shooting an elephant' we are made to feel close to the narrator because he explains things with a convincing air of honesty and circumstantial detail. In 'A hanging' we are thrust into intimacy with a narrator who sounds disturbed. In the terminology of transactional analysis, the 'Orwell' of 'Shooting an elephant' offers us 'I'm OK, you're OK'. In 'A hanging', it is more a case of 'I'm not OK, and soon you won't be either'.

Complicating Action. In 'Shooting an elephant', the shift from orientation to action is clearly announced: 'One day something happened.' But in 'A hanging' it is not clear where orientation ends and action begins. The verbs in the first two paragraphs are oddly ambiguous. The second paragraph begins with a verb in the passive voice and the past perfect tense: 'One prisoner had been brought out of his cell' (ibid). Does this form part of the orientation, or the action? It is notable, too, how many continuous verbs there are in the first three paragraphs: 'was slanting … were waiting … were squatting … were guarding him and getting him ready … was standing' (ibid: 67). This verb form blurs the distinction between state and event, orientation and action. One way of reading the opening is to say that the first two paragraphs form the orientation and that the action only begins with the third paragraph. Read that way, it is striking that the first 'actions' are non-human ones: 'Eight o'clock struck, and a bugle call, desolately thin in the wet air, floated from the distant barracks' (ibid). This contributes to the disturbing quality of 'A hanging', its sense that the human beings in it are not behaving in a purposeful way, but are puppets caught up in a dreadful ritual which they cannot get out of.

Evaluation. This feature of the story is clearly marked. It is one place where 'A hanging' is close to 'Shooting an elephant' in its structure. Both pieces pause the action for the narrator to tell us explicitly about his sudden realisation about what he is doing. They both deploy what Labov calls 'embedded evaluation': 'The first step in embedding the evaluation into the narrative, and preserving dramatic continuity, is for the narrator to quote the sentiment as something occurring to him at the moment' (Labov 1972: 372). In 'Shooting an elephant' it is the narrator's glance behind him at the crowd which produces the crisis and enlightens him about the nature of the white man's dominion in the East. Correspondingly, when the narrator of 'A hanging' sees the condemned man swerve

CRIS YELLAND

to avoid a puddle, he experiences a crisis which lasts from 'It is curious…' at the beginning of the paragraph to 'one world less' at the end of it (ibid: 68-69). The crisis is especially disturbing because of the mysterious atmosphere which has been created earlier in the story. Because we don't know why the narrator is there, nor why the prisoner is being hanged, the distinction between the prisoner and the officials is blurred: 'He and we were a party of men walking together, seeing, hearing, feeling, understanding the same world …' (ibid).

Concluding action. Then we return to the action of the journey to the gallows, the prisoner's repeated calls of 'Ram!' and the climax of the execution, ending with the superintendent confirming that the prisoner is dead (ibid: 70).

Coda. The end of the story does not really have a coda, at least not in the sense that 'Shooting an elephant' does. There is no summing-up, no explanation and no return from the past time when the events happened to the present time of when they are narrated. Instead there is an accumulation of bizarre and disturbing details; lots of people speak, but what they say seems inappropriate: the superintendent is brusque, then quite genial; the Eurasian boy and Francis are ingratiating; the narrator himself 'found that I was laughing quite loudly' (ibid: 71). The 'found that I was laughing', rather than the more purposeful 'I laughed' continues the theme of passivity, of people not being in control of what happens, that pervades the whole piece. The story ends with more inappropriate behaviour, chuckling, laughter and drinking together. It is all rebuked by the material fact 'The dead man was a hundred yards away' (ibid).

The model of natural narrative suggests clearly that, although 'Shooting an elephant' and 'A hanging' are both about experiences in Burma and both quite close together in date, they are actually very different kinds of writing. The crucial structural differences are to do with orientation and coda. In 'Shooting an elephant' these are both clearly marked, and they are two places in the story where the narrator asserts control over the material and demonstrates his understanding of it. This understanding recounts events that happened Then, which made the narrator think, and changed him into the person he is Now. The narrator expresses his understanding in language which is clear and forceful. In 'A hanging', the orientation does not work 'properly', and the coda is a ragbag of disturbing details whose meaning is never stated. The narrator in 'A hanging' cannot articulate the relationship between Then and Now; instead, he is stuck in Then, haunted by it and condemned to relive it. This is because the orientation malfunctions, and because the 'coda' does not do its job of wrapping up and distancing the events of the story. In a disturbed and disturbing way, the story is not safely in the past; it haunts the narrator's present. 'A hanging' has a dream or nightmare quality, not the sense of insight gained through experience which pervades 'Shooting an elephant'.

One can gauge the difference in understanding and control between the two stories by comparing the lengths and structures of the sentences in their final paragraphs. 'Shooting an elephant' has final sentences of 13 words, then 14, 27, 6, 35, 30 and 20 words. There is only one strikingly short sentence, 'Among the Europeans opinion was divided.' This has no emotional charge from the narrator, and simply acts as a menu for the three sentences which follow, which set out people's different views about shooting the elephant, then end with the narrator's superior grasp of the reason for it. These sentences are relatively relaxed and discursive. Apart from the one very short sentence, these concluding sentences have three, four or more clauses, and logical conjunctions which make it clear that the narrator's actions and the others' opinions both have reasons behind them, 'for ... if ... because' and so on. The narrator is in complete control of this material and can see the connections between the different parts of it.

The paragraph has a clear and comprehensible structure; it even starts with its topic sentence 'Afterwards, of course, there were endless discussions about the shooting of the elephant' (Orwell 1970 I [1936]: 272) and goes on to expand on and exemplify it. But the sentences at the end of 'A hanging' are quite different. Their word-counts are 13, 15, then 5, 8, 12 and 8. Cohesion between sentences is weak, and each of these notably short sentences brings one more disturbing detail. The sentences have one clause each, with one exception, a sentence which has two. These sentences are like repeated hammer-blows; the narrator is at the mercy of his own fragmentary perception of events. The only climax is not a climax of superior understanding, as it is in 'Shooting an elephant', but the brutal fact that the dead man is so near.

A 'MODERNIST' ESSAY AND A 'REALIST' ONE
There are lots of ways of describing how different these two stories are. Using one kind of narratological terminology, it could be said that in 'Shooting an elephant' the reader is told what events and situations mean, but that 'A hanging' depends more on narrative 'showing'. Except in the paragraph of evaluation, the fact that the hanging is a foul thing is shown and implied in the accumulation of disturbing detail and the way it has traumatised the narrator. Another way of thinking about the two stories is to do with the literary-historical shift which we began with. 'Shooting an elephant' is a realist story with a conversational reliable narrator who gains

your confidence from the beginning and constructs himself as a straightforward sort of person whose feelings and interpretations are things that the reader can readily share. It is a mode of narration which is common in H.G. Wells, for instance, in stories such as *Aepyornis Island* (1894) and *The Time Machine* (1895). The exotic quality of what is narrated is underpinned by a narrator whom we trust, and that trust builds a bridge between us and the strangeness of the events. The 'Orwell' who narrates 'A hanging' is a device more associated with literary modernism, a profoundly unreliable narrator. This narrator is not capable of telling us what the events mean, except in the central 'evaluation' section. For the most part he is so traumatised by what he has seen that he cannot bring himself to say why he was there, nor explain to us how we should feel about it. 'A hanging' offers itself as a natural narrative, but it is a dysfunctional one. I do not mean that it is in any way unskilful; its deployment of a dysfunctional narrator makes it in some ways a more sophisticated and ambitious piece of writing than 'Shooting an elephant'.

Both essays are what Lodge would call 'historical' discourse, offering themselves as autobiographical natural narratives. But 'A hanging' uses natural narrative dysfunctionally, except in its orthodox evaluation section. The differences between the two essays are part of Orwell's process of trying out modernism, then moving away from it, a process which was incomplete in 1931 but much more advanced by 1936.

REFERENCES

Adams, Tim (2024) George Orwell's Burmese days vibrantly brought to life. Review of Paul Theroux, *Burma Sahib*, *Guardian*, 13 February

Alldritt, Keith (1969) *The Making of George Orwell: An Essay in Literary History*, London: Edward Arnold

Biederstadt, Carol (2022) The elephant in the room: Reassessing the genre of George Orwell's 'Shooting an elephant', *George Orwell Studies*, Vol. 7, No. 1 pp 41-44

Bloom, Lynn Z. (1999) The essay canon, *College English*, Vol. 61, No. 4 pp 401-430

Bluemel, Kristin (2004) *George Orwell and the Radical Eccentrics: Intermodernism in Literary London*, London: Palgrave

Connolly, Cyril (1988 [1938]) *Enemies of Promise*, London: André Deutsch

Cain, William (2007) Orwell's essays as a literary experience, Rodden, John (ed.) *The Cambridge Companion to George Orwell*, Cambridge: Cambridge University Press pp 76-86

Crick, Bernard (1982) *George Orwell: A Life*, Harmondsworth, Middlesex: Penguin

Davison, Peter (ed.) (2017) *George Orwell: The Collected Non-Fiction: Articles, Essays, Diaries and Letters 1903-1950*, London: Penguin

Fowler, Roger (1995) *The Language of George Orwell*, London: Macmillan

Graddol, David, Cheshire, Jenny and Swann, Joan (1996) *Describing Language*, Buckingham: Open University Press

Kerr, Douglas (2022a) *Orwell & Empire*, Oxford: Oxford University Press

Kerr, Douglas (2022b) Reflections on 'St Andrew's day 1935', *George Orwell Studies*, Vol. 7, No. 1 pp 53-60

Kumar, Krishan (2022) Through a Burmese lens. Review of Douglas Kerr, *Orwell & Empire*, *Times Literary Supplement*, 25 November

Kurtz, Cynthia (2014) *Working with Stories in Your Community or Organization*, New York: Kurtz-Fernhout

Labov, William (1972) The transformation of experience in narrative syntax, *Language in the Inner City*, Philadelphia, Pennsylvania: University of Pennsylvania Press pp 354-396

Larkin, Emma (2011 [2005]) *Finding George Orwell in Burma*, Cambridge: Granta Books

Li, Cun, Hu, Jun, Hengeveld, Bart and Hummels, Caroline (2020) Facilitating intergenerational storytelling for older adults in the nursing home: A case study, *Journal of Ambient Intelligence and Smart Environments*, No.1 pp 1-25

Lodge, David (2002 [1966]) *The Language of Fiction*, London: Routledge

Lodge, David (2015 [1977]) *The Modes of Modern Writing*, London: Bloomsbury

Lodge, David (1981) Modernism, antimodernism and postmodernism, in *Working with Structuralism*, London: Routledge & Kegan Paul pp 3-16

Meyers, Jeffrey (ed.) (1975) *George Orwell: The Critical Heritage*, London: Routledge & Kegan Paul

Meyers, Jeffrey (2000) *George Orwell: Wintry Conscience of a Generation*, New York: W.W. Norton and Company

Meyers, Jeffrey (2002) Orwell's elephants, George Orwell Society website, 27 March. Available online at https://orwellsociety.com/orwells-elephants/, accessed on 24 July 2024

Orwell, George (1970 I [1931]) A hanging, *The Collected Essays, Journalism and Letters of George Orwell, Vol. 1, An Age Like This,* Orwell, Sonia and Angus, Ian (eds) Harmondsworth, Middlesex: Penguin pp 66-71

Orwell, George (1970 I [1936]) Shooting an elephant, *The Collected Essays, Journalism and Letters of George Orwell, Vol. 1, An Age Like This*, Orwell, Sonia and Angus, Ian (eds) Harmondsworth, Middlesex: Penguin pp 265-272

Orwell, George (1970 I [1940]) Inside the whale, *The Collected Essays, Journalism and Letters of George Orwell, Vol. 1, An Age Like* This, Orwell, Sonia and Angus, Ian (eds) Harmondsworth, Middlesex: Penguin pp 540-578

Orwell, George (1970 4 [1946]) Politics and the English language, *The Collected Essays, Journalism and Letters of George Orwell, Vol. 4, In Front of Your Nose*, Orwell, Sonia and Angus, Ian (eds) Harmondsworth, Middlesex: Penguin pp 156-170

Pratt, Mary Louise (1977) *Towards a Speech-Act Theory of Literary Discourse*, Bloomington, Indiana: University of Indiana Press

Pope, Rob (1998) *The English Studies Book*, London: Routledge

Rae, Patricia (2009) Orwell, World War I modernism and the Spanish Civil War, *Journal of War and Culture Studies*, Vol. 2, No.3 pp 245-258

Rodden, John (1989) *The Politics of Literary Reputation*, Oxford: Oxford University Press

Rodden, John (1991) Reputation, canon-formation, pedagogy: George Orwell in the classroom, *College English*, Vol. 53, No. 5 pp 503-530

Rodden, John (ed.) (2007) *The Cambridge Companion to George Orwell*, Cambridge: Cambridge University Press

CRIS YELLAND

Rossi, John (2007) 'My country, right or left': Orwell's patriotism, Rodden, John (ed.) *The Cambridge Companion to George Orwell*, Cambridge: Cambridge University Press

Rossi, John and Rodden, John (2007) A political writer, Rodden, John (ed.) *The Cambridge Companion to George Orwell*, Cambridge: Cambridge University Press pp 1-11

Simpson, Paul (2002) *Stylistics*, London: Routledge

Stansky, Peter and Abrahams, William (1974) *The Unknown Orwell*, London: Constable and Company

Sutherland, John (2017) *Orwell's Nose: A Pathological Biography*, London: Reaktion Books

Taylor, D.J. (2023) *Orwell: The New Life*, London: Constable

Woloch, Alex (2017) *Or Orwell: Writing and Democratic Socialism*, Cambridge, Massachusetts: Harvard University Press)

NOTE ON THE CONTRIBUTOR

Cris Yelland graduated from Leeds University in 1971, and later studied under Roger Fowler for his PhD. From 1974 until 2011 he taught English at Teesside Polytechnic/Teesside University. He has published articles on a range of topics, in history and politics journals as well as literary ones. He is the author of *Jane Austen: A Style in History* (Routledge Studies in Romanticism, 2018).

Samuel Butler: The Victorian Orwell

HASSAN AKRAM

Samuel Butler was one of George Orwell's favourite writers. They were both accomplished stylists and outspoken critics of their societies. In this paper I examine the influence on Orwell of Butler's two great novels, and situate Butler as a Victorian precursor to Orwell. I identify Butler's willingness to pursue ideas to absurd conclusions and his scepticism towards institutions as principles that significantly influenced Orwell's most famous works. I compare Erewhon, *a satirical utopia that uses the techniques of fable and science-fiction to critique social institutions, with* Animal Farm *and* Nineteen Eighty-Four. *I then analyse* The Way of All Flesh, *an autobiographical novel and an attack on Victorianism, and the reasons for its appeal to Orwell, inferring that he saw many parallels between his own life and that of Butler's hero Ernest Pontifex. I conclude that Butler, more than any other Victorian writer, closely resembles Orwell in his style, themes and approach to social criticism.*

Key words: Orwell, Samuel Butler, satire, science-fiction, fable, Victorianism

INTRODUCTION

Samuel Butler (1835-1902), the Victorian critic, novelist and evolutionist, wrote prolifically. His literary criticism and notebooks are as much worth reading as the major works, although his reputation rests mainly on two novels. One, his first real success, is a mock-innocent Swiftian allegory; the other, which secured his posthumous reputation, is the bitter masterpiece of a dying man. He was highly outspoken: in spite of his innately conservative tastes, he hated the tyranny and misery of society as he saw it and he possessed an astounding prescience which makes his work as relevant today as it was in his own time. The musical simplicity of his prose style, his clear-sightedness and intellectual honesty, makes everything of his richly readable.

Orwell listed Butler, a formative influence during his time at St Cyprian's and Eton, as one of his favourite writers (*CELJ* 2: 39; Crick 1980: 36). He took a copy of Butler's *Note-Books* with him to Burma, and makes enthusiastic mention of them throughout his articles and essays. In 1945, he scripted broadcasts on both of

HASSAN AKRAM

Butler's well-known novels – *Erewhon* (1872) and *The Way of All Flesh* (1903) – and his piece on the former book throws useful light on his own conception of the utopia novel: 'All Utopia books are satires or allegories. Obviously if you invent an imaginary country, you do so in order to throw light on the institutions of some existing country, probably your own' (*CWGO* XVII: 169). Butler's prose style – simple, fluent, and euphonious – was possibly the most significant reason for Orwell's admiration: '[I]n the narrow technical sense he wrote so well. When one compares Butler's prose with the contortions of Meredith or the affectations of Stevenson, one sees what a tremendous advantage is gained simply by not trying to be clever' (*CEJL* 3: 220-221.). Orwell's high opinion of Butler helps explain the parallels between their works – especially, as I aim to show, in *Erewhon* and *The Way of All Flesh*.

EREWHON

> *It is not our business to help students to think for themselves. Surely this is the very last thing which one who wishes them well should encourage them to do. Our duty is to ensure that they shall think as we do or, at any rate, as we hold it expedient to say we do* (Butler 1933 [1872]: 180).

In October 1950, the American pulp writer and critic P. Schuyler Miller, reviewing *Nineteen Eighty-Four* for a science-fiction magazine, observed: 'The book is in the tradition of *Erewhon* and *Gulliver's Travels*' (Miller 1950: 127-129). Miller, though not alone in comparing Orwell to Swift, was one of the earliest to recognise his debt to Butler, and especially to the 1872 satire about a fictional country – an anagram of 'Nowhere' – where crime is remedied as an illness and illness punished as a crime.

By conventional measures *Erewhon* is a very poor novel. It opens with fifty horrifically dull pages of travel narrative voiced by a Victorian explorer who arrives at an unexplored island, Erewhon, and spends several months recording the absurdities of its society; then, falling in love with a woman there named Arowhena, he elopes with her in a hot air balloon; they make it back to London, marry, have children and establish an Erewhon Evangelization Company, Ltd – keeping the ground fertile for a sequel. (*Erewhon Revisited* was published in 1901, but Butler thought it an inferior work to the original and Orwell also found in it nothing to recommend). The barebones plot and flatness of character go some way in explaining the book's appeal to a pulp writer like Miller; but it has much else to recommend it, such as its freshness of style and imagination, its originality and good humour. 'In *Erewhon* there is little of the personal bitterness and animosity which spoils Butler's later books,' Malcolm Muggeridge, a friend of Orwell's, wrote in his critical study of Butler. 'It is lighthearted and genuinely fanciful' (Muggeridge 1971 [1936]: 205).

Butler focuses his satire on a number of institutions: these include the Musical Banks, the Hospital for Incurable Bores and (one that sounds like something out of *Nineteen Eighty-Four*) the Colleges of Unreason. A 'hypothetical language' (probably Latin) is taught in schools at the expense of practical subjects; texts are translated and retranslated into it, and people who become proficient are given incomes for life. 'The store they set by this hypothetical language can hardly be believed ... it appeared to me to be a wanton waste of good human energy that men should spend years and years in the perfection of so barren an exercise' (Butler 1933 [1872]: 177). Orwell, along with Butler, felt disdain for the persistence of Latin and Greek in schools, and in one of the 'As I Please' columns in *Tribune* he expresses his sympathy for the adults who, like himself, had been 'flogged through the entire extant works of Aeschylus, Sophocles, Euripides, Aristophanes, Vergil, Horace, and various other Latin and Greek authors' (*CEJL* 3: 210).

The most memorable aspect of Butler's satire is his inversion of crime and illness. In Erewhon, the ill and the unfortunate are sent to prison, while criminals are treated with sympathy in the hope that they will recover themselves. Butler carries the crime-illness inversion to its logical end. At Personal Bereavement Courts, for instance, people are tried for having been bereaved, and the case for the defence usually rests on the claim that in some way the defendant benefitted from the death. As Orwell noted, the implication of the inversion, that crime is as much beyond a person's control as illness or poverty, is obvious now, but would have been blasphemously radical in the mid-Victorian era. Yet, in going so far, Butler for some reason refuses to go further. He does not explicitly apply his observations to the real world. He does not synthesise any coherent theory out of them. Another example of this refusal to go too far is his declaration that 'Property *is* robbery' (Butler 1933 [1872]: 105, italics in the original), which, again, is radical, but is spoken with little attempt at elaboration. 'There are innumerable similar passages in Butler's work. You could easily interpret them in a Marxist sense, but the important point is that Butler himself does not do so' (*CEJL* 3: 220). Butler is not a political writer: that is not only his greatest weakness, but his greatest point of difference with Orwell, and the reason why many of his ideas feel underdeveloped.

It also explains why entire chapters of his book, despite their perceptiveness, serve no constructive purpose. Some of the later chapters contain very vivid satire, drawing, like *Animal Farm*, on anthropomorphism and the traditions of fable; but the difference is that Butler, unlike Orwell, seems to be playing for laughs. Take his two chapters satirising vegetarianism. He outlines the 'Views of an Erewhonian prophet concerning the rights of animals' (Butler 1933 [1872]: 220), and the process which leads to the outlawing of all meat in Erewhon unless the animal has died of natural causes. The ban is ineffective: 'Suicidal mania ... which had hitherto been confined exclusively to donkeys, became alarmingly prevalent even among such for the most part self-respecting creatures as sheep and cattle' (Ibid: 224). In the next chapter, whose title speaks for itself, Butler outlines the 'Views of an Erewhonian prophet concerning the rights of vegetables' (ibid: 228). It is the same technique as earlier in the novel of carrying thought experiments to their absurd conclusions, but the difference here, unlike with, say, the Personal Bereavement Court, is that the thought experiments serve no practical purpose. There is absolutely nothing to gain by attacking vegetarianism. According to Orwell: 'Butler chooses to exaggerate his case and gives the impression that he is merely joking' (*CWGO* XVII: 172).

In spite of the chronic flippancy of his attitude, Butler obviously wanted to say something constructive. He, like Orwell who chose to set *Nineteen Eighty-Four* in England of all places, knew that he could bring the story home by emphasising the familiarity of the setting. From the first section he is at pains to do this: 'Had the walls only been passed over with extracts from the *Illustrated London News* and *Punch*, I could have almost fancied myself in [England],' his narrator notes on arriving inside an Erewhonian home (Butler 1933 [1872]: 56). He explicitly roots Erewhon's idiosyncrasies – for example, its sympathetic treatment of crime – in his own observations about contemporary Europe, such as that in Italy where he once heard someone say: 'Poor unfortunate fellow, he has murdered his uncle' (ibid: 86). Without this explicit linkage between the fictional and the real, Butler's novel may not have made so much of an impact; as it is, the book has not been out of print since its publication.

Erewhon's significance today lies, like *Nineteen Eighty-Four's*, in its extraordinary topicality. In recent years many commentators have dubbed it 'Orwellian' to question controversial statues of slave-owners or imperialists (see Anonymous 2020 and Kimball 2023) and, though this is a complete non-issue, they would have been more accurate to have characterised it as Erewhonian, in tune with Butler's refreshing view on statues: '… a simpler plan would have been to forbid the erection of a statue to any public man or woman till he or she had been dead at least one hundred years, and even then to insist on reconsideration of the claims of the deceased and the merit of the statue every fifty years' (Butler 1933 [1872]: 116).

Much more significant, however, is Butler's treatment of what would now be called artificial intelligence. 'The book of the machines', a subsection of the novel, purports to be the document which famously convinced Erewhon to abandon technological development and destroy all of its machines. Its effect is similar to that of Goldstein's Book in *Nineteen Eighty-Four*: they were both originally written as essays and were incorporated clumsily into a novel. The difference is that Orwell writes in earnest, whereas Butler intersperses his essay with ludicrous one-liners such as this: 'Even a potato in a dark cellar has a certain low cunning about him which serves him in excellent stead' (ibid: 192). 'The book of the machines', nonetheless, remains one of the most influential passages in science-fiction, having inspired, among other books, Aldous Huxley's *Brave New World* (1932). Drawing on the then-recent theory of evolution, Butler speculates that machines will develop consciousness and reproductive functions. In the last thousand years, he says, machines have evolved at an exponentially speedier rate than human beings, which will allow them ultimately to supersede us. This is an astonishing forecast for Butler to have made in the 1870s. The idea that machines might be dangerous as well as useful is one that pervades Orwell's writing. Examples include the discussion of machine civilisation in *The Road to Wigan Pier* and, more famously, the omnipresent telescreens in *Nineteen Eighty-Four*.

Some 150 years on from Butler's novel, panicked discussions are underway about the consciousness of AI, and there were definite notes of *Erewhon* in March 2023, when an open letter signed by the luminaries of the field proposed a six-month 'pause' in artificial intelligence research (see Hern 2023). Butler was a visionary. Like Orwell, he is one of those writers who become not less but more relevant as time passes. His groundbreaking blend of social commentary, fable and science-fiction, and his remarkable foresight, establish him as an inspiration to Orwell and his novel as a precursor to *Animal Farm* and *Nineteen Eighty-Four*.

THE WAY OF ALL FLESH

> *This power of cutting logical Gordian knots and fusing two contradictory or conflicting statements into one harmonious whole ... is one without which no living being animal or plant could continue to live for a single day* (Butler 1992 [1964]: 165-166).

After the success of *Erewhon* in 1872, Butler, rummaging around for a theme for another novel, decided to write one about his own boyhood and youth (Furbank 1992: vii). *Ernest Pontifex, or The Way of All Flesh* was completed in 1884, published posthumously with edits in 1903 and only published in full in 1964. The book is a story of four generations of the Pontifex family, with a focus on the great-grandson Ernest (a self-portrait of Butler); and it lacerates

HASSAN AKRAM

every tenet of Victorian society, the physical discipline, the Church, the family, the schooling system and the all-consuming hypocrisy. As a piece of autofiction it was compared by Orwell to Dickens's *David Copperfield* (1850) (*CWGO* XVII: 181) although a more exact comparison would be with D.H. Lawrence's *Sons and Lovers* (1913), which also uses pioneering techniques of psychoanalysis, is not narrated by the hero and is as much family history as plain autobiography.

The first section traces the Pontifexes from 1750 until 1835. In this discussion of family history, especially in terms of the shabby-genteel motif and the force of social convention, there is a foretaste of the history of the Comstocks in Chapter 3 of Orwell's *Keep the Aspidistra Flying* (*CWGO* IV: 39-43). Butler's vision is far bleaker, however. Ernest's grandfather is a horrible man, a cruel, money-loving will-shaker who forces Ernest's father Theobald into a life-long curacy. Theobald is then driven by a series of Trollopean machinations into a marriage with an older woman whom he does not love. Christina is a fiercely loyal wife and a shallow snob. Her head is utterly empty except of prayers to be made happy, united and God-fearing, and of fantasies in which her children become lords or ladies or martyrs or archbishops. Theobald is cruel, though not so cruel as his father before him, and he delights in teasing and tormenting his children. Butler draws his parents – for Theobald and Christina are they – with a degree of savagery which is completely justified. As Bernard Shaw, a great admirer of Butler, puts it: 'He slew the good name ... of his father and mother so reasonably, so wittily, so humorously, and even in a ghastly way so charitably, that he convinced us that he was engaged in an execution and not a murder' (Shaw 1932: 52-71).

Ernest is no sooner born than he 'is bullied and beaten and prayed over – even when he is a tiny child he is beaten because he can't pronounce certain letters of the alphabet properly – he is dosed with calomel and Epsom Salts and stuffed up with Latin and Greek, until at the age of about twelve his spirit is almost broken already' (*CWGO* XVII: 182). It is difficult not to be moved by Ernest's pathetic innocence, all the more so because Butler was drawing on memories of his own childhood. He clearly carried the bitterness of his early life well into adulthood and, at many points in the novel, he remarks that not just he but the entire human race would be better off if the entire parent-child relationship were to be abolished.

Ernest attends boarding-school and Cambridge, then leaves his parents and moves to London. During a brief stint as a clergyman, he lives among the London poor in an effort to convert them. He gets married and cuts off his parents completely, and here the narrative loses its force. It picks up again when he receives a note to say that his mother is dying, and the deathbed and tying-up chapters are a return to the earlier mastery of character and scene. But first Ernest is made to spend six months in prison, become a tailor, marry his former housemaid, have two children, grow miserable, watch his wife become a thief and a drunkard, be informed in the course of a chance encounter with an old friend that she is already married to him (the old friend) and so his (Ernest's) marriage to her is bigamous, give up his children for adoption and accompany the narrator for six months' mourning on the Grand Tour. This string of improbabilities rings completely false. As Orwell correctly noted, the book's greatness lies in its 'honest picture of the relationship between father and son' (ibid: 186), and as soon as Butler begins to describe Ernest's sexual rather than filial relationships, the story collapses. A lifelong bachelor, he is no longer writing from experience. The great flaw of autobiographical novels is that they cease to be believable when they cease to be truthful. A novel, unlike a straight autobiography, must be complete, and so the author must come out with even the most improbable or clichéd ending to complete the story. Examples from Orwell's semi-autobiographical novels include John Flory's suicide in *Burmese Days* and Rosemary's pregnancy in *Keep the Aspidistra Flying*. These events have no basis in reality, but are necessary plot devices for the story to hang together. It is the same with Butler. Ernest's imprisonment and marriage are necessary for his character and the progression of the plot, but they remain thoroughly unconvincing. *The Way of All Flesh* begins, in Bernard Shaw's phrase, as 'one of the great books of the world' (quoted in Furbank 1992: xxxiv); it devolves into the production of a melodramatic hack.

Orwell thought that the ending of *The Way of All Flesh* – in which Ernest inherits a fortune and is able to live alone as a gentleman of leisure – was unconvincing compared with the rest of the novel. The plot device is hackneyed, although, as Butler foreshadows it long in advance, it does not go as far as the prison/marriage subplot in damaging the book's realism. It is also perfectly consistent with Butler's worldview. Orwell saw as much: 'Finally his [Butler's] outlook is that of a Conservative, in spite of his successful assaults on Christian beliefs and the institution of the family. Poverty is degrading: therefore, take care not to be poor – that is his reaction. Hence the improbable and unsatisfying ending of *The Way of All Flesh*' (*CEJL* 3: 220). Muggeridge also picked up on this: 'The bitterness of *The Way of All Flesh* arises [solely] out of a sense of personal grievance. Butler had no general grievance. The constitution of society ... suited him very well' (Muggeridge 1971 [1936]: 228). Butler does not want to change society; he merely wants to be comfortable in it. And so, his ending *is* convincing.

Bachelor's quarters in the Temple, a private income, a library, a desk where he can write his articles and books, luncheons with friends, evening trips to the theatre and, emphatically, no family – this was his ideal. In one sense it is completely Victorian; in another, it is the antithesis of what Orwell and others have identified as the typical Victorian ending – 'a vision of a huge, loving family of three or four generations, all crammed together in the same house and constantly multiplying, like a bed of oysters' (*CEJL* 1: 490). From this contrast it can be seen just how intensely Butler dissonated from all that came before. His last novel embodied anti-Victorianism as definitively as Orwell's embodied the Cold War.

As to the question of why *The Way of All Flesh* appealed to Orwell personally, there are two main reasons. One is the novel's similarity to the work of his favourite George Gissing. Butler wrote a smoother prose than Gissing and he had more of a sense of humour, but he had in common with him a fierce loathing of Victorianism and a gift for character and atmosphere. In Ernest's imprisonment and subsequent abortive marriage to a 'fallen woman', there are definite notes of Gissing, and the most Butlerian of Gissing's novels, *Born in Exile* (1892), centres, like *The Way of All Flesh*, on hypocrisy and the conflict between Christianity and Darwinism.

Second is the fact that, in the character of Ernest Pontifex, Orwell very likely saw something of himself. Biographer D.J. Taylor observes that Butler was one of the strongest influences on Orwell's autobiographical essay 'Such, such were the joys' (see Moore 2023). Then there is the middle-class upbringing, the miserable experience of public school, the start in a conventional career, the time spent among the urban poor in London and the final settling down to a career as a man of letters – all of these experiences were shared by Orwell and Ernest. In the scene towards the end of the novel when Ernest declares his aims as a writer and an essayist, it is difficult not to be reminded of Orwell: 'If I am to come to the fore at all it must be by writing. ... There are a lot of things that want saying which no one dares to say, a lot of shams which want attacking, and yet no one attacks them. It seems to me that I can say things which not another man in England except myself will venture to say, and yet which are crying to be said' (Butler 1992 [1964]: 353).

CONCLUSION

Butler died in 1902, almost exactly a year before Orwell was born. Even in his last writings he never lost his good humour or 'the power to use his eyes and to be pleased by small things' (*CEJL* 3: 220). If he had focused more definitely on novel-writing, his reputation would stand in much higher stead than it does; for the man who wrote two books of such striking originality and power could have done more with his talents than translate Homer and pick fights with Darwin.

His lasting significance lies in his foresightedness, his satirical eye and, most importantly, his flowing and lucid prose style. His hatred of authority and orthodoxy was expressed at the Church and the family rather than at totalitarian regimes, but his radical instinct is the same as Orwell's; and his consistent themes – a willingness to carry ideas to their absurd conclusions and a scepticism towards institutions – are the two overarching principles of Orwell's most famous works. More than Dickens, more than Gissing, he was probably the closest figure imaginable to a Victorian Orwell.

REFERENCES

Anonymous (2020) Orwell was not providing a blueprint. He was issuing a warning. If we do not heed that warning, our country will change forever, *Freedom Association Blog*, 12 June. Available online at https://www.tfa.net/orwell_was_not_providing_a_blueprint_he_was_issuing_a_warning, accessed on 30 August 2024

Butler, Samuel (1933 [1872]) *Erewhon, or Over the Range*, London: Jonathan Cape

Crick, Bernard (1980) *George Orwell: A Life*, Harmondsworth, Middlesex: Penguin

Furbank, P.N. (1992) Introduction, Butler, Samuel (1992 [1964]) *The Way of All Flesh*, London: Everyman's Library

Hern, Alex (2023) Elon Musk joins calls for pause in creation of giant AI 'digital minds', *Guardian*, 29 March. Available online at https://www.theguardian.com/technology/2023/mar/29/elon-musk-joins-call-for-pause-in-creation-of-giant-ai-digital-minds, accessed on 30 August 2024

Kimball, Roger (2023) Woke censors won't stop until every statue is pulled down, *Telegraph*, 6 November. Available online at https://www.telegraph.co.uk/us/comment/2023/11/06/robert-e-lee-charlottesville-statues-censorship/, accessed on 30 August 2024

Miller, P. Schuyler (1950) Reviews: *Nineteen Eighty-Four*, etc., *Astounding Science-Fiction*, Vol. 46, No. 2, October pp 127-129

Moore, Riley (2023) Discovering Orwell: An interview with D.J. Taylor, *Founder*, 24 May. Available online at https://rhulfounder.co.uk/2023/05/24/discovering-orwell-an-interview-with-dj-taylor/, accessed on 30 August 2024

Muggeridge, Malcolm (1971 [1936]) *The Earnest Atheist: A Study of Samuel Butler*, New York: Haskell House Publishers

Orwell, George (1968) *The Collected Essays, Journalism and Letters, Vol. 1: An Age Like This*, Harmondsworth, Middlesex: Penguin

Orwell, George (1968) *The Collected Essays, Journalism and Letters, Vol. 2: My Country Right or Left, 1940-1943*, Harmondsworth, Middlesex: Penguin

Orwell, George (1968) *The Collected Essays, Journalism and Letters, Vol. 3: As I Please, 1943-1945*, Harmondsworth, Middlesex: Penguin

Orwell, George (1998 [1936]) *Keep the Aspidistra Flying, The Complete Works of George Orwell, Vol. IV*, Davison, Peter (ed.) London: Secker & Warburg

Orwell, George (1998 [1945]) *The Complete Works of George Orwell: I Belong to the Left, Vol. VII*, Davison, Peter (ed.) London: Secker & Warburg

Shaw, George Bernard (1932) *Pen Portraits and Reviews*, London: Constable and Company

HASSAN AKRAM

NOTE ON THE CONTRIBUTOR

Hassan Akram is a student and a writer of short stories and essays. In 2018, he picked up a worn copy of *Nineteen Eighty-Four* and he has been a devoted Orwell fan ever since. He has written essays on other topics for publications such as *The Gissing Journal*, and his fiction has also appeared in various places, including several anthologies from Belanger Books. He is currently studying at the University of Oxford where he is a regular contributor and editor on *Cherwell*.

PAPER

Reading Orwell from the Global South

DÉBORA REIS TAVARES

This paper examines George Orwell's works through the lens of the Global South, exploring how his narratives engage with inequalities that resonate with Marxist theories, particularly Dependency Theory. By analysing key texts such as 'Shooting an elephant', The Road to Wigan Pier, Keep the Aspidistra Flying *and* Nineteen Eighty-Four, *the paper highlights Orwell's focus on marginalised individuals, revealing how his literature reflects the experiences of those on the periphery of global power structures. Moreover, this paper draws parallels between Orwell's critique of the inequalities inherent in these systems and the analyses of intellectuals such as David Harvey and Roberto Schwarz. Harvey's concept of accumulation by dispossession and Schwarz's critique of the Brazilian elites' adoption of European ideals without adapting them to local realities both underscore the global and local dimensions of exploitation. Through this comparative analysis, the paper argues that Orwell's work not only critiques power structures within the Global North but also resonates deeply with the struggles of those in the Global South, offering a critique of capitalist inequality.*

Key words: George Orwell, Global South, Global North, Marxism, Dependency Theory, Roberto Schwarz

INTRODUCTION

George Orwell is an author who stands in two different paths, both inside and outside a social sphere, and his choice is to narrate the lives of those outside it. Thus, this paper takes a new approach by examining Orwell's writings within the socio-economic and political framework of the Global South. As he is writing from a position within the Global North, Orwell's books often address issues that resonate with those on the margins – individuals often overlooked by dominant power structures.

Orwell's writing is distinguished by its ability to revitalise narrative through an acute focus on everyday life and the material conditions of human relations. His prose, filled with subtle lyricism, simultaneously reveals inequalities perpetuated by a system that benefits only a privileged few. Despite its apparent simplicity, his

DÉBORA REIS TAVARES

prose is a sophisticated instrument for social critique, dissecting social rules with incisive precision. Indeed, he displays an ability to craft vivid imagery that is not merely aesthetic; it serves a deliberate end: social criticism through the medium of art. For example, his depiction of industrial cities is filled with a critical undertone in *The Road to Wigan Pier*: 'It is a kind of duty to see and smell such places [industrial cities] now and again, especially smell them, lest you should forget that they exist; though perhaps it is better not to stay there too long' (2001 [1937]: 14). This narrative technique exemplifies Orwell's commitment to exposing the harsh realities of societal structures.

Moreover, his work is intertwined with the historical context in which it was written, reflecting his belief that literature cannot be separate from politics: 'No book is genuinely free from political bias. The opinion that art should have nothing to do with politics is itself a political attitude' (2004 [1946]: 8). Orwell's insistence on the inherently political nature of literature serves as a reminder that works claiming to be apolitical are often the most politically charged. His writing, therefore, encourages a heightened awareness of the structures that shape our world.

In essence, Orwell's writings can be seen as a response to the tumultuous events of his time – the crisis of capitalism, the decline of the British Empire after centuries of exploitation – in a way in which his narratives have both historical significance and enduring literary relevance.

THE GLOBAL SOUTH AND THE DEPENDENCY THEORY

The concept of the Global South encompasses more than just a geographical frontier; it means the never-ending exploitation of southern regions by the North, driven by capitalism, colonialism and slavery. This paper applies Marxist Dependency Theory to explore how Orwell's narratives critique these global inequalities. In this analysis, we explore the relationships between the 'centre' (Global North) and the 'periphery' (Global South) as a social place, and how these are depicted in Orwell's literary and non-literary works.

Originating in Latin America during the mid-20th century, Dependency Theory is grounded in Marxist economic thought. It asserts that the global economic system is fundamentally divided between the centre (industrialised, developed nations) and its margins (underdeveloped, often post-colonial nations). This theory suggests that the wealth of the centre is directly tied to the exploitation and under-development of the margins, perpetuating a dependency that stifles economic and social progress in the latter.

Dependency Theory draws heavily on Marxist concepts, particularly those outlined in Karl Marx's seminal works such as *Capital* and *The Manifesto of the Communist Party* (with Friedrich Engels). His theory, for instance, highlights the way that capitalists derive profit by extracting surplus value from labour: 'The need of a constantly expanding market for its products chases the bourgeoisie over the entire surface of the globe. It must nestle everywhere, settle everywhere, establish connections everywhere' (Marx and Engels 2000 [1848]: 6). Applied globally, Dependency Theory suggests that developed nations extract this surplus value not only from their own working classes but also from the global margins, where labour and resources cost less and are more exploited.

Orwell's literary focus on those marginalised by dominant power structures resonates profoundly with Dependency Theory, which critiques the exploitation of the Global South by the Global North. Orwell's depictions of individuals abandoned by the system – yet being himself inherently part of it – mirror the economic and social dependencies described in Marxist thought, particularly how wealth in the developed centre relies on the continued underdevelopment of the periphery.

His narratives, such as the vivid portrayal of industrial decay in *The Road to Wigan Pier*, subtly critique the unequal global structures, where the prosperity of a few is built upon the suffering of many. Orwell's insistence on intertwining literature with politics, therefore, aligns with the Dependency Theory's assertion that the exploitation of the periphery is an inescapable reality of global capitalism, much like the systemic injustices he exposes through his prose.

ORWELL AND THE DEPENDENCY THEORY

There is, then, a connection between Orwell's critique of systemic inequalities and Dependency Theory, which finds a parallel in Roberto Schwarz's analysis of Brazilian society. Schwarz critiques the Brazilian elites' superficial adoption of European liberal ideals which, much like Orwell's depiction of those abandoned by the system, highlights a deep dissonance between ideology and reality.

While Orwell exposes the exploitation and marginalisation within the capitalist system, Schwarz reveals how Brazil's intellectual and social elites perpetuated a facade of modernity and progress, masking the brutal exploitation of slavery and inequality. Both Orwell and Schwarz, therefore, can illuminate contradictions inherent in systems that claim to uphold universal ideals, but in practice perpetuate deep-seated injustices, whether through the global exploitation critiqued by Dependency Theory or through the local distortions Schwarz identifies in Brazilian society.

DÉBORA REIS TAVARES

Schwarz, in his critical analysis of Brazilian society, emphasises the dissonance between European liberal ideals and the Brazilian context, particularly during the era of slavery. In his view, the Brazilian elites have adopted European concepts such as free labour, equality before the law and universalism without adapting them to the local reality, creating what he describes as 'misplaced ideas'. This superficial mimicry of European ideas, which obscured the exploitation inherent in Brazilian society, particularly of slave labour, highlighted the inauthenticity of intellectual discourse in Brazil. The ideas arrive from the Global North and cannot find their real place within the contradictions of Brazilian society: they are out of place, left out (1992: 12).

Roberto Schwarz's analysis connects deeply with the broader critique of intellectual and cultural authenticity in the Global South. He argues that Brazilian elites, by adopting European liberal ideas without adapting them to the local context – where slavery and economic dependency were still pervasive – have created a distorted and inauthentic intellectual discourse. This misalignment between imported ideologies and local realities serves as a critique of how global power dynamics are mirrored and perpetuated in literature, much like Orwell's exploration of class and power struggles in his works.

This concept of 'misplaced ideas' highlights the consequences of applying foreign intellectual frameworks without considering the socio-economic realities of the local context. Hence, this critique resonates with Orwell's depictions of marginalised people struggling under the weight of oppressive systems imposed by distant powers. By connecting these ideas, Schwarz's analysis underscores the importance of intellectual authenticity and the dangers of uncritically adopting foreign ideologies, particularly in contexts marked by exploitation and dependency.

Similarly, David Harvey's analysis in *The Enigma of Capital* (2010) aligns with this perspective. His critical comments on capitalism, particularly his concept of accumulation by dispossession, intersects meaningfully with Roberto Schwarz's critique of how Brazilian elites adopted European liberal ideas without contextual adaptation. Both scholars examine the dynamics of power and exploitation, albeit in different contexts – Harvey in the global capitalist system and Schwarz within Brazilian intellectual history.

Harvey's idea of accumulation by dispossession, which describes how capitalism continually generates wealth through the expropriation of resources from less powerful regions, resonates with Schwarz's observation of how European ideologies were superficially imposed on Brazil, masking the exploitation inherent in the local context. Schwarz's critique of the Brazilian elites' uncritical adoption of European liberalism mirrors Harvey's analysis of how global capitalism perpetuates inequality by imposing Western economic practices on the Global South:

> Capital accumulation has also played a crucial role, as we have seen, not only in reshaping places with ancient names like London, Rome and Edo (Tokyo), but also building vast new cities with names like Chicago, Los Angeles, Buenos Aires and Shenzhen, while colonial practices have shaped Johannesburg, Kinshasa, Mumbai, Jakarta, Singapore and Hong Kong in ways that feed into the ever-expanding demands located in the main centres of capital accumulation for means of production, markets, for new productive activity and for ruthless accumulation by dispossession (2010: 192).

In essence, both scholars highlight the dangers of adopting foreign ideologies without addressing the underlying exploitation and inequalities they perpetuate. Harvey's global perspective and Schwarz's national focus converge on the critical examination of how power and wealth are maintained by perpetuating dependencies and inequalities, whether through economical means or intellectual frameworks. This connection underscores the importance of contextually grounded critiques in understanding and resisting global and local forms of exploitation.

Putting into perspective, it's possible to connect the point of view of Orwell, David Harvey and Roberto Schwarz, despite their differing contexts. They seem to converge on a critical examination of power, inequality and exploitation. Orwell's focus on the marginalised within capitalist systems parallels Harvey's analysis of accumulation by dispossession, where global capitalism expropriates resources from weaker regions to perpetuate wealth in dominant centres. Similarly, Schwarz's critique of Brazilian elites adopting European liberal ideals without contextual adaptation exposes a localised form of this global exploitation, where foreign intellectual frameworks mask the inherent inequalities and dependencies in Brazilian society. Orwell's literary critique of these dynamics, through his portrayal of those abandoned by the system, underscores the universal relevance of these ideas, making the connection between the intellectual, economic and social critiques of these three thinkers essential for understanding the perpetuation of global and local inequalities.

While Orwell's works predate the creation of the Dependency Theory, they can be interpreted through its lens, in an analytical exercise. His writings frequently delve into the dynamics between the oppressors and the oppressed, reflecting the core-periphery relationship central to Dependency Theory.

In the context of Orwell's work, this critique can be extended to the way his narratives, though centred on the Global North,

DÉBORA REIS TAVARES

resonate with similar themes of exploitation and marginalisation that are acutely felt in the Global South. Orwell is in the centre looking towards the margin, the forgotten, the dispossessed; his aim is not to reflect the struggles of the oppressed from a distance but to understand the world from their standpoint.

Throughout his works, Orwell consistently highlights characters and stories forgotten by the system, individuals who bear the brunt of systemic exploitation. *Burmese Days* and *The Road to Wigan Pier* provide depictions of people imprisoned in the machinery of imperialism and capitalism. Orwell's deep empathy for these characters underscores his commitment to addressing the perspective of the marginalised, a theme that strongly resonates with the experiences of the Global South.

LOOKING OUTSIDE THE SYSTEM FROM INSIDE

To further elucidate the tension between the centre and the margins, this paper examines four of Orwell's key works, chronologically. First, his essay 'Shooting an elephant' in which Orwell's portrayal of a British colonial officer struggling with his role in the imperial system marks the beginning of his exploration of double consciousness – a recurring theme in his nonfiction: 'In Moulmein, in Lower Burma, I was hated by large numbers of people – the only time in my life that I have been important enough for this to happen to me. ... I was a sub-divisional police officer of the town, and in an aimless, petty kind of way anti-European feeling was very bitter' (2009 [1936]: 36).

This passage shows Orwell's early expression of what would later be named by Raymond Williams as 'double consciousness' (1971: 52). This concept, rooted in the experience of holding power and at the same time feeling alienated, is key to understanding the tension between the centre and the margins.

Orwell places the colonial officer at the core of the imperial system – the centre – while also capturing the hostility from the colonised population. This double perspective highlights the contradictions within colonialism and sets the beginning of Orwell's critique of English imperialism. By positioning himself in the narrative, he embodies the centre but is keenly aware of the margins, creating an internal conflict that reflects broader societal tensions.

BELONGING TO A CLASS AND TAKING THE OTHER SIDE

Later on, in *The Road to Wigan Pier*, he confronts the realities of working-class life in industrial England, revealing his internal conflict between his middle-class background and his empathy for the working class.

Which class do I belong to? Economically I belong to the working class, but it is almost impossible for me to think of myself as anything but a member of the bourgeoisie. And supposing I had to take sides, whom should I side with, the upper class which is trying to squeeze me out of existence, or the working class whose manners are not my manners? It is probable that I personally, in any important issue, would side with the working class. But what about the tens or hundreds of thousands of others who are in approximately the same position? And what about that far larger class, running into millions this time – the office-workers and black-coated employees of all kinds – whose traditions are less definitely middle class but who would certainly not thank you if you called them proletarians? All of these people have the same interests and the same enemies as the working class. All are being robbed and bullied by the same system. Yet how many of them realise it? When the pinch came nearly all of them would side with their oppressors and against those who ought to be their allies. It is quite easy to imagine a middle class crushed down to the worst depths of poverty and still remaining bitterly anti-working-class in sentiment; this being, of course, a ready-made Fascist Party (2001 [1937]: 145).

When questioning his class affiliation, the narrative voice offers an objective Orwellian insight: 'Which class do I belong to? Economically I belong to the working class, but it is almost impossible to think of myself as anything but a member of the bourgeoisie.' Thus, he appears to occupy two positions, yet is not fully in either. Economically, he is part of the working class, bound by the market and book club rules. However, culturally, he sees himself as part of the bourgeoisie, despite needing to sell his labour. The narrator is both an employee and someone who identifies with those who control the means of production.

Even as he critically examines his own condition, the narrative voice goes further: whose side would he take?: 'Whom should I side with, the upper class which is trying to squeeze me out of existence, or the working class whose manners are not my manners?' He faces the dilemma of siding with those who seek to eliminate him or those who do not share his habits.

In response, the narrator says: 'I personally, in any important issue, would side with the working class.' He says this because he knows economic concerns dominate society. The narrator recognises his connection to miners, manual labourers and farmworkers. The limitations of his wage-earning life place him alongside those whose surplus product slips through their fingers. In the narrative, the pen and the pickaxe occupy the same place in the class struggle.

However, the middle class position interferes with the narrator's decision. He occupies two positions simultaneously. The ideologically conditioned path splits when action is required. In the case of social unrest, the path presents two options: becoming aware of material conditions or emphasising cultural differences between him and manual workers.

In the first case, the narrator sees himself as similar to miners in economic terms. He states: 'Economically, I am in the same boat with the miner, the navvy and the farm-hand; remind me of that and I will fight at their side' (ibid: 145). The narrator needs to be reminded of his economic similarity to the workers. The verb 'remind' is passive, suggesting that the narrator and the middle class he represents will not remember their connection to the working class on their own. This needs to be prompted externally. This reflects a typical middle-class complacency that refuses to acknowledge its similarity to the working class. Once reminded the narrator quickly aligns himself with the workers, walking alongside them, recognising their shared material conditions and limitations.

Thus, the domination of capital has created a common situation and common interests between manual and intellectual workers. The narrator recognises himself as part of the working class, but has not yet critically examined his surroundings and the process of exploitation. This is an early stage of class consciousness, where workers only recognise each other. However, a transformative perspective still seems out of reach.

The second path of the ideological split involves culture. Culture separates intellectual workers from manual workers, and customs and traditions prevent the narrator from aligning with them in their struggles. This is reflected in the action suggested by the verb: 'culturally I am different from the miner, the navvy, and the farm-hand: lay the emphasis on that and you may arm me against them'. The imperative verb 'lay' reinforces the passive role of the narrative voice. Again, an external element needs to emphasise this cultural difference for the middle class to arm itself against the workers.

This action subtly pits middle class members against other workers. By emphasising cultural differences, a middle class person can be set against their peers. Once again, the action needs to be prompted externally: something must act on the narrator's consciousness. However, this emphasis on cultural habits easily distracts the narrator from economic similarities, focusing instead on abstract ideological differences.

This reflects the reality of much of the middle class: 'If I were a solitary anomaly I should not matter, but what is true of myself is true of countless others. ... These are the sinking middle class, and most of them are clinging to their gentility under the impression that it keeps them afloat' (ibid: 145). Some undergo a process of awareness, aligning themselves with the workers, while others cling to their superior status, immersed in the world of appearances, consumption and the illusion of belonging to the bourgeoisie, unable to resist the ideological tide.

In *The Road to Wigan Pier*, Orwell delves into the harsh realities of working-class life, exposing the economic inequalities that define society. This exploration of poverty and class struggle sets the stage for *Keep the Aspidistra Flying*, where Orwell shifts focus to the middle class, particularly through the character of Gordon Comstock. While the first critiques the systemic forces that trap the working class, the second one examines the psychological and ideological struggles of those caught between rejecting and conforming to the materialism that defines their existence. Through this transition, Orwell continues to dissect the pervasive influence of economic forces, now through the lens of a disillusioned individual battling the very societal norms he previously sought to escape.

GORDON'S REBELLION IS A BATTLE OF ONE

Orwell's 1936 novel *Keep the Aspidistra Flying*, in which a flawed Gordon Comstock rebels against the capitalist system but ultimately returns to middle-class comforts, satirises the contradictions within middle-class consciousness.

> He had declared war on money but that did not prevent him from being damnably selfish. Of course he dreaded this business of going to work. What boy wouldn't dread it? ... [His uncles and aunts] seemed to want to see every young man in England nailed down in the coffin of a 'good' job. ... But he grasped now what was the matter with them. It was not *merely* the lack of money. It was rather that, having no money, they still lived mentally in the money-world – the world in which money is virtue and poverty is crime. It was not poverty but the down-dragging of *respectable* poverty that had done for them. They had accepted the money-code, and by that code they were failures. They had never had the sense to lash out and just *live*, money or no money, as the lower classes do. How right the lower classes are! Hats off to the factory lad who with fourpence in the world puts his girl in the family way! At least he's got blood and not money in his veins (1956 [1936]: 45, italics in the original).

The normalisation of female sacrifice for male success reveals the privileged position of our protagonist. While Julia, Gordon's sister, endures a gruelling twelve-hour workday, Gordon 'dreaded this business of going to work. What boy wouldn't dread it?' From a young age, he is spared from this burden, as the sexual division of

DÉBORA REIS TAVARES

labour grants him access to education through his sister's sacrifice. This is a legacy of the industrial revolution's labour distribution, where much of the work was assigned to women and children, allowing for a significant transfer of earnings from labour to capital.

Gordon's selfish attitudes are reflected in the literary form. The narrator almost becomes a character, passing judgement on the protagonist's actions. We see this in the use of the adverb and adjective at the end of the sentence: 'He had declared war on money but that did not prevent him from being damnably selfish.' Gordon behaves selfishly, refusing to seek work and relying on his sister for support. The narrator not only labels Gordon's comfortable attitude but also provides justifications: 'Of course he dreaded this business of going to work. What boy wouldn't dread it?' The narrative, told from a certain point of view, offers access to the protagonist's consciousness, which drives much of the novel.

We are led by Gordon's narrow logic: 'What boy wouldn't dread it?', but at times the narrative voice distances itself from him to criticise 'being damnably selfish'. This creates a sense of agreement with Gordon at one moment and distance at another, allowing for judgement. This transition between the narrator's evaluation and apparent agreement with the protagonist's thoughts is skilfully constructed through free indirect discourse.

This discursive technique means that when the narrator seems to agree with Gordon, the protagonist's thoughts replace the selective omniscient narrator's voice. This can be seen in detail when the narrative subtly shifts its perspective and adopts linguistic markers signalling a change in internal focalisation. We witness an oscillation of opinion, evident in the use of the phrase 'damnably selfish' and the verb 'dreaded'.

Thus, the irony here portrays Gordon as immature, not having fully considered all the implications of his beliefs. By refusing to live under the rule of money, he seeks employment without considering the practical consequences, which fall on his sister, who is forced to sacrifice for the brother deemed the most intelligent in the family. However, this is a burden for both: on the one hand, there is the imposition of Gordon's supposed intellectual potential which, if realised, could mean better days for the family; on the other, there is the imposition of financial responsibility on Julia, seen as inferior and treated as an object rather than a subject. She faces the pressure of practical demands, while he experiences a different kind of tension – the pressure on his intellectual abilities, another aspect of the privilege of being outside the labour market.

Gordon is spared the sacrifices his sister Julia assumes and remains unaware of his mother's illness, something kept secret between the two women. When he realises this, his reaction is to equate their behaviour regarding the lack of money: 'It was rather that, having no money they still lived mentally in the money-world – the world in which money is virtue and poverty is crime.' Although they lack financial means, the family persists mentally within the logic of money, a logic that seems to apply to the protagonist, even without his awareness. He excludes himself from those who agree with the logic of money: 'they still lived', hence the use of the third-person plural pronoun.

Thus, poverty, while not abstract, only affects Gordon's mind, as it only impacts certain aspects of his life. Reflecting on his mother's and sister's precarious condition, he reveals aspects of himself. After Julia's sacrifice, Gordon secures a job at an advertising agency, a place that catalyses his break with the monetary exchange system. Consequently, he resigns and embarks on his journey against money, going to work in a bookshop. Thanks to Julia's selflessness, Gordon has choices unavailable to his sister and mother.

Provided with opportunities, without assuming any responsibilities, our protagonist begins his attempt to isolate himself from money, seeking to live on the margins of society. He chooses not to be completely destitute, where poverty takes over the body and all material life. We begin to understand how he embarks on an endeavour in which he will be the only one to suffer the consequences.

In such a money code, poverty is a crime. In the logic of capital, those who lack it are those who sustain it. On this threshold, Gordon places himself in a limbo that allows him to escape absolute destitution. But there is a distinction between two types of poverty, one generalised and one considered respectable: 'It was not poverty but the down-dragging of *respectable* poverty that had done for them' (italics in the original). We encounter a value judgement, an idealisation of the condition of those who truly live in poverty, something seen as respectable and dignified.

Gordon's family had accepted the rules of money 'and under the terms of that code they were failures', meaning they could not be seen as the poor who adhered to the criteria of idealised poverty: 'How right the lower classes are!' Perhaps in the details of the sentence, we can see the construction of an idealised view regarding the lower classes, especially in the punctuation, with the use of an exclamation mark. Gordon's argument remains emphasised, conveyed through free indirect discourse once again.

Our protagonist fetishises poverty to hide his own condition. According to him, his family lacks 'the sense to lash out and just *live*', like the lower classes (italics in the original). But this line of reasoning is flawed. Gordon constantly avoids reflecting on his role in his network of relationships. In his logic, the lower classes seem carefree and full of common sense for not having 'money in their veins'. But this has nothing to do with detachment. It is instead a reality of need, scarcity and deprivation.

Consequently, it is the result of a historical process in which a vast segment of the population has been deprived of any emancipatory possibility: their labour sustains the production of surpluses appropriated by a minority. The discourse on 'detachment' is an instrument of ideological domination, an attractive fallacy for Gordon and a whole sector of intellectual workers who, out of ignorance or interest, do not admit that 'classes constitute ... a system of relations in which each class presupposes the existence of another or others; there can be no bourgeoisie without a proletariat, and vice versa' (2018: 12). In other words, this so-called 'detachment' is nothing more than exclusion disguised by the veils of exploitation.

BREAKING THE SYSTEM FROM WITHIN: WINSTON AND THE PROLES

Finally, in Orwell's dystopian vision, Winston Smith's failed rebellion against the Party highlights the difficulty of dismantling a deeply entrenched system. The proles, representing the oppressed masses, echo Marxist theories of class struggle and the role of the proletariat in instigating change. As Winston writes in his secret diary:

> If there was hope, it *must* lie in the proles, because only there, in those swarming disregarded masses, 85 per cent of the population of Oceania, could the force to destroy the Party ever be generated. The Party could not be overthrown from within. Its enemies, if it had any enemies, had no way of coming together or even of identifying one another. Even if the legendary Brotherhood existed, as just possibly it might, it was inconceivable that its members could ever assemble in larger numbers than twos and threes. Rebellion meant a look in the eyes, an inflexion of the voice; at the most, an occasional whispered word. But the proles, if only they could somehow become conscious of their own strength, would have no need to conspire. They needed only to rise up and shake themselves like a horse shaking off flies. If they chose they could blow the Party to pieces tomorrow morning. Surely sooner or later it must occur to them to do it? And yet...! (2009 [1949]: 80, italics in the original).

It is quite clear how narrative is functioning to externalise the character's thoughts. However, since these thoughts are not verbalised, this externalisation is directed towards the reader, transcending the boundaries of the work itself. These thoughts do not affect the closed plot of the work but instead reach beyond it.

Winston's expression of the importance of the proles as potential agents of change suggests his detachment from the vast majority of the population. He is not a proletarian but an intellectual member of the Party, aware of who can truly bring about change. Thus, he positions himself outside this process, merely aware of how things should happen. It is not his role to incite rebellion, as he belongs to the minority of the population that, despite being repressed, enjoys privileges the proles do not have. Winston's only action within the 'class struggle' is to express his indignation through his diary, which could incriminate him for opposing Big Brother, but nothing more.

The next diary entry, along with the previous one, sets the tone that will guide the entire book: '*Until they become conscious they will never rebel, and until after they have rebelled they cannot become conscious*' (italics in the original) (ibid: 90). Here, the narrator directly reflects Winston's thoughts in the diary. By referring to the proles as 'they' Winston excludes himself; otherwise, he would have used the first-person plural pronoun, 'we'. This subtle evidence is significant in placing the protagonist far from the potential of the mass population.

After all, when, and if, the population takes power, it will overthrow the system in which Winston is involved and from which he benefits. In a sense, when the proletarians become aware of their power, they could destroy a part of his way of life, much more than Big Brother has done. If Winston does not break free from the many chains that privilege him, he risks being excluded from a new order – an order that paradoxically would be the realisation of his true awakening.

In this excerpt, the issue of class consciousness emerges clearly and becomes a theme throughout the novel, not through Winston's rebellion, but through the proles' revolt against the system created by the Party. The diary entry is merely the character's observation of what others must do, positioning him as a distant observer who is aware but does not put this awareness into action.

The issue faced by Winston, the one regarding class consciousness, is inherent to the capitalist system, as the division into social classes subjected to the means of production is a unique characteristic of this system. Thus, for Marxism, the notion of class consciousness is embedded within the concept of class itself, stemming from the material bases of common labour relations and the means of production. At the same time, the notion of class only solidifies when there is an awareness of its existence.

Therefore, it is necessary for an individual and/or group of individuals (that is, a class) to recognise the position they occupy in this process, considering that this condition often remains unknown for a long time, leading to the alienation of the individual, who lives for years being exploited by the system without realising it. In other words, upon becoming aware of this entire process, the notion of class emerges and, dialectically, the act of awakening to consciousness only happens because of the division of society into classes within the production process.

The highlighted passage from Orwell's work is a clear example of the dialectical manifestation of class consciousness, one of the central discussions in the book. This is evident from the beginning, due to the way the author chooses to present the discussion: through a metalinguistic device, where the character creates a parallel writing within the novel, in the form of a diary. This writing appears prominently on the page, like a citation, drawing the reader's attention to the moment when the character expresses himself in the most direct way possible.

Considering the context of the plot, the diary form is the most explicit and intimate way for the reader to access the character's thoughts since, in the dictatorship in which Winston lives, dialogues are artificial, mechanical and, most importantly, monitored, preventing the use of direct discourse. If the character expressed himself aloud, he would be caught and arrested by the police.

Further grammatical analysis of the sentence reveals that the verb tense in each clause differs. In the first clause, the verb is in the present tense but has the value of a future tense sentence ('until they become conscious'); in the second clause, the verb is in the future tense ('they will never rebel'); in the third clause, the verb is in the past participle ('and until after they have rebelled'); and finally, the fourth clause is again in the present tense ('they cannot become conscious'). It is possible to see a cycle of verb tenses in this passage, beginning and ending in the present, as if it were a movement with a beginning, middle and end; a completed cycle. The act of class consciousness is always presented in the present and is linked to the act of rebellion, both in the future and the past, culminating in consciousness in the present. This could suggest that the act of becoming aware is linear and constant, while what truly changes is how the result of this awareness (rebellion) manifests within the proletariat.

The construction of the sentence invites a parallel to the way society is presented: most of the time there is an awareness of class belonging, either in an individual or a group of individuals, but this may or may not lead to rebellion. Here, the process of rebellion does not run alongside consciousness; it oscillates between the past and the future, as if past revolutions did not impact the present, while this present is on the verge of organising a rebellion that will only occur in the near future.

Finally, syntactically, the use of the conjunction 'until' is noteworthy. As an invariable word that links two clauses, the conjunction equalises the value of the clauses, meaning that the clauses hold the same level of importance and develop together. This syntactic relationship can be observed in the semantics of the sentence, that is, in the dialectical relationship between class consciousness and rebellion. The paradox of Winston's reflection may seem insoluble unless dialectical reasoning is applied, allowing for rebellion to occur simultaneously with the working class's awakening to its precarious living conditions.

Rosa Luxemburg, in *Reform or Revolution* (2020 [1898]), highlights the role of social experience and class struggle in forming class consciousness and, consequently, in the possibility of instituting historical change in society. In other words, through the perception and experience of social inequalities, a fundamental characteristic of the capitalist system, the working class begins to organise and demand its rights, with the aim of imposing substantive changes on the social order.

This is a process where rebellion occurs alongside the awakening of consciousness; if one were to happen without the other, no social transformation would be possible. However, Winston, as an intellectual, remains solely on the level of awareness, placing the working class on the opposite side, responsible for the concrete aspect of rebellion. This issue is problematic because those who recognise the importance of class consciousness should join the exploited majority, since, like the proletariat, the intellectual worker is also exploited – albeit deceived by the real material comforts they receive as payment for aiding in the propagation of hegemonic ideology. In other words, Winston should act according to his reflections and join the proles, identifying himself as equal to them and contributing to the rebellion's realisation.

By remaining passive and acting only in his self-interest, Winston perpetuates the Party's ideology – even incompletely, as he does not become the perfectly adapted intellectual like O'Brien – rather than opposing it. Thus, the diary serves as a formal device, ostensibly for the awakening of consciousness but, in reality, it reveals Winston's character limitations, expressed in the narrative.

Another passage from Chapter 7, of Part One, '*I understand* HOW: *I do not understand* WHY' (italics in the original) demonstrates Winston's limitation as a rebel. By acknowledging that his social understanding is limited to the 'how,' he admits ignorance of the reason behind all the motivations needed to overthrow the Party. This diary excerpt is connected to the end of the second part, where Winston receives from O'Brien the black book of the organisation opposing the Party, *The Theory and Practice of Oligarchical Collectivism*, supposedly written by Goldstein, in reality, a tool of the Party written by O'Brien to identify rebels. Here, Goldstein's book reinforces the idea that Winston functions merely as a cog in such a vast production line that it is impossible to grasp the whole process or its deep-rooted motives.

Moreover, the content of this diary entry relates to the final part of the book, where Winston is tortured and, in order to escape death, professes his love for Big Brother. In other words, he chooses to abandon any form of questioning, precisely because he never understood the 'why' of how things work, and thus saves his own life. Winston's rebellion seems to extend only to the point where it might benefit him. When it no longer suits him, he abandons it, also for his own gain.

Finally, the sentence that ends Chapter 7 is Winston's last diary entry: '*Freedom is the freedom to say that two plus two equals four. If that is granted, all else follows*' (italics in the original) (2009 [1949]: 101), a passage that plays an essential role in the third part of the novel, where Winston is tortured by O'Brien. Winston seeks a form of freedom that is different from the reality imposed by Big Brother. However, after undergoing brainwashing, asserting freedom is of no use to him. He confronts the power of the Party, which is capable of distorting and relativising all information and is forced to accept it or face death.

Throughout the novel, the main character becomes aware of the severity of the system in which he lives and tries to rebel against it, as long as it is convenient for him. We can see the workings and consequences of this repressive society in detail, but it is impossible to understand the reason behind everything that happened.

Winston is incapable of reflecting deeper about the world around him and this incapacity seems to be a deep critique of oppressive systems and the results it brings on the oppressed. Orwell meticulously deconstructs the mechanisms of control, surveillance and ideological manipulation employed by totalitarian regimes, as seen through Winston's struggles in *Nineteen Eighty-Four*. However, Winston's inability to grasp fully the underlying reasons for these systems' existence reflects a broader challenge within Marxist and Dependency Theory critiques – understanding not just the mechanisms of exploitation, but the deeper, often elusive motivations that sustain such structures globally. Thus, the question of 'why' remains central to the critique of global power structures, highlighting the complexities of alienation by not only recognising but also dismantling deeply entrenched systems of inequality, whether on a global scale or within specific national contexts.

LEGACY AND THE GLOBAL SOUTH

Orwell's nuanced exploration of the relationship between the margins and the centre continues to resonate in the context of the Global South. His works not only critique the power structures that exploit the periphery but also suggest the potential for resistance and transformation. By engaging with Orwell's writings through the lens of the Global South, we gain a richer understanding of his relevance to contemporary socio-political issues.

His legacy, particularly his focus on the marginalised, remains a crucial tool for analysing the socio-economic and political structures that shape the Global South. By connecting Orwell's work with Marxist theories and the lived experiences of those on the periphery, this paper contributes to a deeper comprehension of the global dynamics at play in his writing.

REFERENCES

Eagleton, Terry (2018) *Why Marx Was Right*, New Haven: Yale University Press

Harvey, David (2010) *The Enigma of Capital: And the Crises of Capitalism*, New York: Oxford University Press

Luxemburg, Rosa (2020 [1898]) *Reform or Revolution*, Paris: Foreign Languages Press

Marx, Karl and Engels, Friedrich (2000 [1848]) *The Manifesto of the Communist Party*, Marxists Internet Archive. Available online at https://www.marxists.org/archive/marx/works/1848/communist-manifesto/

Orwell, George (1956 [1936]) *Keep the Aspidistra Flying*, New York: Harcourt Publishing Company

Orwell, George (2001 [1937]) *The Road to Wigan Pier*, London: Penguin Classics

Orwell, George (2004 [1946]) *Why I write*. London: Penguin Great Ideas

Orwell, George (2009) *Shooting an Elephant and Other Essays*, London: Penguin Books Ltd

Orwell, George (2009 [1949]) *Nineteen Eighty-Four*, London: Penguin Books

Schwarz, Roberto (1992) *Misplaced Ideas: Essays on Brazilian Culture*, London: Verso

Williams, Raymond (1971) *Orwell*, New York: The Viking Press

NOTE ON THE CONTRIBUTOR

Débora Reis Tavares has a Master's and a PhD degree in English Literature from the University of São Paulo, where she specialised in 20th-century British literature and Marxist studies. Her research focuses on the intersections of literature, politics and social theory, with a particular emphasis on the works of George Orwell. She has published extensively on Orwell's reception in Brazil and is the founder of *Livre Literatura®*, an independent online institution dedicated to teaching literature and society.

PAPER

Orwell's Middle Age Anxiety

CARRIE KANCILIA

This paper investigates the prominence of ageing as a theme – and locus of anxiety and disgust – in Orwell's work, noting that he pays particular attention to unsettling portrayals of middle age in his inter-war canon. A cataloguing and analysis of ageing rhetoric in Orwell's inter-war work illuminates a consistent fixation on the age of his characters and the corresponding value he confers upon them. In A Clergyman's Daughter *(1935) and* Coming Up For Air *(1939), depictions of the ageing woman emerge as especially heinous though ageing appears as a significant theme in his later, more famous, novels. This paper, therefore, argues that ageing is a major theme in Orwell's work on par with those issues for which he is most known, such as imperialism, totalitarianism and socialism.*

Key words: *A Clergyman's Daughter, Coming Up For Air*, disgust and ageing, middle age, spinsters, inter-war fiction, gender

While Orwell is best known for warnings about the future, meditations on wealth and poverty, and critiques of imperialism and totalitarianism, ageing was as important an issue to him as any other, and recently scholars have begun to turn towards it as an important theme when analysing his work.[1] His often savage depictions of ageing are especially excoriating for women characters whose advancing age represents personal and disgusting failure.

In a way, Orwell's conservative and fixed attitudes towards ageing align with the demands for newness extolled by modernity. Baudelaire acknowledges the 'ephemeral, the fugitive, the contingent' (1964 [1863]: 13) and his depiction of modernity centres on the new, the momentary, and the individual's ability to adapt continually to fresh circumstances. Further, Baudelaire contends that resisting the natural flow of ever-changing circumstances enables one 'to tumble into the abyss of an abstract and indeterminate beauty, like that of the first woman before the fall of man' (ibid). The expression 'Make it new', attributed to the poet Ezra Pound, is, according to Michael North, 'the most durably useful of all modernist expressions of the value of novelty' (2013: 162). Similarly, Peter Gay comments:

'In short, modernists considered Ezra Pound's famous injunction: "Make It New!", a professional, almost a sacred obligation. And it was the avant-garde painters who were first, and the most highly visible, cultural revolutionaries' (2010: 106).

Even the Spanish Civil War (1936-1939), where Orwell fought in a Republican militia against Franco's fascist forces and whose experiences would later be reported in *Homage to Catalonia* (1938), ushered in a novel geopolitical shift. In *The Origins of Totalitarianism*, Arendt notes that this conflict, in its move from a domestic matter to one with geopolitical implications, was 'almost as frightening as these new dangers arising from the old trouble spots of Europe' and that it reflected an entirely *new* kind of behaviour 'of all European nationals in "ideological struggles"' (1973: 282; italics added). Throughout Orwell's work, there is a perceptible dispensing with the old in favour of the new, both in terms of global systems and with respect to ageing, human bodies.

Publishing novels, journalism and essays roughly from the early 1930s to 1949, Orwell's writing consistently grapples with oppositions between old and new; his tactic for reconciling this tension in his inter-war canon, and in *A Clergyman's Daughter* in particular, reveal persistent age-related anxieties and his tendency to eviscerate his women characters. While Daphne Patai's seminal *The Orwell Mystique: A Study in Male Ideology* (1984) does not expressly engage with ageing as a concept, it provides a useful framework with which to consider Orwell's pathological disparagement of women characters. Patai locates despair at the core of this tendency:

> Orwell's uncritical embrace of misogyny and his hostility to feminism are among his most serious shortcomings as a moral witness to his times. But they explain his despair. *Clinging* to an inherently dangerous, and *presumably inescapable*, notion of the masculine, while aware of its deadly, potentiality, Orwell can see no way out. In *his adherence to a conventional notion of manhood*, he cannot discern that the characteristics he lends, and the ones he promotes, are united by the demands of the male gender role (Patai 1984: 264, italics added).

Philip Goldstein highlights a central contradiction in the work of Orwell, a man who 'condemned imperialist oppression in Burma, the suffering of impoverished city dwellers, the exploitation of British coal miners, the fascist victory in Spain, and the Stalinist influence on the left' while also holding some conservative views, including the denunciation of feminism and intellectualism (2000:44).

CARRIE KANCILIA

AGEING IN ORWELL'S 1930S NONFICTION

In Orwell's ethnographic nonfiction of the 1930s, *Down and Out in Paris and London* (1933) and *The Road to Wigan Pier* (1937), peppered observations about age arise. In *Down and Out*, we see one of the first examples of what will become a standard mode of description in Orwell's subsequent works when we encounter 'a horrid, fat, Frenchwoman with a dead-white face and scarlet lips, reminding me of cold veal and tomatoes' (1961 [1937]: 51). Orwell also describes 'an old, skull-faced woman' (ibid: 56) in the laundry, and a dishwasher of 'quite sixty years old' (ibid: 69) whose demoralising life of toil he acknowledges while castigating her in this way: 'It was so strange to see that in spite of her age and her life she still wore a bright wig, and darkened her eyes and painted her face like a girl of twenty' (ibid). Later, he will admit to calling another 'poor old woman' a 'cow' and 'jeer' at her as she cries, owing this behaviour to 'fatigue' (ibid: 113). He describes a fellow tramp at the spike, a man, as a 'toothless mummy of seventy-five' (ibid: 143). The young men in *Down and Out* worry about the prematurely ageing effects of poverty, especially Charlie, who laments: 'At twenty-two, I am utterly worn out and finished' (ibid: 10).

There is also much age-related commentary in *The Road to Wigan Pier*. For instance, he describes a young woman: 'She had a round pale face, the usual exhausted face of the slum girl who is twenty-five and looks forty, thanks to miscarriages and drudgery' (1958 [1937]: 18). While we may take the premature ageing of coal miners in the industrial north of England as self-evident, the adult men observed by Orwell also suffer from an impish, stalled maturity. As Michael Amundsen notes: 'Joe [is] a middle-aged man who, lacking in all responsibility, seems more of a boy' (2016: 17). Orwell's treatment of ageing in nonfiction consistently shows poverty and toilsome workdays as both accelerants of physical manifestations of age and barriers to traditional markers of adulthood, such as spouses and children.

AGEING IN *BURMESE DAYS*

Each of Orwell's novels, especially those in his inter-war canon, relies on tropes and rhetoric about ageing to develop story and characters. Fatma Kalpakli notes the binary divide between the coloniser and the colonised in *Burmese Days* (1934), a novel that explores the declining strength of British colonialism: 'Throughout the novel, the "us and them" attitude is prevalent and the Indians, being non-white and non-Christian, are perceived as the other. There are clear-cut distinctions and borders between the English and the Indians in *Burmese Days*' (Kalpakli 2015: 1215). Kalpakli reminds us that the first representative of the British Empire we see in the novel is the district superintendent of police, Westville, 'a sandy-haired Englishman, with a prickly moustache, pale grey eyes too far apart, and abnormally thin calves to his legs' (1962 [1934]: 52). We then see the conflation of racism and ageism later in an allusion to thin calves when Dr Veraswami, himself Indian, comments to Flory on the appearance of an old Indian doorman: 'Look at the wretchedness of hiss limbs. The calves of hiss legs are not so thick ass an Englishman's wrists' (ibid: 97). Not only does this passage suggest that thinness is a detriment in the aged, Lieskounig remarks that 'it nevertheless represents an early example in the text of the ridiculing of the pretended superiority of a representative of both the master-race and British Imperialism by means of a precise and telling physical detail' (2012: 52-53). In the scene with the 'old' Indian man of slight physical frame, we see how this malicious attitude of the British officer towards the Indians has been internalised as self-hatred from one Indian to another. With Dr Veraswami castigating the old Indian doorman for his age and slight frame (especially when such an appearance is praised among the British) we see one of Orwell's first attempts to locate ageism as an 'othering' mechanism; the familiarity with and similarity to the older Indian doorman unearths in Veraswami the reaction of immediate animosity.

Orwell carefully details the ages of the characters in *Burmese Days*, typically to point out their resistance to rapidly changing attitudes or to the colonial pressure to Europeanise; for example, we learn that Ma Kin 'was a simple, old-fashioned woman, who had learned even less of European habits than U Po Kyin' (1962 [1934]: 15). The novel's main protagonist receives an extended description in which his age is highlighted in this way:

> Flory was a man of about thirty-five, of middle height, not ill made. He had very black, stiff hair growing low on his head, and a cropped black moustache, and his skin, naturally sallow, was discoloured by the sun. Not having grown fat or bald he did not look older than his age, but his face was very haggard in spite of the sunburn, with lank cheeks and a sunken, withered look round the eyes (ibid: 16-17).

As we will see later with his women characters, Orwell highlights the late twenties as the point at which his characters' anxiety about ageing peaks.

> [Flory] celebrated his twenty-seventh birthday in hospital, covered from head to foot with hideous sores which were called mud-sores, but were probably caused by whisky and bad food. They left little pits in his skin which did not disappear for two years. Quite suddenly he had begun to look and feel very

much older. *His youth was finished.* Eight years of Eastern life, fever, loneliness and intermittent drinking, had set their mark on him (ibid: 68; italics added).

The sense of despondency suffered by Flory on his twenty-seventh birthday and the feeling of having been prematurely aged by life's circumstances harkens back to Charlie, the tramp Orwell meets in Paris, who deems himself 'finished' at twenty-two. The young men we meet through Orwell, by observation or creation, express persistent terror about getting or feeling old.

AGEING IN *KEEP THE ASPIDISTRA FLYING*

In *Keep the Aspidistra Flying* (1936), with the novel's core focus on the evils of money and the would-be prolific author/protagonist's lack thereof, Orwell still manages to lament ageing, if briefly. At twenty-nine, Gordon Comstock winces at his own reflection, musing: 'Not a good face. Not thirty yet, but moth-eaten already. Very pale, with bitter, ineradicable lines' (1956 [1936]: 5-6). He also makes passing but notable references to the crushing drudgery of middle age with allusions to the 'rather undesirable middle-aged marriages' (ibid: 39-40) of pitiable women in his family to men whose 'incapacity to earn a proper living … were the kind of "can't afford" to marry' (40). Of Gordon's sister, Julia, he writes:

> Julia was a tall, ungainly girl, much taller than Gordon, with a thin face and a neck just a little too long – one of those girls who even at their most youthful remind one irresistibly of a goose. But her nature was simple and affectionate. She was a self-effacing, home-keeping, ironing, darning, and mending kind of girl, a natural spinster-soul. Even at sixteen she had 'old maid' written all over her (ibid: 41).

In *Keep the Aspidistra Flying*, Orwell makes many other interesting observations about age, including that old age begins at sixty[2] and that grey hair in a woman of thirty suggests premature maturing. He notes: 'Julia was nearly thirty now, and looked much older. She was thinner than ever, though healthy enough, and there was grey in her hair' (ibid: 48). He also gives a humorous if snarky depiction of one lascivious Mother Meakin: '[She] was not the type to interfere. She was a dishevelled, jelly-soft old creature with a figure like a cottage loaf. People said that in her youth she had been no better than she ought, and probably it was true. She had a loving manner towards anything in trousers' (ibid: 207). Elsewhere Gordon reflects on the signs of ageing on his face and hair, or at least as a state of being 'non-young': 'He was shabby to the point of raggedness, his face had grown much thinner and had the dingy, greyish pallor of people who live on bread and margarine. He looked much older –

thirty-five at the least' (ibid: 224).³ Orwell weaves anxiety around middle age into *Keep the Aspidistra Flying* linking it to the ability (or otherwise) to attract a spouse and marry, but also as a gauge for artistic accomplishments; Gordon's observations about premature ageing suggest vanity, but pointedly accentuate the fear of time running out to make his name as a writer.

AGEING IN *COMING UP FOR AIR*

Like *A Clergyman's Daughter*, *Coming Up For Air* (1939) provides an extended commentary on the anxieties of becoming middle aged. In the novel's opening section, the first-person narrator, also named George, takes out his false teeth and, looking at his face in the mirror, proclaims: 'I've never gone grey or bald, thank God, and when I've got my teeth in I probably don't look my age, which is forty-five' (1950 [1939]: 3). The narrator goes on: 'When your last natural tooth goes, the time when you can kid yourself that you're a Hollywood sheik is definitely at an end. And I was fat as well at forty-five' (ibid: 5).

This preoccupation with teeth evokes Freud's *Interpretation of Dreams*. Teeth figure highly in that work; for Freud, dreams of lost teeth are the most common along with flying and appearing publicly nude (1915 [1899]: 31) and he cites teeth as 'beyond all possibility of being compared with anything' (ibid: 234) making teeth 'suitable for representation under pressure of sexual repression' (ibid). Additionally, Freud suggests that teeth can be viewed as replacements for the genitals and the imagined loss of them as a reflection of the castration complex (ibid).

Much of the first half of *Coming Up For Air* continues this reflection on lost teeth, going so far as to link false teeth with the unstable state of modernity itself. George recalls having bit into a sausage made of fish with his temporary teeth: 'It gave me the feeling that I'd bitten into the modern world and discovered what it was really made of. That's the way we're going nowadays. Everything slick and streamlined, everything made of something else' (1950 [1939]: 27). As though self-conscious about his fixation on teeth, the narrator acknowledges to the reader that 'very likely it sounds absurd to say that false teeth can make you feel younger, it's a fact that they did so. ... There's life in the old dog yet' (ibid: 28).

Even though George is older than his wife, he still speaks uncharitably of her, again in ageist terms: 'Hilda is thirty-nine ... she's gotten very thin and rather wizened, with a perpetual brooding, worried look in her eyes ... like an old gypsy woman over her fire' (ibid: 7). George's disparagement of Hilda escalates towards the close of the novel. He conjectures cruelly of wives in general: 'They don't want to have a good time, they merely want to slump into middle age as quickly as possible. After the frightful battle of getting her man to the altar, the woman kind of relaxes, and all her youth, looks, energy and joy of life just vanish overnight' (ibid: 159). George then bemoans the inevitable rapid physical decay, noting that his wife Hilda had 'settled down into a depressed, lifeless, middle aged frump' (ibid: 160). Not only does Hilda's entry to middle age read as a personal attack on the narrator, the nature of marital relationships emerges as a nefarious and intentional ruse to lure unsuspecting men into permanent unions with women with one chief goal: 'relaxing' into a less appealing appearance as rapidly as possible.

SOME ALLUSIONS TO AGEING IN *ANIMAL FARM* AND *NINETEEN EIGHTY-FOUR*

While Orwell's inter-war canon places most persistent value judgment on ageing people, systems and things, the trend can be found to a slightly less degree in the later novels and more celebrated works. In *Animal Farm*, it is an 'old' boar who utters the call to arms and it is his advanced age, twelve, that legitimates the wisdom of his message: '[Old] Major, the prize Middle White boar, had had a strange dream on the previous night and wished to communicate it to the other animals… Old Major … was so highly regarded on the farm that everyone was quite ready to lose an hour's sleep in order to hear what he had to say' (2001a: 13). When his rapt audience gathers, Old Major delivers a speech that decries capitalism as a system, but highlights the particular expendability of the aged in that system: 'The very instant that our usefulness has come to an end we are slaughtered with hideous cruelty. No animal in England knows the meaning of happiness or leisure after he is a year old' (ibid: 14). Old Boar reminds his comrades that ageing is a process by which you lose perceived value and that death is the consequence of that lost worth: 'You, Boxer, the very day that those great muscles of yours lose their power, Jones will sell you to the knacker, who will cut your throat and boil you down for the foxhounds. As for the dogs, when they grow old and toothless, Jones ties a brick round their necks and drowns them in the nearest pond' (ibid: 15).

While Orwell uses Old Boar's age to position him as an elder statesmen who can rally the like-minded to his cause, he also introduces Benjamin the donkey, 'the oldest animal on the farm, and the worst tempered' (ibid: 13), devoid of the enthusiasm for engaging in new ideological frameworks. In the same opening address, Old Boar questions the value of the farm's ageing hens and horses, citing the ability to reproduce as their core value on the farm: 'And you hens, how many eggs have you laid in this last year, and how many of those eggs ever hatched into chickens?' (ibid: 15) The anthropomorphisation of the female animals evokes the reference to menopause by Margaret Gullette as a 'false decline narrative' (2011: 88): 'Clover was a stout motherly mare approaching middle life, who had never quite got her figure back after her fourth foal' (2001a [19045]: 13). On the horses, Orwell writes: '... the retiring age had been fixed for horses and pigs at twelve, for cows at fourteen, for dogs at nine, for sheep at seven, and for hens and geese at five. Liberal old-age pensions had been agreed upon. As yet no animal had actually retired on pension, but of late the subject had been discussed more and more' (ibid: 54). V.C. Letemendia suggests the condensed lifespans in *Animal Farm* facilitate nuanced conversations about ageing: 'Unlike men, the majority of the beasts are limited naturally by their brief lifespan and the consequent shortness of their memory' (1992: 129). Using animals as conduits for complex political discussion might engage an otherwise reluctant audience, and it also implicates a microcosmic view of ageing as bestowing wisdom on men and marginalisation on women the further they move from their peak fertility.

Significantly, in *Nineteen Eighty-Four*, Winston Smith, the novel's anti-hero, is 'thirty-nine and had a varicose ulcer above his right ankle' (2021 [1949]: 617) and turns forty at the point of acceptance of Big Brother by the novel's close. Stressing Orwell's tendency to write 'hyper-conscious anti-heroes', Roger Fowler identifies the similarities between his early protagonists and Winston Smith: '[He] has ancestors: John Flory in *Burmese Days*, Gordon Comstock in *Keep the Aspidistra Flying*, George Bowling in *Coming Up For Air*. All these "little men", petty clerk-like figures of no worldly success and of unenviable physique; somewhat educated ... *no longer young*, sexually frustrated; self-conscious and self-pitying' (1995: 184, italics inserted). Also in *Nineteen Eighty-Four*, Mrs Parsons is described as 'a woman of about thirty, but looking much older. One had the impression that there was dust in the creases of her face' (2021 [1949]: 626).

ORWELL ON GENDERED AGEING: *A CLERGYMAN'S DAUGHTER*

Although *A Clergyman's Daughter* was Orwell's second-published novel, I conclude this paper with it since the entire novel centres on ageing. As Daphne Patai argues, the novel best captures Orwell's 'nostalgia for the past, his misogyny ... and the conservatism apparent in his carefully circumscribed challenge to hierarchy and inequality' (1984: 14). With *A Clergyman's Daughter,* Orwell introduces the archetypal spinster, Dorothy Hare, who aligns perfectly with Emma Liggins's description of 'women outside marriage between 1850 and the Second World War ... as abnormal, threatening, superfluous and incomplete, whilst also being hailed as "women of the future"'

(2014: 147). Indeed, unwed women, spinsters or 'unnecessary women' as they are often called in modernist literature, represented a threat to heteronormative domesticity and stability. Orwell's *A Clergyman's Daughter* offers a narrative in which Dorothy Hare, an unmarried woman of twenty-eight, suffers a bout of amnesia for eight days after suffering a sexual attack by Mr Warburton, during which she is mistaken for a sex worker and denied lodging. One of the many interesting elements of Dorothy's mysterious dissociative episode is that it places her outside of the possibility of domesticity, marriage and familial responsibility. The life she leads now presents multiple challenges in terms of securing housing and food, but the precarity around obtaining basic necessities is accompanied by the excitement Dorothy feels about being at last surrounded by people in her age group.

Interestingly, Orwell's depiction of Dorothy is similar to that of the spinster, Lolly Willowes, in Sylvia Townsend Warner's novel of the same name:

> It was thick, fine, exceedingly pale hair, and it was perhaps as well that her father had forbidden her to bob it, for it was her only positive beauty. For the rest, she was a girl of middle height, rather thin, but strong and shapely, and her face was her weak point. It was a thin, blonde, unremarkable kind of face, with pale eyes and a nose just a shade too long; if you looked closely you could see crows' feet around the eyes, and the mouth, when it was in repose, looked tired. Not definitely a spinsterish face as yet, but it certainly would be so in a few years' time (1936: 8).[4]

In her late twenties and frequently waylaid by fears about spinsterhood, Dorothy, for the first half of *A Clergyman's Daughter*, is surrounded by much older individuals, with unenviable lives who make her daily existence a terrible drudge. In addition to tending to a demanding and fickle father, she must confront her guilty disgust over Miss Mayfill's aged appearance, defend herself against Mr Warburton's unwanted sexual advances, indulge Mrs Semprill's lonely nosiness, deal with Mr Tombs's many cats and endure Mrs Pither's complaints about the physical ailments of her ageing body.

Early on in the novel, Orwell's focus on ageing begins with the narrator harshly critiquing the ageing features of older women in Dorothy's circle; the corresponding disgust Dorothy displays at their ageing features seems to be a mechanism by which to distance herself, however impossibly, from her own inevitable ageing.

Orwell begins with Miss Mayfill, who 'was very old, so old that no one remembered her as anything but an old woman. A faint scent radiated from her – an ethereal scent, analysable as eau-de-

Cologne, mothballs and a subflavour of gin' (2001a [1936]: 12). It is presented as a tragedy that Mayfill's current physical state is the only one remembered; her preferable youthful state has been woefully scrubbed from the minds of the town's inhabitants. With the suggestion that Mayfill emanates the scent of mothballs and gin, we encounter stereotypes around 'old age smell' and alcoholism among senior citizens. Dorothy punishes herself for drifting off with disparaging thoughts about Mayfill's advanced age and 'quasi-pork-pie hat and tremulous jet earrings' (ibid: 12) by puncturing her forearm with the point of 'long glass-headed pin' (ibid). Orwell continues: 'She made it a rule, whenever she caught herself not attending to her prayers to prick her arm hard enough to make the blood come. It was her chosen form of self-discipline, her guard against irreverence and sacrilegious thoughts' (ibid: 13). Dorothy punishes herself for indulging in an internal monologue about Mayfill's ugliness, and then later for admiring the beauty of her own handiwork. While men pinch women as a sexual provocation, Dorothy only pinches *herself* when overwhelmed by disgust for the older women in her community.

While a few of the inhabitants of Knype Hill are men, most are women. What follows are a sort of 'greatest hits of insults' Orwell provides for the ageing women. For instance, when describing Mrs Mayfill, the narrator remarks: 'In her ancient bloodless face, her mouth was surprisingly large, loose, and wet. The under lip, pendulous with age, slobbered forward... On the upper lip was a fringe of dark, dewy moustache. It was ... not the kind of mouth that you would like to see drinking out of your cup' (ibid: 14). Later on, we are introduced to the archetype of bored widowed gossip with Mrs Semprill, 'the town scandalmonger' (ibid: 50): 'She was a slender woman of forty, with a lank, sallow, distinguished face, which, with her glossy dark hair and settled melancholy, gave her something the appearance of a Van Dyck portrait' (ibid). Mrs Semprill 'began to pour forth a stream of libel involving Molly Freeman and six young men who worked at the sugar-beet refinery' (ibid: 52). Her inflated tales of sexual intrigue provide the otherwise sleepy town with tabloid entertainment: 'Compared with the ordinary scandalmongers of a country town, she was as Freud to Boccaccio. From hearing her talk you would have gathered the impression that Knype Hill with its two thousand inhabitants held more of the refinements of evil than Sodom, Gomorrah and Buenos Ayres put together' (ibid: 53). When Semprill's neighbours provide a distracted audience to her tales, they are punished with freshly spun gossip with them in the title role: 'An unwillingness to listen to her scandals was taken as a sign of depravity, and led to fresh and

PAPER

worse scandals being published about yourself the moment you had left her' (ibid: 55).

With Mrs Pither, Orwell introduces the archetype of the overly dependent and effusive grandmother figure whose ageing body, riddled with various maladies, acts as a cautionary example of the inevitable challenges to come for Dorothy. Similar to Dorothy's reactions to other aged women in Knype Hill, the narrator reveals the guilty disgust experienced by Dorothy in her interactions with Mrs Pither, 'a large, stooping, grey woman with wispy grey hair, a sacking apron and shuffling carpet slippers' (ibid: 58), who asks Dorothy to massage her with 'a bottle of Elliman's'; Dorothy obliges, but pinches herself as punishment for her disgust (ibid: 63). Dorothy endures additional revulsion as Mrs Pither attempts to show Dorothy affection: 'She took Dorothy between her large, gnarled hands, whose knuckles were as shiny as skinned onions from age and ceaseless washing up, and gave her a wet kiss' (ibid: 59). These grotesque characterisations of the aged women continue with Dororthy speculating that 'Mrs Pither led a dreary, wormlike life of shuffling to and fro' (ibid: 59). Acknowledging the older woman's needs but nauseated by the task nonetheless, Dorothy agrees to message Mrs Pither while savagely describing her body: 'The room reeked of urine and paregoric. Dorothy took the bottle of Elliman's embrocation and carefully anointed Mrs Pither's large, grey-veined, flaccid legs' (ibid: 63).

Central to the narrative is Warburton's traumatic sexual assault on Dorothy[5][6] providing the catalyst for her extended dissociative episode. Dorothy 'awakens' in London with no recollection of who she is. In time, Dorothy begins to regain her memory. After she becomes a teacher, Mrs Creevy, who runs the school, is described as 'a woman somewhere in her forties, lean, hard, and angular, with abrupt decided movements that indicated a strong will and probably a vicious temper' (ibid: 216). Although still in her forties, Mrs Creevy's body betrays her when attempting the most routine of physical movements: 'There were even times when she produced a grimace that was intended for a smile; her face, it seemed to Dorothy, creaked with the effort' (ibid: 282). Orwell writes of Mrs Creevy: 'She was one of those people who experiences a kind of spiritual orgasm when they manage to do somebody else a bad turn' (ibid: 236). In a book devoid of consensual sex or discussions of pleasure, the use of the word 'orgasm' stands apart, suggesting that an unmarried schoolmistress in her forties is most likely to climax at the misfortune of others than from physical contact.

As with the elders at Knype Hill, Dorothy seems to absorb the wilted essence of the ageing educators surrounding her: 'She had grown, quite suddenly it seemed, much tougher and maturer.

Her eyes had lost the half-childish look that they had once had, and her face had grown thinner, making her nose seem longer. At times it was quite definitely a schoolmarm's face' (ibid: 281). In his characterisation of Dorothy, Orwell demonstrates how 'premature cognitive commitments, or the mindless acceptance of information' work (Nelson 2002: 285); they 'can lead people to form, and then fall victim to, stereotypes about ageing' (ibid: 285). Nelson adds: 'When a younger person who has initially mindlessly processed stereotypes about ageing becomes elderly and finds himself or herself forgetting things, he or she may attribute this forgetfulness to senility, and begin to behave as if senile' (ibid: 287). Having internalised her disgust for ageing women, Dorothy's own ageing process appears to hasten.

When Dorothy regains her memory, Warburton pays to retrieve her belongings and for first-class tickets for the four-hour trip from Liverpool Street Station in London back to Knype Hill. The duration of Dorothy's exile from Knype Hill is a mere eight months and yet the resulting change in her appearance moves Warburton to remark: 'You look older' (ibid: 293). While a comment of this sort may have shocked and silenced Dorothy before her sojourn, she answers coolly: 'I am older' (ibid) and commits to a life of reflection and adaptability, noting: 'It's the things that happen inside you that matter... Oh – things change in your mind. And then the whole world changes, because you look at it differently' (ibid: 294). Seemingly challenged by Dorothy's newfound introspection and disregard for external conventions, Warburton snaps: 'I call that perfectly scandalous in a girl of your age' (ibid: 297). Warburton goes on to caution her that a husband twenty years her senior and whom she does not love is far preferable to none at all: 'You would be happier married, even to a husband with a bald head and a clouded past. You've had a hard, dull life for a girl of your age, and your future isn't actually rosy. Have you really considered what your future will be like if you don't marry?' (ibid: 302). He ends his rant with pointed, age-related insults: 'And remember that you won't always be twenty-eight. All the while you will be fading, withering, until one morning you will look in the glass and realise that you aren't a girl any longer, only a skinny old maid. You'll fight against it, of course. You'll keep your physical energy and your girlish mannerisms – you'll keep them just a little too long' (ibid: 303). While Dorothy Hare refuses to succumb to Warburton's tactics, she is to be viewed essentially 'not as an individual in her own right but rather in terms of her relationship to a man, a clergyman, her father' (Patai 1984: 96).

CARRIE KANCILIA

CONCLUSIONS

Orwell's preoccupation with characterising gendered differences in ageing is undeniable: for Orwell's men, ageing is unpleasant and alienating, but for his women characters, ageing is grotesque and unforgiveable. Why is Orwell's inter-war work, specifically, so overwhelmingly rife with detailed and often horrifying descriptions of middle age and old age? Orwell's own poor health escalated after being shot by a sniper while serving with anarchists in the Spanish Civil War in 1937. Sylvia Topp records Orwell's severely weakened physical state the month following the incident: 'Orwell's neck wound was mostly healed, but he was weak from all the freezing months on the front, his voice was reduced to a near whisper, and lingering blood poisoning in his right hand kept his arm in a sling for weeks to come' (2020:190). Later, he would be treated for – and finally succumb to – tuberculosis. Yet, these threats to Orwell's personal health occur after having written much of his ageist fictional passages and, therefore, a neat link from personal experience to creative motif cannot be logically drawn.

Is Orwell's 'hypertrophied masculinity', in Patai's words (1984: 19), to blame for his seeming inability to consider the ageing woman as worthy of respect? Or is Orwell's disgust at ageing best seen as reflecting Baudelaire and Pound's edicts to elevate the new over the old?

NOTES

[1] Nathan Waddell's 2021 introduction to *A Clergyman's Daughter* notes how the eponymous clergyman serves as a symbol of decay: 'Charles's false teeth broadly align him with another denture-sporting Orwellian character: George Bowling in *Coming Up For Air* (1939). They also suggest that his ageing body is of a piece with the crumbling Rectory he calls home' (2021a: xxi)

[2] *Keep the Aspidistra Flying*'s Gordon notes of the older generations' distaste for revolution: 'Meanwhile the old – *those over sixty, say* – were running in circles like hens, squawking about "subversive ideas". He did not hate and despise his relatives now – or not so much, at any rate. They still depressed him greatly – those poor old withering aunts and uncles, of whom two or three had already died, his father, worn out and spiritless' (1956 [1936]: 43, italics added)

[3] This is one of the many mentions in modernist literature pinpointing the age of thirty-five as the end of youth; other examples can be found in the work of James Joyce, Jean Rhys and Thomas Mann. Molly Bloom, of Joyce's *Ulysses*, momentarily forgetting her age, points to thirty-five as a type of ending: 'The men won't look at you and women try and walk on you because they know you've no man then will all the things getting dearer every day for the *4 years more I have of life up to 35* no I'm what am I at all I'll be 33 in September will I' (1986: [1922] 18 470-475, italics added). The narrator of Mann's *Death in Venice* comments on the protagonist's early professional success noting of Gustav Aschenbach that 'he had never known the carefree recklessness of the young' (Mann 1995 [1912]: 6). It is during a rare respite from creative output while on a vacation when 'at about the age of thirty-five, he [Aschenbach] fell ill in Vienna' (ibid). In Jean Rhys's *Voyage in the Dark*, the young year-old Anna Morgan meets her stepmother, Hester, at a restaurant. As she waits, she begins to read distractedly another patron's newspaper. She recounts that 'there was an

advertisement at the back of the newspaper: "What is purity? For thirty-five years the answer has been Bourne's Cocoa"' (1982 [1934]: 58). The 'thirty-five' in the advertisement inspires her meditation on ageing. Anna observes: 'There were two middle aged women at our table. ... Everybody took one mouthful and then showered salt and sauce out of a bottle on it. Everybody did this mechanically, without a change of expression, so that you saw they knew it would taste of nothing' (ibid). In contrast, Rebecca West, in *Return of the Soldier*, offers the age of thirty-six as a symbol for loss. Chris Ellis, having left to serve the British army at twenty, returns home at thirty-six with no recollection of the intervening years or the wife he left behind. Margaret Allington, presumably of a similar age, is described as 'old', 'not beautiful any longer' and 'drearily married'. Chris's realisation of his age is explained as follows: 'Chris was looking at himself in a hand-mirror, which he threw on the floor as I entered. "You are right," he said: "I'm not twenty-one, but thirty-six"' (1918: 39).

[4] Compare to Warner's description of Lolly Willowes: 'Laura's hair was black as ever, but it was not so thick. She had grown paler from living in London. Her forehead had not a wrinkle, but two downward lines prolonged the drooping corners of her mouth. Her face was beginning to stiffen. It had lost its power of expressiveness, and was more and more dominated by the hook nose and the sharp chin. When Laura was ten years older she would be nut-crackerish' (1926: 59)

[5] For example, Rodden and Rossi, in *The Cambridge Introduction to George Orwell*, suggest Warburton is a friend whom Dorothy finds 'attractive' and her horror-struck reaction to Warburton is characterised as the result of sexual frustration: 'Orwell also makes her sexually frustrated. She only has one male friend, a middle-aged, semi-roué, Mr Warburton, who serves to stand for everything Dorothy is not. ... He is worldly, financially well-off, but most importantly he is romantically interested in her. While she finds him attractive, the thought of sex with "horrible furry beasts", as she describes men, disgusts her' (Rodden and Rossi 2012: 36). *The Cambridge Introduction to George Orwell* goes on to explain Dorothy's fugue state – essentially a trauma response to unwanted sexual attention – in this way: 'Orwell has Mr Warburton try to seduce her, which brings on a bout of amnesia' (ibid: 37).

[6] Douglas Kerr's *Orwell & Empire* highlights sexual assaults in some of Orwell's works: such as Charlie's rape of an 'infantilized, brutalized, powerless, and silenced' young woman 'crying out for mercy' in *Down and Out in Paris and London* (2022: 98) and he also acknowledges that 'Elizabeth's uncle' of *Burmese Days* 'tries to rape her and her aunt wants rid of her' (ibid: 99).

REFERENCES

Amundsen, Michael (2016) George Orwell's ethnographies of experience: *The Road to Wigan Pier* and *Down and Out in Paris and London*, *Anthropological Journal of European Cultures*, Vol. 25, No. 1 pp 9-25

Arendt, Hannah (1973) *The Origins of Totalitarianism*, New York: Harcourt, Brace, Jovanovich

Baudelaire, Charles (1964 [1863]) *The Painter of Modern Life and Other Essays*, Greenwich, CT: Phaidon Publishers, Inc

Fowler, Roger (1995) *The Language of George Orwell*, New York: St. Martin's Press

Freud, Sigmund (1915 [1899]) *Interpretation of Dreams*, New York: Macmillan

Freud, Sigmund (2010 [1930]) *Civilization and Its Discontents*, New York: Norton

Gay, Peter (2010) *Modernism: The Lure of Heresy*, New York: W.W. Norton & Company

Goldstein, Philip (2000) Orwell as a (neo)conservative: The reception of *1984*, *The Journal of the Midwest Modern Language Association*, Winter, Vol. 33, No. 1 pp 44-57

Gullette, Margaret Morganroth (2011) *Agewise: Fighting the New Ageism in America*, Chicago: University of Chicago Press

Joyce, James. (1986 [1922]) *Ulysses*, New York: Vintage Books

Kalpakli, Fatma (2015) Representation of the Other in George Orwell's *Burmese Days*, *Procedia: Social and Behavioral Sciences*, Vol. 174 pp 1214-1220

Kerr, Douglas (2022) *Orwell & Empire*, Oxford: Oxford University Press

Letemendia, V.C. (1992) Revolution on *Animal Farm*: Orwell's neglected commentary, *Journal of Modern Literature*, Vol. 18 pp 127-138

Lieskounig, Juergen (2012) The power of distortion: George Orwell's *Burmese Days*, *Journal of the Australasian Universities, Language and Literature*, No. 117 pp 49-68

Liggins, Emma (2014) *Odd Women?: Spinsters, Lesbians and Widows in British Women's Fiction, 1850s-1930s*, Manchester: Manchester University Press

Mann, Thomas (1995 [1912]) *Death in Venice*. New York: Dover

Nelson, Todd D. (ed.) (2002) *Ageism: Stereotyping and Prejudice Against Older Persons*, Berkeley: MIT Press

North, Michael (2013) *Novelty: A History of the New*, Chicago: University of Chicago Press

Orwell, George (1961 [1933]) *Down and Out in Paris and London*, San Diego: Harcourt Brace

Orwell, George (1962 [1934]) *Burmese Days*, New York: Harcourt, Inc.

Orwell, George (1936 [1935]) *Clergyman's Daughter*, San Diego: Harcourt Brace

Orwell, George. (1956 [1936]) *Keep the Aspidistra Flying*, San Diego: Harcourt Brace

Orwell, George (1958 [1937]) *The Road to Wigan Pier*, San Diego: Harcourt Brace

Orwell, George (1950 [1939]) *Coming Up For Air,* New York: Harcourt Brace

Orwell, George (2021) *The Complete Novels of George Orwell*, Oxford: Benediction Classics

Patai, Daphne (1984) *The Orwell Mystique: A Study in Male Ideology*, Amherst: University of Massachusetts Press

Rodden, John and Rossi, John (eds) (2012) *The Cambridge Introduction to George Orwell*, Cambridge: Cambridge University Press

Rhys, Jean (1982 [1934]) *Voyage in the Dark*, New York: Random House

Topp, Sylvia (2020) *Eileen: The Making of George Orwell*, London: Unbound

Waddell, Nathan (2021) Introduction, Orwell, George, *A Clergyman's Daughter*, Oxford: Oxford University Press pp ix-xliv

Warner, Sylvia Townsend (1926) *Lolly Willowes*. New York: Grosset and Dunlap

West, Rebecca (1918) *Return of the Soldier*, New York: Century

NOTE ON THE CONTRIBUTOR

Carrie Kancilia received her PhD in English from Purdue University and currently works as Lecturer of English and Writing Center Director at the University of Southern Maine. Her work has been published in *James Studies Annual*, the *James Joyce Literary Supplement* and *The Modernist Review*. Her research interests include European modernism with a focus on inter-war narratives, film and representations of the ageing process in media. Her enduring love of Orwell began by reading her stepfather's worn copy of *Down and Out in Paris and London* as a child.

INTERVIEW

'Orwell's Thorough Understanding of Russia'

L.J. Hurst interviews Masha Karp, author of the widely-acclaimed *George Orwell and Russia*, about her book, her researches and her thoughts since its publication in June 2023.

LJH: Orwell described an incident towards the end of his time at school when his class were asked: 'Whom do you consider the ten greatest men now living?' Orwell recalls, in *The Road to Wigan Pier*. 'Of sixteen boys in the class (our average age was about seventeen) fifteen included Lenin in their list.'

Firstly, since Orwell does not explicitly say he was one of the fifteen, do you think he was, or was he the odd-man-out?

Secondly, as well as *George Orwell and Russia*, you have written and published an enormous biography of Orwell in Russian. Did you follow up what happened to the other boys in Orwell's class? What did they think or say about Lenin and Russia then, or later in their lives? Was Orwell an outlier, or did others match his life and career?

MK: To answer your first question: I am pretty sure that he was one of the fifteen, otherwise he would not have missed an opportunity to say that he was of a different opinion. Moreover, he famously says: 'I was both a snob and a revolutionary' but a bit earlier also: '*We* retained, basically, the snobbish outlook of our class … but also it seemed natural to *us* (emphasis added – MK) to be "agin the government"' (*CWGO* V: 130) – so he does think of himself as part of a larger group of boys. For all of them Lenin was a revolutionary and therefore one of 'the greatest men now living'.

As far as the other boys are concerned, I did not follow the fates of his classmates in the Russian biography – thank you, by the way, for mentioning it: it was published in 2017 by a St Petersburg publisher Vita Nova – although obviously I quote from Steven Runciman's, Roger Mynors's and Denys King-Farlow's reminiscences of Eric Blair in Eton. But these people did not seem to be particularly interested in politics in later life, nor did Orwell keep a close relationship with any of them.

L.J. HURST
MASHA KARP

However, for most of his contemporaries on the left the October revolution of 1917 was a major – and positive – event of the century, and it took them years and years to realise that something had gone wrong there. One of the most sincere and active politicians of the time, Fenner Brockway, was shocked in 1936 by the First Moscow Trial and the confessions made by Lenin's former comrades. He felt that they might have been extracted under duress. Yet still he and other ILP – and Labour Party – members were full of admiration for the Soviet economy, while ordinary people in the Soviet Union were hungry and impoverished. It was Orwell's ability 'to face unpleasant facts' that enabled him to see through 'the Russian myth'.

LJH: If we stay on *The Road to Wigan Pier* for a moment, there is a mention in both Orwell's Wigan diary, and in his published book, of Prosper Olivier Lissagaray's *Histoire de la Commune de 1871* (*The History of the Paris Commune of 1871*). Orwell returned to the Commune in his 1941 review of *The Friends of the People*, by Alfred Neumann. In between he made the connection through Frank Jelinek who wrote books on both the Commune and the Spanish Civil War. Was Orwell's thinking shaped from an early age by the Commune? That is, did he have no need to realise what Stalin might do? Orwell had French relatives – did they influence him?

MK: Orwell's review of Alfred Neumann's book starts with a wonderful sentence, and I read here from the *Complete Works*: 'Although history does not repeat itself it is constantly producing situations so alike in general outline that at certain moments one ought to be able to predict, merely by rule of thumb, what the next move will be.' This is, of course, Orwell's sociological approach to history which he had learnt from Austrian sociologist Franz Borkenau, who became his friend. The crushing of the Commune therefore was for him 'an extreme and terrible example' of the revolution where 'the moderates will overthrow the extremists and proceed to set up a tyranny of their own, always better but never very much better, than the original tyranny which the revolution destroyed'. This definition, however, does not describe the Soviet history where, despite all the noble aims proclaimed by the revolution, the post-revolutionary life for ordinary citizens was definitely not better but in many respects much worse than the life under the tsars. This is basically what *Animal Farm* is about. But I do not think that it was specifically the Commune that made Orwell expect the Soviet history to go this way.

LJH: In a moment I would like to go on to the individual chapters of your book. First, though, I notice that it is organised chronologically.

Was that always your intention, or did you consider in its early days organising the book in a different way: for instance, in chapters by theme?

MK: The book is organised chronologically, especially the first part, but in the second there are chapters devoted to this or that theme, for example 'As I understand it' – about socialism or 'Over the heads of their rulers' – about translations of banned Orwell's books getting to Soviet readers. But the chronological approach was necessary because one of my aims was to explore the sources of Orwell's thorough understanding of Russia. The common knowledge is that he first encountered Soviet communism in Spain – and this is true of course. However, I thought it was very important to stress that in 1928-1929 in Paris he was closely connected with Esperantist Eugene Lanti, his Aunt Nellie's partner, and that was exactly the period of Lanti's deep disappointment and frustration with the way things had developed under the communist government in Russia. Orwell's exposure to the views of the ILP and meeting some Trotskyists in the early 1930s also made him sceptical about the Soviet Union. In *The Road to Wigan Pier* there is not a single positive assessment of it. All this had happened before Spain. After Spain he was mostly terrified that the lies issued by communist propaganda were proving powerful and affecting civilised people in free countries.

LJH: Lanti had experience in Russia, as your book makes clear. I don't recall Bernard Crick giving him much time – have we discovered more about him, or did Crick not understand the width of Orwell's experience?

MK: Crick mentions Lanti, but he certainly did not realise what important role Lanti played in the relationship with the Soviet Esperantists and how strong and powerful was his original 'desire to put Esperanto at the service of the world revolution' (Ulrich Lins, *Dangerous Language – Esperanto under Hitler and Stalin*, London: Palgrave MacMillan, 2016: 160). According to Crick, Lanti and Aunt Nellie 'were, if not full-blown cranks, certainly crankish' (Bernard Crick. *George Orwell. A Life,* Harmondsworth, Middlesex: Penguin Books, 1982: 190), which might be true, but Crick obviously did not have any idea about Lanti's essay about his trip to Russia, about his books or about his fate. And yet scholars of the history of Esperanto, like Ulrich Lins, were aware of this. Bernard Crick was not really particularly interested in Orwell's attitude to Russia. The first biographer who paid serious attention to Lanti's influence was Gordon Bowker.

INTERVIEW

L.J. HURST
MASHA KARP

LJH: A later figure of importance was Franz Borkenau, an intellectual driven into exile by the nazis. How important was he to the development of Orwell's thought? As an intellectual political analyst Borkenau should be the sort of figure appreciated by Crick.

MK: Borkenau's impact is hard to overestimate. Orwell was first attracted to *The Spanish Cockpit* (1937) – Borkenau's book about Spanish Civil War – not only because both he and the Austrian sociologist assessed the Spanish situation in a similar way and stressed the need to be honest about it but also because of Borkenau's detached, analytical and yet lively style of writing. Borkenau had had an experience of working for the Comintern and that is why his next book *The Communist International* (1938) taught Orwell, as he admitted, 'more than any other about the general course of the revolution' (Orwell's letter to Dwight Macdonald, 15 April 1947). As a pioneer of the theory of totalitarianism, Borkenau was convinced that Russia was much more totalitarian than Germany – the view that was not widely supported then and is not now. Between 1937 and 1940 when Orwell and Borkenau saw each other in London regularly they discussed lots of important things and, in particular, an imminent revolution in Britain. Borkenau, like Orwell, was a man who firmly stood on the left, but could not ever support Soviet communists, whom he continued attacking until the end of his days – he died in 1957.

As far as Crick is concerned, he appreciated Borkenau, but he was writing a biography – rather than a book about Orwell and Russia.

LJH: I notice that among Borkenau's books other than *The Totalitarian Enemy* is one on the philosopher Pareto. Pareto's name appears only once in Orwell's non-fiction, and then it is in a list. As you worked, how much evidence did you find of Orwell's researches, conversations and reading that indicate he was aware of much more than he repeated in his writings? Can it be taken on trust that Orwell knew more about Pareto than just his name, for instance? What is the evidence?

MK: Pareto's name appears at least twice in Orwell's writings and both times it is related to James Burnham. In his review of Burnham's *Machiavellians*, published in January 1944, Orwell stresses that Burnham follows Pareto when he 'points out that a ruling caste decays if it is not renewed from time to time by able recruits from the masses' (*CWGO* XVVI: 71). And in 'Second thoughts on James Burnham' (1946), he calls Pareto a modern disciple of Machiavelli and says that 'Burnham lays much stress on Pareto's theory of the "circulation of the elites"' (*CWGO* XVIII: 269-270). There is absolutely no evidence that Orwell read Pareto or Borkenau's book about him. He was not a scholar but a talented writer who could explain to others rather complicated subjects, which probably were argued about in learned circles. Orwell naturally was aware of the debates of his day and James Burnham was one of the people widely discussed in the 1940s. I believe that Orwell probably knew more than just the name of Pareto, but how much more – that is impossible to say.

LJH: And can you remind us of the importance of the Russian exile Gleb Struve to Orwell's education, please.

MK: Struve was the first person to learn about Orwell working on *Animal Farm* ('a little squib which might amuse you') and planning to write *Nineteen Eighty-Four* – having read about Zamyatin's novel *We* in Struve's book *Twenty Five years of Russian Literature*, Orwell wrote to Struve: 'I am interested in that kind of book and even keep making notes for one myself which might get written sooner or later.' Zamyatin's book was out of print and it was with Struve's help that Orwell obtained a copy in French translation. There is no doubt that Struve told Orwell a lot about what was going on in Russia including the 'striking out of history' in 1944 of the Molotov-Ribbentrop Pact of 1939 – as if it had never existed. It was also he who reassured Orwell that Zamyatin's book was written about Russia.

LJH: But now we must come to the two figures who dominate any discussion of Orwell and Russia: Stalin and Trotsky. Winston Churchill's essay on Trotsky in *Great Contemporaries* (1937) was little more than a stream of abuse while he had little to say about Stalin. What was it that made so many figures ignore Stalin for so long?

MK: The lack of understanding of what was actually happening in Russia. For too long people who did not live there – especially those on the left – were telling themselves that with all the scary information about Soviet citizens being arrested and shot, still the socialist economy was functioning, there was no unemployment and it was the state of workers and peasants, which was fair and flourishing. People did not want to part with their dreams and they did not want to agree with what their political opponents were saying.

A similar situation occurred in the 21st century when the West was happy to believe that Russia was gradually becoming a capitalist democracy, law-based society and a 'normal' country. Only some individuals saw that under Putin the country – slowly but steadily – was returning to its old imperial and oppressive self. Propaganda

L.J. HURST
MASHA KARP

and wishful thinking achieved their results both in 1930s and 1940s and after 2000.

Orwell saw through Stalin very early but he was not enchanted by Trotsky either – he was sure that had Trotsky stayed in the Soviet Union, as a leader, he would not have been very different from Stalin. One thing he admitted, though: Trotsky, he said, was a much more interesting writer.

LJH: Among his contemporaries did Orwell show much awareness of Russian literature? I know he did read Chekhov – he had a question about Chekhov unanswered when he died. Did he ever say anything about Mikhail Sholokhov, for instance, the author of *And Quiet Flows The Don*?

MK: Orwell liked Russian literature. In his 'As I Please' column of 10 March 1944, he wrote with great feeling about Tolstoy's *War and Peace*, regretting that the book was not long enough: 'It seemed to me that Nicholas and Natasha Rostov, Peter Besukhov, Denisov and all the rest of them were people about whom one would gladly go on reading forever. The fact is that the minor Russian aristocracy of that date, with their boldness and simplicity, their countrified pleasures, their stormy love affairs and enormous families, were very charming people' (*CWGO* XVI: 117). This obviously did not stop him from exposing the reasons for Tolstoy's antipathy for Shakespeare. He read – and reviewed – other famous Russian writers – Lermontov, Chekhov and Korney Chukovsky's book about Chekhov. He tried to learn something about the poetry of Blok and Mandelstam – and here once again it was Struve and his book that guided him. Thinking about literature under totalitarianism he understood how the Soviet literature worked. I don't think he wrote about Sholokhov, but he called official Soviet writers Alexey Tolstoy and Ilya Ehrenburg 'literary prostitutes' and was indignant about Zhdanov's 1946 attack on Akhmatova and Zoshchenko, feeling sorry for the satirical writer unable to write under the constant pressure from the party. He found an earlier satire, *Diamonds to Sit On*, by Ilya Ilf and Evgeny Petrov, hilarious and thought that it was in a way 'reassuring to read a novel about modern Russia which is so essentially good-tempered'.

LJH: You end *George Orwell and Russia* by discussing Russia in the twenty-first century under Vladimir Putin. Orwell was afraid of slave societies persisting for centuries – should we apply that concern to Russia now?

MK: The Russian situation today is too gloomy for words. It is difficult to imagine how under present circumstances the best that we have always had in Russia and have been proud of can survive. I mean not only the Russian art and literature, but also some talented and brave individuals who are ready to oppose the oppressive government for the sake of making Russia free and democratic. The current war – with so many Ukrainians killed and maimed, with their children taken away from the country and their identity stolen from them, with the ordinary Russians, who either are so brainwashed that they support the war or are oblivious to it or profoundly scared and therefore reluctant to protest – is a real and lasting tragedy. It is impossible to predict what will happen next. Too much needs to change for the country to reinvent itself. That is why Orwell's concern is still legitimate and yet I do hope that people in Russia will gradually realise how they have been duped and will try and build a new life for themselves. One thing, though, is of primary importance – Russia should part with its imperial ambitions.

LJH: Going back to Orwell's reading of Lissagaray, was the revolution always doomed to be betrayed?

MK: The revolution of 1917 – yes, the Bolsheviks just wanted power for themselves. In 1991, Russia had a chance but lost it and probably not so much due to a betrayal, but because the resistance of the old regime was too strong. Now something really dramatic should happen for the revolution to take place at all.

LJH: Masha Karp – thank you.

- *George Orwell and Russia*, by Masha Karp, was published by Bloomsbury Academic, in 2023

Captain Robinson: 'The Most Disreputable Englishman in Mandalay'

PHIL BAKER

When it comes to phrases with a period ring, 'the most disreputable Englishman in Mandalay' (Shelden 1991: 97) is up there with the best of them. Capt. Herbert Reginald Robinson (1896-1965) was that man, and if his bad reputation has been saved from total oblivion it is largely because he was a sometime friend of George Orwell: he has been suggested as the model for Flory in *Burmese Days*, he has a prominent role in Paul Theroux's recent novel *Burma Sahib* (loosely based on Orwell's years in Burma) and he has an insubstantial, flitting, rumour-like presence in a number of Orwell biographies.

The son of a young solicitor, Edward Robinson, and his wife Rose, Robinson was born on 6 July 1896 in Stoke Newington, in those days a respectably Pooterish expanding suburb of north east London. In 1900, Robinson's father died from typhoid and he moved with his mother to Norfolk, later boarding at Pocklington School, in Yorkshire.

After applying to Sandhurst he embarked, in April 1915, with other 'gentleman cadets' for the staff college at Quetta, north west India (now Pakistan). Appointed to the Indian army, he was at different times with the 90th and 91st Punjabis, at one point becoming adjutant for the 2nd Battalion 90th Punjabis, and he served in Mesopotamia and Waziristan during the Third Anglo-Afghan War in 1919, before being seconded to the Burma military police.

In 1921, Robinson became assistant commandant, Putao Battalion, at Konglu on Burma's north-eastern frontier, where he exercised considerable responsibility virtually alone. He acted as magistrate and arbitrator with jurisdiction over tribespeople including Kachins, Nungs, Marus and Lisus, and when the plant-hunter Frank Kingdon-Ward encountered him in 1922 he noticed 'he liked the people, and was obviously respected by them' (1924: 257).

Robinson's Indian army service ended in July 1923, seemingly not cashiered in scandal over a native mistress or similar (as has been suggested by several Orwell biographers, e.g. Stansky and Abrahams 1972: 157-158) but as part of a cost-cutting exercise known as 'the Geddes axe' (from the committee on public expenditure chaired by Sir Eric Geddes), which fell heavily on officers who had been commissioned during World War One.

It was also in 1923 that Robinson first visited an opium den and found it fatally congenial. In Orwell's words, after being 'axed … he settled down for a couple of years in Mandalay, where he devoted himself almost exclusively to smoking opium… [along with] unsuccessful attempts to float a gold-mine and run a car-hiring business' (Orwell 1997 [1942]: 34).

Facing addiction, Robinson sought refuge in Buddhism and later, in 1923, joined Mandalay's Ma Soe Yein Nu Kyaung monastery (the monastery 'Free of Anxiety'). He was ordained as a monk that September with the name U Nipuna ('the Gentle Monk'). Now living in the monastery, he went out in the streets daily with his begging bowl (by which point, as a former British colonial magistrate, he may have been considered to have 'let the side down').

Unfortunately, he still felt the pull of opium, especially in the evenings when he knew the little opium lamps were being lit in dens all over the city (Robinson 1942: 89). He made a final attempt to escape the temptation of Mandalay by wandering as a mendicant monk in the countryside, but before the year was out he 'gave in' (ibid: 90) and took a riverboat back to the city. A three-month trip to England in 1924 failed to break his addiction, suffering withdrawal on board ship but finding supplies in Colombo and Port Said. Returning to Mandalay, he rented a house, fitted a room out as a simple 'den' and gave himself up to smoking.

This life continued until 18 March 1925, when the police came to arrest him for debt. Remembering his Kipling – 'Just roll to your rifle and blow out your brains, / And go to your God like a soldier' (Kipling 1893) – and his old Browning pistol, Robinson made an excuse to go upstairs, where he shot himself in the head. After the shattering bang, followed by darkness, he thought for a few disorientated moments he was now in an afterlife, before realising he had succeeded only in blowing both eyes out (ibid: 143). He was groping around on the floor for the gun when the police broke through the door and led him 'very tenderly' downstairs (ibid.).

FOUR DECADES

The next forty years of Robinson's life, so unexpected when he put the gun to his head, are like another incarnation. Returning

PHIL BAKER

to Britain, he retrained as a masseur: something blind people were encouraged to do. He practised for almost four decades, first privately in Worthing and Balham (as Robinson, Capt. Herbert Reginald, masseur, 229 Balham High Road, SW17; tel. Streatham 7897) and later for the NHS, chiefly at the Fountain Hospital, in Tooting, which was for severely disabled and mentally handicapped children.

In July 1931, he married an older neighbour in Wandsworth, Emily Adey, 44 to his 35 (he was living at 131 Church Lane, and she was across the road at number 144) but in 1934 she had the marriage annulled for non-consummation (for divorce, see National Archives: J 77/3368/2817). Around 1936, he may have been in love with his receptionist Doreen Manby, writing her a poem:

> Deep lie the smould'ring passions of my youth
>
> O'erladen with the ashes of the years.
>
> Rouse not the dying embers with thy tears
>
> Else I must needs relearn the bitter truth…
>
> Exquisite blooms in shadow never throve
>
> Nor ever yet was pity kin to love.

The initial letters of the lines spell out 'DOREEN', while 'Exquisite blooms in shadow never throve' addresses the underlying subject of his blindness (and the final rhyme, perhaps coincidentally, is an 'eye-rhyme'). She married another man in 1939.

A MODERN DE QUINCEY

Robinson could touch-type, and in 1942 he published his autobiography – taking the story up to the events of 1925 – *A Modern de Quincey*. It is a fascinating book, rich with period detail and sensational incident, and the overall drift is unmistakably authentic although it is possibly embroidered in places. One lonely New Year's Eve, his last in Burma, he shares his smoking through the night in silent companionship with an intruder, a man he soon realises has just committed a murder; he has already seen the almost decapitated corpse (1942: 134-137). On an earlier occasion, during his days as a magistrate, he has a night of passion with a manacled female murderer who has poisoned her elderly husband. After she gets off lightly – tribal elders decide murder is unproven, but she is guilty of infidelity and her village has to a pay a fine of cooking pots and chickens to the village of the deceased – he fancies (or 'was it my imagination …') that she winks at him as she leaves the court room (ibid: 32-35).

As the de Quincey title suggests, the book is also of interest as drug writing. Robinson is 'thrilled, but a little disappointed' (ibid: 66) with his first experience of opium, bereft of whatever exotic thrills he was expecting and only making him 'perfectly content – which is not a good state for any man to be in' (ibid: 65). There are accounts of paraphernalia and procedures (scenting the inside of a bamboo pipe with musk, for example, ibid: 94) and in his opium reveries Robinson is repeatedly tantalised by the secret of existence, glimpsed and lost. He realises he must write it down, before he forgets it yet again, and it turns out to be 'The banana is great, but the skin of the banana is greater' (ibid: 70).

At one stage, Robinson has a large rock of cocaine to try to get him through opium withdrawal, and there is a memorable moment when he is in Port Said, looking for an opium den, and there doesn't seem to be one. Instead, he has to go to a hashish den where he is appalled by the people ('a strange assembly of cut-throats'). It was a weird spectacle, he says, so very different from the 'refinement, cleanliness and comfort' of the polite and peaceful opium dens he has known. He has fallen among cannabis smokers (ibid: 125-126).

Buddhism also plays a central role. Before shooting himself, Robinson fixes his gaze on his little Buddha (ibid: 143): not a very Buddhist act, if true. More particularly, the book is written from an understated Buddhistic perspective. The acquisition of 'merit' by good deeds is several times noted, and the narrative is laced with small ironies and meaningful coincidences to show the workings of karma in one lifetime. Robinson remembers that when he was at prep school, taking the church collection, he deliberately loitered in front of a teacher who had no money instead of discreetly moving on: this comes back to him when he is out on the streets of Mandalay with his begging bowl (ibid: 10-11).

Robinson also allows a Burmese sorcerer, 'the Purveyor of Charms', to give him a magic tattoo against death by bullet wounds (ibid: 101-102): not in itself unlikely; Orwell also had some magical Asian tattooing, in his case against snake bite, perhaps accepted partly to show goodwill. The book's great over-arching coincidence comes when Robinson applies for massage school, and has to provide his birth certificate. He applies for it and discovers he was born in 'Burma Road', Stoke Newington (ibid: 150). Suddenly, he feels his life fall into place as a pre-destined journey. His original title for his book, as in his 1941 contract with the publisher Harrap, was *Burma Road*, which would have made it more of a spiritual autobiography; the later title, with its narrower and more sensational drug emphasis, may have been the publisher's.

There is also a strange strand in the book; less a subtext than a straightforward minor theme on the surface. Robinson's smoking companion Ba Ohn seems to him not only 'the incarnate spirit of Opium', but 'beauty incarnate' and reminds him of 'boys at school whose faces had been a source of perpetual disquiet to me' (ibid: 65,

ARTICLE

PHIL BAKER

64; and more in the same vein). In a lighter episode, he is captivated by the charms of a transvestite Gurkha (ibid: 28). He is also deeply sentimental about his little friend Ba Set, a ten- or twelve-year-old cousin of Ba Ohn, who is devoted to Robinson: when his life hits rock bottom, Ba Set and his mother offer to take him in, but he declines although he is moved: 'Poor as they were, they had come to offer me a home for as long as I cared to stay. I could have wept' (ibid: 139). And after Robinson shoots himself, Ba Set waits outside the hospital every day with flowers, in case it should be the day Robinson is discharged, but as a low-status, non-white person he is never allowed in. Robinson only learns of this back in England, in a letter from the Mandalay Buddhist Association, and writes: 'I never knew of this, and can you blame me if it hardened my heart against the Christian belief? Little Ba Set, the ever-faithful, surely he must have attained to great merit' (ibid: 149-150).

'I have said that I have never loved,' Robinson writes, 'but in that I was wrong because here [contemplating the loyalty of Ba Set on an earlier occasion] … I felt within me the love that passeth the love of women (ibid: 139, alluding to the Biblical David and Jonathan: 2 Samuel 1: 26). It is tempting to remember Robinson's admiration for Ba Ohn when considering the failure of his marriage, but it may be a false lead, while his gratitude for Ba Set, compared to the love of women, may be sharpened by the failure of that marriage itself; he is writing not so long after it. And if his night of passion with the shackled murderess is uncorroborated, his nostalgia for Auntie's – a Rangoon brothel run by a former teacher in a Catholic girls' school, who employed her former pupils and decorated the place with religious texts, such as 'The Lord watcheth beside thy bed' – seems unfeigned (ibid: 19-20).

So Robinson's sexuality remains a mystery, as does the scarcity of his book (one of those 'warehouse bombed' stories could yet emerge). He signed a contract for *Burma Road* with Harrap on 1 September 1941, at which point his address is given as 41 Marine Parade, Worthing, with an advance of £50 (about £2,000 today, probably in the widespread arrangement of thirds on signature, delivery and publication). He was with the then-eminent firm of literary agents, James B. Pinker and Son Ltd, based on the Strand, whose clients had included Conrad, Arnold Bennett and Henry James. Founded by J.B. Pinker (1863-1922), the firm passed to his sons Eric and Ralph but foundered in the 1940s: Ralph was declared bankrupt in 1941 and imprisoned for embezzlement of clients' money in 1943. *A Modern de Quincey* was, nevertheless, published in the autumn of 1942 and received a modest spread of reviews in newspapers including the *Times Literary Supplement* and – most notably – one in the *Observer* by George Orwell.

HIS LATER YEARS

With service abroad and blindness, it is easy to imagine that the clock may have stopped for Robinson sometime around World War One, but in his later years he had a surprisingly modern interest in sound-recording technology; magnetic tape was still relatively new in the 1950s. He went to the audio trade fair at Earl's Court (the annual National Radio Show), and owned a number of machines including an Elpico, a Ferrograph, a Wyndsor and two state-of-the-art Grundigs, sending and receiving recordings as well as typing letters.

He was universally known as 'Robbie' and much loved by most who knew him, particularly the later families of two boys who helped him with errands and became lifelong friends – Monty Silsby, in Worthing, and Tommy Rogers, in south London – to whom he became a kindly, funny and philosophical 'eccentric uncle' figure. His worldview was still influenced by Buddhism – he had a gilt wooden Buddha, after the brass one he mentions in *A Modern de Quincey* – and when he thanks Monty Silsby for remembering his birthday he writes: 'There was much Merit in the deed, Monty' (letter, 8 July 1943).

Nevertheless, he remained the black sheep of his own family, and his great-nephew, Jeremy, remembers him being outnumbered in a stand-up row at a family gathering, his mother's golden wedding anniversary in 1957, fortified by the contents of his hip flask and 'giving as good as he got'. He drank and could be confrontational, and was apparently barred from one or more of the Tooting pubs he frequented, which included the Fountain Hotel, the Trafalgar Arms, the Castle and the Queen Victoria or Little House at 13 Tooting Grove, close to the Fountain Hospital. Writing to Tommy Rogers about the latter and its landlord Hughie, he says: 'I have not been near Hughie since we last met. I do feel that I have been abominably rude to him. I cannot say that this keeps me awake at nights but I regret my capacity to be so unpleasant' (letter, 19 July 1951).

Robinson ceased to work at the Fountain Hospital in autumn 1959, before it closed altogether in 1963. His mother was still alive, and by this time she seems to have been a formidable matriarch, with property and hotel interests in the Worthing area; she owned two hotels, the Cumberland and the Clearview. In October 1959, Robinson writes to Monty from 67 Longley Road, Tooting, mentioning that he is now 'definitely retired' and draws his 'dole' money on Fridays, asking him not to mention this to his mother: 'Not a word to my Mother if you should meet her as she still thinks that I am on part-time' (7 October 1959).

PHIL BAKER

Robinson's mother died in 1962 (her second husband, Robinson's step-father, Douglas Finden-Crofts, followed her in 1963). And on 2 March 1965, now living at 187 Crowborough Road, Tooting, Herbert Reginald Robinson, 'retired hospital physiotherapist', aged 68, died from 'hypnotic poisoning due to sodium amytal' – an overdose of barbiturates – 'self administered', apparently 'while suffering from depression'. It was forty years to the month from his attempted suicide in Burma.

THE ORWELL/ROBINSON RELATIONSHIP

The sole evidence for Orwell and Robinson having known each other seems to lie in Orwell's *Observer* review of his book which appeared on 13 September 1942, with its references to those 'who knew the author in Mandalay in 1923' and those 'who knew Captain Robinson in the old days' and who 'will be glad to receive this evidence of his continued existence'. The warmth of this strongly suggests Orwell is among them, although (if I can act as devil's advocate for a moment) he could be writing of mutual acquaintances.

But following the common-sense reading that Orwell did know Robinson, Orwell biographers tend to note Robinson's scandalous reputation, sometimes suggesting this is why Orwell got to know him in the first place. Shelden suggests Orwell 'made a point' of getting to know him (1991: 97) and Bowker says Orwell 'sought out such men as this [referring to Eric Frank Seeley, another friend], as he had Robinson' (2003: 86). However, it seems possible that Orwell and Robinson were acquainted before Robinson's slide into disreputability. This is suggested by a closer reading of his review, where he writes that those who knew Robinson in 1923 'were completely unable to understand why a young, healthy and apparently happy man should give himself up to such a debilitating and – in a European – unusual vice…'. This suggests that 'they' (and, by implication, Orwell among them) knew Robinson in pre-opium days.

The late Gerry Abbott went further than other writers on this subject by arguing that the character of 'the Poet' in Robinson's book is, in fact, Orwell (2004, 2006). If this were true it would mean the Burmese Orwell was a rather effete poet (perhaps of the aesthetic, 1890s-ish variety) who conceives a mad passion to shoot an elephant just for the fun of it. Instead, he shoots a man in a terrible accident, gravely wounding him, and then funks dealing with the aftermath, which Robinson has to clear up. I have considered this unlikely identification in more detail (Baker 2019), and although it is difficult to agree that 'the poet' in *A Modern de Quincey* is Orwell in any meaningful sense – and the whole episode may be a fiction

– it is possible that Eric Blair had a role in the initial inception and moniker of the Poet, who then rapidly becomes a fictional character. If this is true, it may be relevant to the chronology of their friendship to consider that one evening in April 1923 the pre-infamy Robinson is in the Upper Burma Club, talking with his friends 'the Poet' and 'the Padre', when the Poet suggests that they should go out and eat at a Chinese restaurant (1942: 60). And this, in fact, becomes the night when Robinson gives his friends the slip and first tries opium.

Biographers have also tried to fill in how Orwell felt about Robinson. For Bowker he was 'bemused' by him, but 'identified' with him (2003: 81; 86) while, in Meyers' account (2010: 67), he is 'morbidly fascinated' by him. There are certainly curious links between Robinson and the story of Flory, protagonist of Orwell's novel *Burmese Days* (1934). Stansky and Abrahams (1979: 29) suggest that 'very likely Flory, as a character, had his roots in Captain Robinson' although, as a disaffected Englishman in Burma, we could also say he had his roots in Eric Blair. More specifically, there is an odd overlap in the circumstances of the suicide. Robinson was going to shoot himself with the gun in his mouth, then thought of the unsightly mess it would leave (1942: 142-143) and tried to shoot himself in the temple. Flory shoots his dog in the head before shooting himself, and after seeing the mess this makes he decides to shoot himself in the heart instead of the head.

Reviewing the book, Orwell stresses: 'It is profoundly interesting to know what the mind can still contain in the face of apparently certain death – interesting to know, for instance, that a man can be ready to blow his brains out but anxious to avoid a disfiguring wound' (*CWGO* XIV: 34). Abbott suggests that Orwell and Robinson may have discussed this subject. It is certainly possible, at the very least, that a memory of the Robinson case, which Orwell must surely have known about, may be present in the episode of Flory shooting himself – rather than, say, taking poison or cutting his wrists – as something at the back of Orwell's mind when he wrote *Burmese Days*.

It is also interesting to wonder if Robinson knew anything of Orwell's later life, from listening to the wireless or being read to. Robinson was certainly not averse to talking about his past, and even talking it up a little (saying that he had smuggled rubies in his empty eye sockets, for example) but no one with whom I have been in contact (four people, with a fifth at second-hand) remembers him ever mentioning Orwell. Did he know that the man he had known as Eric Blair became the famous George Orwell? Did anyone ever read the *Observer* review to him, and if so, what did he make of those 'who knew Captain Robinson…'?

PHIL BAKER

IN HIS OWN RIGHT

The Orwell link has simultaneously preserved Robinson's name while overshadowing his historical and literary interest in his own right. While researching Robinson I dreamed that I was in a south London park, and there I found a bench with a plaque dedicated to his memory by former hospital colleagues. No such bench exists. Instead, he has his memorial in his unrepentant book: 'If my life has been a failure, I am prepared to accept the full responsibility. … I have been down in the mud, but my experiences there have not been without value. There are, stored away in my heart, one or two memories the fragrance of which is ever with me, and, if only for these, I would not have had it otherwise' (1942: v).

REFERENCES

Abbott, Gerry (2004) Introduction, Robinson, Captain H.R., *A Modern de Quincey: Autobiography of an Opium Addict*, Bangkok, Orchid Press, second edition pp ix-xv

Abbott, Gerry (2006) Robbie and the Poet, *SOAS Bulletin of Burma Research*, Vol.4, No.1 Spring

Baker, Phil (2019) Orwell and Captain Robinson's 'Poet': A more than cautionary note, *George Orwell Studies*, Vol. 2, No. 2 pp 47-54

Bowker, Gordon (2003) *George Orwell*, London: Little, Brown

Kingdon-Ward, Frank (1924) *From China to Hkamti Long*, London: Edward Arnold

Kipling, Rudyard (1893) The young British soldier, *Ballads, and Barrack-Room Ballads*. Available online at https://www.gutenberg.org/files/2819/2819-h/2819-h.htm

Meyers, Jeffrey (2010) *Orwell: Life and Art*, Urbana, Illinois, University of Illinois Press

Orwell, George (1997 [1942]) Review of *A Modern de Quincey*, Davison, Peter (ed.) *Complete Works of George Orwell* (*CWGO*), *Vol. XIV*, London: Secker & Warburg pp 34-35; first published in *Observer*, 13 September 1942

Robinson, Captain H.R. (1942) *A Modern de Quincey: An Autobiography*, London: George G. Harrap

Shelden, Michael (1991) *Orwell: The Authorised Biography*, London: Heinemann

Stansky, Peter and Abrahams, William (1972) *The Unknown Orwell*, London: Constable and Company

Stansky, Peter and Abrahams, William (1979) *Orwell: The Transformation*, London: Constable and Company

Theroux, Paul (2024) *Burma Sahib*, New York and London: Mariner Books

PERSONAL SOURCES AND ACKNOWLEDGEMENTS

The late Gerry Abbott shared an email from Josephine Felton, daughter of Doreen Manby, including Robinson's poem. Robinson and Doreen kept in touch after her marriage, and Josephine remembers visiting him in the early 1950s. Her mother remembered that he drank and would hide whisky. It was to Josephine's brother that he said he had smuggled gemstones in his eye sockets (email to Gerry Abbott from Josephine Felton, 25 January 2010).

Doris Rogers remembered him as a 'wonderful character' and a 'contented man' who 'had his philosophy' and 'a terrific sense of humour'. Her husband, Tommy, met Robinson in the 1930s when he was a boy running errands: 'Robbie' was working from home as a masseur and physiotherapist and Tommy would go to the chemist for him. Over the years they became friends and would go to the pub on Friday nights (telephone conversation with Doris Rogers, 2 May 2005).

I am particularly grateful to Jeremy Robinson, Robinson's great nephew, for nearly two decades of intermittent correspondence and meetings in London and Worthing. Jeremy very generously shared Robinson's correspondence with Tommy Rogers and Monty Silsby (in which, among other things, he urges the young Monty to read Kipling's *Kim*), gave me a recording of his voice (measured, a little orotund, almost Victorian) and showed me his publisher's contract and his gilt-wood Buddha.

Through Jeremy I met Pearl Silsby, Monty's widow, and her daughter, Jane, in Worthing (25 October 2014). Monty first met Robinson when he was a boy of about ten after answering an advertisement in Lyndhurst Road post office, Worthing: 'Elderly blind gentleman wants help' for errands. Pearl and Jane could imitate Robinson's 'drawn out' voice ('Hell-ooo Jane; Hell-ooo [so-and-so]'). He was generous with toys and boxes of chocolate, and when he stayed with the family the children would go into his room in the mornings and jump up and down on his bed. They remembered his eyes just looked closed, with little or no disfigurement, and that he would sit contentedly by the fireside. He was very talkative, chatting to Monty until midnight. He seemed to have adjusted to blindness, and would not be patronised about it; when someone asked him, perhaps a little fatuously, if he would like his sight back, he said: 'I'd have to give it careful consideration.'

Visiting him in London, they remembered he lived in two rooms, with a landlady, and that his rooms were 'rather dark'. Pearl believed his death was an accident, as did his brother Frank, who reasoned that he would not have killed himself without leaving a note or having made a will; he died intestate.

I also want to give a tip of the hat to indefatigable Orwell researcher Darcy Moore. He has traced the ship Robinson came home on after his suicide attempt (the S.S. *Sagaing* of the Henderson Line, Rangoon to London, arriving on 29 June 1925) and found that his medals were sold at Bonhams, Knightsbridge, in 2015 (Medals, Bonds, Banknotes and Coins, 19 November: see darcymoore.net). It would be interesting to know where they have been in the intervening years, but the vendor's identity is protected.

NOTE ON THE CONTRIBUTOR

Phil Baker wrote an Oxford DPhil. on the work of Samuel Beckett, later published as *Beckett and the Mythology of Psychoanalysis* (1997), and came to Orwell late. He writes and reviews for a number of papers and journals including the *Times Literary Supplement*, and his books include *Austin Osman Spare: The Life and Legend of London's Lost Artist* (2011, expanded third edition 2023), and *City of the Beast: The London of Aleister Crowley* (2022)..

'A Disillusioned Little Middle Class Boy': George Orwell, Harry Pollitt and *The Road to Wigan Pier*

JOHN NEWSINGER

Harry Pollitt's review of *The Road to Wigan Pier* appeared in the *Daily Worker* on 17 March 1937. It was, of course, quite unusual for the general secretary of the Communist Party to review books in the party newspaper; one can almost count it an honour, even if the review was patronisingly hostile. Indeed, when Orwell finally received a copy of the review while he was fighting in a Republican militia in the Spanish Civil War, he wrote to his 'wonderful wife' Eileen, recently arrived in the country, describing it as 'pretty bad, tho' of course good as publicity'. He put the nature of the review down to the fact that Pollitt 'must have heard I was serving in the Poum militia'. What is particularly interesting, however, is that, despite Pollitt's review, Orwell was still very much thinking of joining the communist-run International Brigades on the Madrid front. He asks Eileen to have a word with John McNair, the Independent Labour Party's man in Barcelona: 'You might at some opportune moment say something to him about my wanting to go to Madrid etc' (*CWGO* XI: 16). Clearly at this point, the bad review did not precipitate for Orwell any fundamental breach with the communists. He was already critical of communist politics, but he was still broadly sympathetic to what he believed to be their strategy in Spain and hoped to make a contribution on what was clearly the decisive front in the war, fighting in the ranks of the International Brigades.

It is worth here briefly rehearsing how Orwell had ended up joining the POUM militia rather than the International Brigades. He had approached John Strachey, one of the key figures behind the Left Book Club, for his help in getting to Spain. Strachey, at the time, a committed and determined Communist Party fellow-traveller, had duly taken him to meet Harry Pollitt.[1] One can safely assume that this was with the intention of pointing him in the direction of the International Brigades. Orwell has provided his own account of that meeting in his 'Notes on the Spanish Militia'. He writes of how Pollitt 'after questioning me evidently decided that I was politically unreliable and refused to help me, also tried to frighten me out of going by talking a lot about Anarchist terrorism'. Nevertheless, Pollitt still asked him if he were prepared to join the International Brigades to which Orwell replied that he 'could not undertake to join anything until I had seen what was happening. He then refused to help me…' Pollitt advised him that if he were determined to go to Spain he should get a safe conduct from the Spanish Embassy in Paris. Pollitt's rejection led him to approach Fenner Brockway, general secretary of the ILP, and his fateful enlistment in the POUM militia. But as Orwell points out, if he had understood the situation in Spain better then, he would have joined the anarcho-syndicalist militia, the CNT. Pollitt's emphasis on 'anarchist terrorism' at this meeting would suggest that Orwell did, indeed, make clear his sympathies were with the anarchist cause in Spain at this time (ibid: 136).

While Orwell was, initially, not too put out by Pollitt's review, this was before the May uprising in Barcelona. As we have seen, when he received the review, he was still thinking of transferring to the International Brigades, but what he saw and experienced in Barcelona and the communist-orchestrated repression of the revolutionary left that followed, irrevocably changed all that. He and his POUM comrades were now denounced as, at best, 'fascist dupes' and, at worst, 'fascist agents'. They were condemned as 'Trotskyists' and he and Eileen were both lucky to escape from Spain in June 1937. Once he was back in Britain, Pollitt's review took on the appearance of the opening shot in a campaign of abuse and slander intended to cover-up the extent of communist repression in Spain.

Orwell can hardly have been surprised by Pollitt's hostile review of *The Road to Wigan Pier* given his references to 'Bolshevik commissars' as 'half gangster, half gramophone'. The sneering, patronising style is still something of a surprise today – though Pollitt does praise Orwell's account of the miners' working conditions and of working class housing conditions. But rather than engage with Orwell's political arguments, Pollitt, instead, attempts to discredit him by claiming that Orwell thought working class people 'smell', indeed 'the chief thing that worries Mr Orwell is the "smell" of the working class, for smells seem to occupy the major portion of the book'. Pollitt describes his review as being written in a 'fatherly way', but goes on to dismiss Orwell as knowing nothing about and contributing nothing to the socialist cause, dubbing him the 'disillusioned little middle class boy'.

While Orwell thought the review was probably provoked by Pollitt knowing that he was serving with the POUM militia, in fact it reads more as if his main objection is that Orwell does not celebrate the Popular Front. This was the Communist Party's overriding priority at the time. It must have been all the more galling that *The Road to Wigan Pier* was such a success – indeed, was the Left Book Club's most popular volume, selling 44,000 copies of the club edition. The other great concerns that gripped British communists were support for the Soviet Union, wholehearted endorsement of the ongoing Moscow trials and celebration of the genius of Joseph Stalin. Orwell's *The Road* was distributed by the Left Book Club in March 1937 and nothing better demonstrates communist support for the Soviet Union than that month's other choice, Dudley Collard's *Soviet Justice and the Trial of Radek*. This eulogy of the so-called trial of Karl Radek, Yuri Piatakov and fifteen others that lasted from 23 to 30 January 1937 is truly sickening to read. Collard tells his readers that all the victims pleaded guilty, 'as far as could be seen, quite voluntarily and spontaneously' to crimes of treachery, sabotage and murder, spying for the nazis and blowing up mines, factories and the railways, all presided over by Leon Trotsky. The prosecutor, Vishinsky was masterly in his presentation of the case: 'He never once lost his temper or bullied a defendant. …He invariably behaved with restraint and courtesy.' And his final speech, calling for the death penalty was greeted with prolonged applause. Not all those on trial were sentenced to death which, as Collard observes, 'was more merciful than I would have been' (Collard 1937: 33, 36, 79). Thirteen were shot immediately and the others including Radek were all later murdered in various labour camps.

After the May insurrection in Barcelona, Orwell's attitude towards the communists changed. He went from regarding them as being on the same side while disagreeing with them on some issues to being a deadly enemy. The reality that the Popular Front aimed not to advance the cause of socialism but was designed to serve the interests of Soviet foreign policy had to be covered up, along with the communist readiness to use torture and assassination against its opponents on the left in Spain. As far as he was concerned, far from advancing the socialist cause in Spain, they had brutally repressed the left in an effort to restore capitalism. This truth had to be suppressed. In Britain, this involved attempting to silence and discredit the likes of George Orwell and others by means of a campaign of slander and intimidation.

On 20 August 1937, Orwell wrote to publisher Victor Gollancz to complain about the way he was being smeared in the *Daily Worker*. Three times the paper had asserted that he thought working class people 'smell'. But he had rather written that middle class people were brought up to believe that. The smear was all about labelling him a 'vulgar snob' and thereby discrediting him and 'the political parties with which I have been associated'. He warned Gollancz that if the communists continued with this lie, then he would 'publish a reply with the necessary quotations, and in it I shall include what John Strachey said to me on the subject just before I left for Spain (about December 20th). Strachey will no doubt remember it, and I don't think the CP would care to see it in print'. What Strachey said we are, sadly, never likely to know. Orwell went on to complain to Gollancz about what he thought was the more serious intimidatory treatment being meted out to Stafford Cottman, who had fought in the ranks of the POUM militia and had had his home picketed by CP members on his return. He threatened libel action over claims that the POUM was 'in the pay of Franco' and told him that 'I am taking counsel's opinion'. He was very reluctant to go down this road, but 'I think one has the right to defend oneself against these malignant personal attacks'. Gollancz had to do something about it (*CWGO* XI: 72-73).

The following month (15 September) Orwell wrote to his friend Geoffrey Gorer[2] complaining about how the communists had behaved in Spain:

> For instance, they have succeeded in breaking up the workers' militias, which were based on the trade unions and in which all ranks received the same pay and were on a basis of equality, and substituting an army on bourgeois lines where a colonel is paid eight times as much as a private etc. All these changes, of course, are put forward in the name of military necessity and backed up by the 'Trotskyist' racket, which consists of saying that anyone who professes revolutionary principles is a Trotskyist and in Fascist pay (ibid: 80-81).

He could not believe the lies that were being told and went on about how the *Daily Worker* 'had been following me personally with the most filthy libels, calling me pro-Fascist etc'. He had asked Gollancz 'to silence them, which he did, not very willingly I imagine' (ibid). This was, of course, just the beginning of Orwell's 'war' with the communists, the opening shot so to speak.

One last point worth briefly exploring is the Harry Pollitt conundrum. How was it that a man who had been fighting for the workers' class since the early days of the First World War, had been a leading member of Sylvia Pankhurst's Workers' Socialist Federation and had played a crucial role in the 1920 'Hands Off Russia' campaign came to end up a determined supporter of Stalin's murderous tyranny? Pollitt had been one of the Communist

JOHN NEWSINGER

Party leaders imprisoned for twelve months in October 1925, conveniently out of the way during the General Strike of May 1926. Somewhere along the way this working class rebel was transformed into an enthusiastic Stalinist. In August 1929, he was installed as the general secretary of the British Communist Party, faithfully implementing the ultra-sectarian Third Period strategy. He was, of course, to embrace wholeheartedly the Popular Front strategy when it was imposed by the Kremlin and was second to none when it came to celebrating the achievements of the Soviet Union and the genius of Joseph Stalin. He was also fervent in his support for the Moscow trials. In 1937, for example, he published his own account of the Radek trial, *The Truth about Trotskyism: Moscow Trial January 1937*. This 2d pamphlet included the complete text of the official indictment. Trotsky, Zinoviev, Kamenev and now Radek and co. had always been enemies of socialism and had been trying to bring down the Soviet regime, allying with and working for the nazis to restore capitalism in Russia. There was no ambiguity in his argument: 'Trotskyism is terrorism. Trotskyism is anti-working class. Trotskyism is a foul conspiracy against the interests of all who want to ensure the preservation of democracy, peace and Socialism. The Moscow trial will serve to strengthen a world-wide fight against Trotskyism' (Pollitt 1937: 8, 11). During the 1930s, the Stalin regime executed more German communists who had mistakenly fled to the Soviet Union for safety than the Hitler regime executed in Germany. How a man like Pollitt, a working class socialist, came to support such a regime – and he was far from alone in this – has never been properly nor adequately explained.[3]

There is plenty of evidence to show that if a Stalinist regime had ever been installed in Britain, Pollitt would almost certainly have been one of its victims, confessing to 'Trotskyism' or 'Titoism', naming others, before being shot. He had come under suspicion when he attempted to intervene following the arrest of Rose Cohen, a British communist whom he knew well enough to have proposed marriage to. She had married a Russian and went to live with him in the Soviet Union in 1929. She was arrested in August 1937. Unknown to him, she was executed at the end of November 1937. More dangerous was the fact that when the veteran Hungarian communist, Bela Kun, was being interrogated and tortured in the summer of 1937, he had named Pollitt as a Trotskyist and a British spy. Kun was himself executed. What seems to have saved Pollitt from at best expulsion from the Communist Party and at worst an unfortunate fatal illness or accident when visiting the Soviet Union was that another prisoner, Osip Pianitsky, a party member since 1901 and prominent Comintern official, refused to name him under torture. Pianitsky was shot on 30 October 1938. These concerns regarding Pollitt's reliability resurfaced in the early summer of 1942 when Georgi Dimitrov recorded in his diary that the NKVD had received reports on Pollitt's 'strange behaviour. English intelligence is using him to plant its people in the party and also in the apparatus of Sov organs'. A 'most scrupulous study of Pol [sic] and what is taking place in the leadership of the English CP' had been ordered (Dimitrov 2003: 219). Pollitt had refused to support the Hitler-Stalin Pact of August 1939 and, for a while, had been replaced as general secretary! He would certainly have been purged if the communists had taken power in the late 1940s, executed when the Titoite purges that had engulfed Eastern Europe were imposed on the country. He would not have been alone. In this respect, it is always important to remember that Stalin executed tens of thousands of Communist Party members, actions that loyal communists such as Pollitt always supported, but that Orwell opposed and condemned. Nevertheless, Pollitt's support for Stalin remained firm. Even after Khruschev's revelations in February 1956 in which he denounced Stalin's crimes and the cult of personality surrounding him, he still kept a portrait of Stalin on the wall in his living room. Those communist critics of Orwell have only the fact that the Stalinists never took power in Britain to thank for never having experienced themselves the murderous realities that informed *Nineteen Eighty-Four*. Orwell would surely have appreciated the irony.

ARTICLE

NOTES

[1] John Strachey had a remarkable political trajectory. He was elected a Labour MP in 1929, went with Oswald Mosley to found the New Party in 1931, but broke with him when he embraced fascism and was a communist fellow-traveller throughout the 1930s. He broke with the communists in 1940, rejoined the Labour Party and was elected as a Labour MP in 1945, serving in the Attlee government first as Minister of Food and then Minister for War and later in the 1950s embracing the Gaitskellites. He was by now staunchly anti-Stalinist. In 1960, the journal *Encounter* published his 'The strangled cry' which included an assessment of Orwell and fulsome praise for both *Animal Farm* and *Nineteen-Eighty Four* (see https://www.marxists.org/archive/strachey/1961/strangled-cry.htm). He describes Orwell as embodying 'the England of the major eccentrics, the major satirists. Lean and long of body, cadaverous, ravaged in face, with shining quixotic eyes, you might easily have taken him for one more English idealist crank. And so he nearly was. But in the end he became for good and ill, far more than that. He was a major writer, and by means of his pen, he became one of the most effective men of his generation' (Strachey 1962: 23)

[2] In 1934, Gorer had published his first book, *The Revolutionary Ideas of the Marquis de Sade*. Just saying!

[3] For a discussion of Communist Party historiography see Newsinger 2006

REFERENCES

Banac, Ivo (2003) *The Diary of Georgi Dimitrov*, New Haven: Yale University Press

Collard, Dudley (1937) *Soviet Justice and the Trial of Radek and Others*, London: Gollancz

Newsinger, John (2006) Recent controversies in the history of British communism, *Journal of Contemporary History*, Vol. 41, No. 3, pp 557-572

Orwell, George (1998 [1937a]) Letter to Eileen Blair, *CWGO, Vol. XI*. p 16

Orwell, George (1998 [1937b]) Letter to Victor Gollancz, *CWGO, Vol XI* pp 72-73

Orwell, George (1998 [1937c]) Letter to Geoffrey Gorer, *CWGO, Vol. XI* pp 80-81

Orwell, George (1998 [1938]) Notes on the Spanish militia, *CWGO, Vol. XI* pp 136

Pollitt, Harry (1937) *The Truth about Trotskyism: Moscow Trial January 1937*, London: Communist Party of Great Britain

NOTE ON THE CONTRIBUTOR

John Newsinger is a retired academic. He is the author of *Orwell's Politics*, *Hope Lies in the Proles: George Orwell and the Left* and *Chosen by God: Donald Trump, the Christian Right and American Capitalism*.

ARTICLE

The Two Arthurs

DARCY MOORE

Why did George Orwell join the Indian Imperial Police? He told his second wife, Sonia Brownell, who was curious as to why he had pursued this career rather than 'Oxbridge', that it was a 'long and complicated story' (Fyvel 1982: 36). Darcy Moore reconsiders this question with new research into an unknown paternal uncle who served as a district superintendent of police in Bengal.

Except for Jacintha Buddicom's testimony that her childhood friend wished to study at the University of Oxford, there is little evidence Orwell wanted to follow the traditional academic and social path from Eton College to Oxbridge (Buddicom 2006 [1974]: 77; Coppard and Crick 1984: 52-54; Moore 2023; Taylor 2023: 102-104). Buddicom recounted that their family matriarchs were supportive of the idea but Orwell's father, Richard Walmsley Blair (1857-1939), employed in the Opium Department from 1875 until his retirement in 1912, was 'adamant' his son would follow the Blair family footsteps into the 'Indian civil' (Buddicom 2006 [1974]: 77, 119). Mr Blair did consult with Andrew Gow (1886-1978), his son's tutor at Eton, enquiring if a scholarship was possible, only to be told poor academic results made this unrealistic (Meyers 2000: 43). The ingenuousness of Gow's advice has been questioned but, either way, Orwell never received a university education and joined the Indian Imperial Police in 1922 as a probationary assistant district superintendent (ibid).

Eric Arthur Blair (1903-1950) was born in Motihari and his parents married in Nainital. One school friend, the historian Steven Runciman (1903-2000), recalled Orwell being sentimentally entranced by 'the allure of the East' and was not 'the least bit surprised' he decided on this option rather than university (Wadhams 1984: 21). Buddicom also understood this was 'a sort of tradition with his father's family' believing it was entirely Mr Blair's idea and that Eric just 'fell in with it' (ibid: 22). One biographer, finding it challenging to imagine the 'unassuming' Mr Blair being 'adamant' about anything, surmised it was 'perfectly reasonable that he would want to stop spending his limited income on educating a son who was old enough to begin a suitable career' (Shelden 1991: 85). This

DARCY MOORE seems like case closed but recently uncovered primary sources shed more light on his father's personal context and ambitions for his son.

The youngest of the ten children born to Thomas Arthur Richard Blair (1802-1867) and Frances 'Fanny' Catherine Blair (1823-1908), Orwell's father was no stranger to family tragedy. By 1874, before he reached adulthood, Richard's five sisters were dead. The only one of his brothers who survived into the twentieth century was Horatio Douglas Blair (1854-1939) also employed in the Opium Department (Thacker, Spink & Co. 1873: 142). All his other siblings had died childless by 1884. In one of Orwell's early novels, *Keep the Aspidistra Flying*, the protagonist's family is reminiscent of his own:

> Gran'pa Comstock, for instance, himself one of a litter of twelve, had produced eleven progeny. Yet all those eleven produced only two progeny between them, and those two – Gordon and his sister Julia – had produced, by 1934, not even one. Gordon, last of the Comstocks, was born in 1905, an unintended child; and thereafter, in thirty long, long years, there was not a single birth in the family, only deaths. ... Every one of them seemed doomed, as though by a curse, to a dismal, shabby, hole-and-corner existence (Orwell 1997 [1936]: 41).

Orwell's great-grandfather, Charles Blair (1776-1854), and great-uncle, Henry Charles Blair (1775-1794), had received privileged educations at Westminster School where students were prepared for Oxford and a career in the Anglican Church (Westminster School Archive n.d.; Moore 2024b). In his correspondence, the Poet Laureate, Robert Southey (1774-1843), who was expelled from the school, provided a rare insight into the privileged lives of these aristocratic, slave-owning Blairs (Southey 1849: 152-154). Charles Blair's son, the Rev. Thomas Arthur Richard Blair M.A., appears to be the only one of Orwell's ancestors to attend university, albeit briefly, at Pembroke College, Cambridge, in 1833 (*Western Daily Press* 1867: 31 August; Pembroke College Archives: 91; Venn 1940: 286). Orwell was a clergyman's grandson.

The Rev. Blair also served with the 72nd (Duke of Albany's own Highlanders) Regiment of Foot (National Archives 2024: 93-94). In an eleven-year career, starting when he enlisted as an ensign in 1819, Blair served abroad at the Cape of Good Hope for three years, 282 days and at home for six years, 223 days (ibid). Blair's regiment was engaged in the ongoing colonial warfare against the Xhosa people of the Eastern Cape when he arrived (ibid). Ensign Blair was promoted to lieutenant in 1820 and then captain in 1825 (*English*

Chronicle and Whitehall Evening Post 1823; National Archives 2024: 93-94). Both of those promotions were 'by purchase', a system, until reformed in 1871, which ensured the officer class would predominantly be gentlemen of means (Spiers 1980: 2, 177-182). His own father, Charles Blair, had been a captain in the 4th Royal Irish Dragoon Guards (Westminster School Archive n.d.). Charles Blair was later stationed at the Cape of Good Hope as a collector of customs c. 1808-1826 and owned at least two 'enslaved' people during this time (UCL 2024; Westminster School Archive n.d.). His brother Henry Charles Blair, who had purchased a commission in the 23rd Regiment of Foot at sixteen years of age, died of yellow fever while his regiment was endeavouring to quell the slave revolt on Saint-Domingue (now Haiti) in the West Indies (Moore 2024b; Southey 1849: 152-154; Westminster School Archive n.d.).

Why Orwell's parents settled on 'Arthur' as a middle name for their only son rather than the traditional Blair choices – Horatio, Charles, Henry and Thomas – seems to be a nod towards this grandfather he never met. However, the career of a paternal uncle, unknown in Orwell scholarship, is an interesting one; Arthur Blair (1846-1879) was a district superintendent of police in Bengal (General Register Office 1879).

THE BLAIR BROTHERS IN INDIA

Richard W. Blair's imperial service as an assistant sub-deputy opium agent in Bengal began on 4 August 1875. He was first stationed near Motihari, at Mozzuferpore (Muzaffarpur) in the year his wife-to-be, Ida Limouzin (1875-1943), was born. When he arrived, Horatio Douglas Blair and Arthur Blair were already stationed in India. Horatio was in the Opium Department at Kheree (Khere) and Arthur, based at Noakholly (Noakhali), was making good career progress in the police department (*Englishman's Overland Mail* 1875: 6 July; *Indian Statesman* 1875: 22 December). In 1873, Horatio had been appointed to the Benares Agency, subject to passing Chemistry and Surveying exams, as an assistant sub-deputy opium agent (*Englishman's Overland Mail* 1875: 12 December). Horatio and Richard were reunited, in March 1876, when they sat these examinations together in Patna, Bihar:

> The Opium Assistants have, properly speaking, to be examined by the Central Committee of Examination. However, to save the extra cost to Government of fresh examination papers in Botany, Chemistry, and Surveying, it was arranged that the Opium Assistants should appear to be examined in the above subjects along with the Native Civil Service candidates, on condition that the Central Examination Committee should share the cost from funds at their disposal (1876: 5).[1]

Twenty-three candidates were examined, including five 'assistants in the Opium Department' who were required to pass the special subjects of Surveying, Botany and Chemistry (ibid: 3). Both Blairs did very poorly, with the examiner mentioning, in his report to the secretary of Bengal, that 'the Opium Assistants have not passed in any subjects' (ibid: 4). He was dismissive of complaints suggesting 'the failure to advertise the new examination rules' prevented adequate preparation and commented that there was 'a general paucity in quality candidates' (ibid). One 'native' candidate, by some mistake of the 'local committee' was examined in Hindustani instead of Bengali but still managed a pass on one of the subjects, although he understandably failed the others (ibid). Richard Blair did particularly poorly, achieving just 15/150 for Surveying and Measurement; 15/60 for Botany and 11/60 for Chemistry: a grand total of 41/270 (ibid: 6).

Following the First War of Indian Independence, what Orwell's father and uncles would have called the Mutiny of 1857, superintendents of police, with rare exceptions, were to be European (La Bouchardiere 1985). They were recruited in several ways during this period but from 1893, it was only possible if one sat a competitive examination in England, as Eric Blair did in 1922 (ibid). Blair sat challenging exams, often identical to those attempted by officer candidates for the military services, over an eight-day period:

> The passing grade for the examination was 6,000 marks out of a possible 12,400. This did not mean, however, that all the numerous applicants who had received a passing grade would be accepted as candidates. From this particular group only the top twenty-six were; and Blair with a score of 8,463 was seventh on the list. In September he and the twenty-five other successful candidates were required to take a riding test, for which he prepared himself during the summer at a stable in or near Southwold, and was placed twenty-first on the list of twenty-three who passed (Stansky 1972: 155).

Although it is generally thought that Richard Blair and his siblings were 'privately tutored' at home, Arthur Blair had been well-educated at a reputable grammar school (Bowker 2004 [2003]: 5; National Archives 1861). He is listed on the 1861 census as a scholar attending 'East Street Grammar School' (Milton Abbey School) at Blandford Forum (National Archives 1861). No records of any of his siblings participating in formal schooling have been located and it would have been particularly unaffordable for a widow with few means to formally educate the youngest child of such a large family at a quality school. Possibly Arthur showed more potential.

In 1859, he attended a fête with his father and two sisters which a local newspaper trumpeted, under the headline, OPENING OF THE NATIONAL SCHOOLS, as celebrating 'the completion and opening of a beautiful group of buildings in which it is intended to give the rising generation in the locality the full advantage of our national system of education' (*Dorset County Chronicle* 1859: 6 October). It is evident that his education prepared him more than adequately for his career as a district superintendent of police. Arthur Blair successfully passed his 'police paper' in 1864, when he was eighteen years of age (*Friend of India and Statesman* 1864: 29 December).

The newspaper and government records of Arthur Blair's promotions, transfers and furloughs during the decade before his brothers joined him in Bengal are extensive. The list of districts, towns and cities where Arthur was stationed (1864-1878) included: Bancoorah (Bankura), Berhampore (Baharampur), Bogra (Bogura), Burden, Calcutta (Kolkata), Chittagong Hill Tracts, Cuttack, Gaya, Howrah, Jessore, Lohardugge (Lohardaga), Mymensingh, Nadiya (Nadia), Nuddea (Nabadwip), Rungpore and Tirpoot (Tirhut). In the year Richard W. Blair joined his two brothers in Bengal, Arthur was appointed 'justice of the peace' and promoted temporarily, although his substantive rank was that of a district superintendent (fourth grade) to be an additional deputy commissioner of police in Calcutta (*Indian Daily News* 1875: 17 December; *Indian Statesman* 1875: 22 December). This role continued into the following year. In 1877, he was appointed to act as assistant inspector-general of railway police for the Bengal Division after the previous incumbent was suspended from duties (*Friend of India and Statesman* 1877: 28 August). These are reasonably sound indicators that his superiors recognised his talent.

On 21 July 1878, Blair began three months' leave, sailing five days later from Bombay on the *Cathay*, a P&O Steamship bound for Southampton (*Times of India* 1878: 27 July; *Friend of India and Statesman* 1878: 13 August). The following year, he is granted furlough, from 15 May for '1 year, 4 months and 22 days' but never returns to India, where his two brothers continue serving in the Opium Department into the 20th century (*Friend of India and Statesman* 1879: 9 May).

Arthur Blair died of phthisis,[2] once thought to be a hereditary disease, in the presence of a servant, on 13 October at 7 Paragon, Bath (General Register Office 1879; Byrne 2013 [2010]: 23). Probate records show his personal estate was under £450 and that he was employed as a 'district superintendent of police in the province of Bengal in the East Indies' (England and Wales Government Probate Death Index 1858-2019). His mother, also residing at the

ARTICLE

same address, was 'the sole executrix' (ibid). Horatio had married a month after Arthur's death, on 14 November 1879, to an American, Millicent O'Donnell (1854-1940) in Mussoorie[3] (MacGregor 2023 [2016]: 233). Richard and Horatio (with his wife) return to this same apartment for the next two decades while on leave from the Opium Department (*Bath Chronicle* 1889: 30 May; *Bath Chronicle* 1891: 11 June).

Horatio and Millicent had three children (all born in India) and the 1901 census (taken on 31 March) reveals that one of their daughters, Margaret Rosabel Blair (1890-1984), along with Orwell's mother and sister, are all residing with Fanny Blair in Bath (National Archives 1901). Their eldest son, Robert Cuthbert Blair (1880-1911), was educated the Royal Military College, served with the East Lancashire Regiment in South Africa before transferring to the Indian Army in 1902 (MacGregor 2023 [2016]: 233). He was a captain in the 6th Gurkha Rifles by 1909 (ibid; *London Gazette*, 26 March 1909: 2354). He appears to have suicided, throwing himself overboard from a mail steamer in 1911 (ibid; *London Gazette*, 15 September 1911: 6821). The remaining four members of the family emigrated to New Zealand before the outbreak of World War One (MacGregor 2023 [2016]: 233).

Arthur Blair's grave at Landsdown Cemetery
(©Bath Record Office – Bath Burial Index, taken 2012)

Although Arthur Blair was dead nearly a quarter-of-a-century before Orwell was born, he seems likely to have been in Richard W. Blair's mind when he named his first-born son after his own father, who died when he was ten.[4]

REFLECTIONS

Orwell's family were extremely focused on his academic progress which practically meant one had to be able to sit exams successfully. Mr Blair understood the challenges, through personal experience. His mother and her siblings attended good schools in Bedford, an epicentre of Anglo-Indian education during the second half of the 19th century, where girls were encouraged to sit public examinations (Moore 2024a: 5-15). Orwell was enrolled at St Cyprian's, a noted 'scholarship factory', with the support of a maternal uncle, Charles W. Limouzin (1868-1947), and well-prepared by a 'cramming' school in Southwold during 1922 to pass the civil service examinations (Wadhams 1984: Moore 2024a).

Orwell, in his *Observer* review of *India Called Them*, by Lord Beveridge, clearly valued the 'picture of British India' that his parents also experienced, 'in the forgotten decades between the Mutiny and Kipling's *Plain Tales from the Hills*' (Orwell 1998 [1947-1948]: 261). He noted that the author was 'one of the very first batch of "competition wallahs"' admitted to the Indian civil service by competitive examination instead of through influence and property (ibid). Steven Runciman had observed the young Eric Blair's nostalgic attachment to this world nearly thirty years previously (Coppard and Crick 1984: 54).

The reasons why Orwell decided to join the Indian Imperial Police in 1922 have been widely discussed but never satisfactorily settled, mostly due to the information included in the second edition of Jacintha Buddicom's memoir (Buddicom 2006 [1974]: 169-189; Moore 2023). It is not difficult to imagine two adolescents, in love with literature, making romantic plans to attend university together – nor to understand the impact of Blair's shameful behaviour which – in Buddicom's own words, 'by trying to take us the whole way before I was anywhere near ready for that' – ruined their relationship (Davison 2013: 9). The wishes of a father, adamant about the direction of his only son's future career, are also easily understood.

This new biographical information, connecting the three Blair brothers – Richard, Arthur and Horatio – to shared experiences of imperial service in Bengal, deepens our knowledge of the 'tradition with his father's family' mentioned by Buddicom (Wadhams 1984: 22). It also goes some way to explaining why Mr Blair was so adamant his son would join the Indian Imperial Police and follow in Arthur Blair's footsteps.

ARTICLE

NOTES

[1] This crumbling document was located while researching in the West Bengal Archives in late 2023. At the time, it was exciting to find a primary source about Blair's work in the Opium Department but later it led to reflection on the effort he and Ida had made to ensure Eric Blair was extremely well-educated

[2] The myths abounding about phthisis, more commonly known as consumption or tuberculosis, during the 19th century are well covered by Katherine Byrne in *Tuberculosis and the Victorian Literary Imagination*

[3] Blanche Evelyn Limouzin (1872-1903) died in Mussoorie shortly before her sister gave birth to Orwell in Motihari. Blanche attended school with two of her sisters in Bedford and was the only relative to attend Richard and Ida's wedding in Nainital during 1897 (Moore 2024a: 8-13)

[4] Orwell's maternal grandfather, Francis Limouzin (1835-1915) had lost an infant son named Arthur (1862-1865) from his first marriage

[5] A photograph of Arthur Blair, aged about 19, in a distant relative's photo album (compiled as a gift for Christmas 1869) was discovered too late to be included in this article but can be viewed at darcymoore.net

REFERENCES

Bath Chronicle and Weekly Gaze (1889) 30 May

Bath Chronicle and Weekly Gaze (1892) 25 August

Bath Record Office (n.d.) Arthur Blair. Available online at https://www.batharchives.co.uk/cemeteries/lansdown-cemetery/arthur-blair, accessed on 10 September 2024

Bowker, Gordon (2004 [2003]) *George Orwell*, London: Abacus

Buddicom, Jacintha (2006 [1974]) *Eric & Us*, Chichester: Finlay Publishers, Postscript by Dione Venables

Byrne, Katherine (2013 [2010]) *Tuberculosis and the Victorian Literary Imagination*, Cambridge: Cambridge University Press

Coppard, Audrey and Crick, Bernard (1984) *Orwell Remembered*, London: Ariel Books/BBC

Crick, Bernard (1992 [1980]) *George Orwell: A Life*, Harmondsworth, Middlesex: Penguin, second edition

Davison, Peter (2013) *George Orwell: A Life in Letters*, New York: Liveright

Dorset County Chronicle and Somersetshire Gazette (1859) 6 October

General Register Office (1879) *Death Certificate for Arthur Blair*, died 13 October 1879, Registered December Quarter 1879, Bath District 05C/416, Sub-district of Walcot, County of Somerset, Entry No. 20

England and Wales Government Probate Death Index (1858-2019) *Probate Record for Arthur Blair*, UK Government, HM Courts & Tribunals Service

English Chronicle and Whitehall Evening Post (1823) 5 August

Englishman's Overland Mail (1875) 6 July

Friend of India and Statesman (1864) 29 December

Fyvel, T.R. (1982) *George Orwell: A Personal Memoir*, London: Weidenfeld and Nicolson

General Register Office (1879) *Death Certificate for Arthur Blair*, Registrar's District of Bath, Registrar's Sub-District of Walcot, County of Somerset, Entry No. 20

Grimley, W.H. (1876) Superintendent, subordinate civil service examination, government of Bengal, appointment department, Branch III – examinations, proceedings for July. Proceedings 1-3, File No. 8, No. 35

Indian Daily News (1875) 17 December

Indian Statesman (1875) 22 December

La Bouchardiere, Basil R.E. (1985) *Roll of Indian Police Officers 1861-1947: Superintendents & Assistant Superintendents (Incomplete)*, FBIS. Available online at https://search.fibis.org/bin/aps_browse_sources.php?mode=browse_components&id=955&s_id=287

London Gazette (1909) 26 March

London Gazette (1911) 15 September

MacGregor, Gordon (2023 [2016]) *The Red Book of Scotland, Vol. 2: Bai-Bru*, Scotland: Tanner Ritchie

Mason, Philip (1985) *The Men Who Ruled India*, New York: W.W. Norton & Co.

Meyers, Jeffrey (2000) *Orwell: Wintry Conscience of a Generation*, New York: W.W. Norton & Co.

Moore, Darcy (2023) The map & the territory, *Darcy Moore's Blog*. Available online at https://www.darcymoore.net/2023/09/24/orwell-the-map-the-territory/

Moore, Darcy (2024a) Orwell and Bedford, *History in Bedfordshire* (*HIB*), Vol. 10, No. 5, Summer. Available online at https://www.bedfordshire-lha.org.uk/letters/#flipbook-df_9336/7/

Moore, Darcy (2024b) Orwell's ancestors & Robert Southey', *Darcy Moore's Blog*. Available online at https://www.darcymoore.net/2024/08/19/orwells-ancestors-robert-southey/

National Archives (1861) *England Census*, RG 9; Piece: 1333; Folio: 57; Page: 17; GSU roll: 542797, Kensington, London

National Archives (1901) *England Census*, Class: RG13, Piece: 2343, Folio: 104, Page: 15, Kensington, London

National Archives (2024) *Thomas [Arthur] Blair*, WO 25/799/47, Folio 93. Available online at https://discovery.nationalarchives.gov.uk/details/r/C17355339, accessed on 8 August 2024

Orwell, George (1998 [1903-1936]) *A Kind of Compulsion: The Complete Works of George Orwell, Vol. X*, Davison, Peter (ed.) London: Secker & Warburg

Orwell, George (1997 [1934]) *Burmese Days, The Complete Works of George Orwell, Vol. II*, Davison, Peter (ed.) London: Secker & Warburg

Orwell, George (1997 [1936]) *Keep the Aspidistra Flying, The Complete Works of George Orwell, Vol. IV*, Davison, Peter (ed.) London: Secker & Warburg

Orwell, George (1998 [1947-1948]) *It Is What I Think: The Complete Works of George Orwell, Vol. XIX*, Davison, Peter (ed.) London: Secker & Warburg

Pembroke College Archives, Admissions Book, GBR/1058/COL/4/3/1/2

Shelden, Michael (1991) *Orwell: The Authorised Biography*, London: Heinemann

Southey, Rev. Charles Cuthbert (ed.) (1849) *The Life & Correspondence of the late Robert Southey, Vol. I*, London: Longman, Brown, Green and Longmans

Spiers, Edward M. (1980) *The Army and Society 1815-1914*, London and New York: Longman

Stansky, Peter and Abrahams, William (1972) *The Unknown Orwell*, New York: Alfred A. Knopf

Taylor, D.J. (2023) *Orwell: The New Life*, London: Constable

Thacker, Spink & Co. (1873) *Thacker's Directory*, Thacker, Spink & Co.

Times of India (1878) 27 July

UCL Department of History (2024) Charles Blair junior, *Legacies of British Slave-Ownership Database*, Centre for the Study of the Legacies of British Slave-Ownership, University College London. Available online at https://wwwdepts-live.ucl.ac.uk/lbs/claim/view/2120016474, accessed on 6 September 2024

DARCY MOORE

Venn, J.A. (1940) *Alumni Cantabrigienses: A Biographical List of All Known Students, Graduates and Holders of Office at the University of Cambridge from the Earliest Times to 1900, Part 2: From 1752 to 1900. Vol. I Abbey-Challis*, Cambridge: Cambridge University Press

Wadhams, Stephen (1984) *Remembering Orwell*, Harmondsworth, Middlesex: Penguin

Western Daily Press (1867) 31 August

Westminster School Archive (n.d.) Blair, Charles (1776-1854). Westminster School Collections. Available online at https://collections.westminster.org.uk/index.php/blair-henry-fl-1785, accessed on 8 August 2024

NOTE ON THE CONTRIBUTOR

Darcy Moore is a deputy principal at a secondary school in New South Wales. He blogs at *darcymoore.net* and his X/Twitter handle is @Darcy1968. His Orwell Studies Library can be accessed at darcymoore.net/orwell-collection/.

ARTICLE

How I Constructed the Newspeak Language from Orwell's *Nineteen Eighty-Four*

BRENNAN CONAWAY

INTRODUCTION

You know about Newspeak, of course, the language George Orwell invented in *Nineteen Eighty-Four*. Winston and Syme discuss it in the Ministry of Truth cafeteria, with gin in metal cups and cigarettes held vertically so the tobacco doesn't fall out. It's doubleplus goodthinkful! You may even have a false memory (oh, the irony) that parts of the book are written in Newspeak, or O'Brien spoke it, or Winston read it. All untrue, comrade.

The truth is that Orwell wrote only three (3!) sentences in Newspeak, and those sentences are not in the narrative but in the Appendix titled *The Principles of Newspeak*. *The Principles* appear to be straightforward instructions for constructing the language, but they are not. *The Principles* are just … principles. They are also not as specific as they first seem, and at times they are downright contradictory, so it's unsurprising that in the decades since the book's publication, nobody has followed those principles and constructed the Newspeak language.

When I began working on my book *year84*, I, too, had the vague feeling that Newspeak already existed somewhere, fully formed and functional, and I assumed I could employ it for my idea: translating *Nineteen Eighty-Four* into Newspeak. But the language didn't exist. To make that translation, I first had to construct the Newspeak language from Orwell's *Principles* and clues within *Nineteen Eighty-Four*. Then, and only then, could I use this newly-created language to reword the original text, a process that I refer to as 'a metalinguistic ouroboros' in the Introduction to *year84* (Conaway 2023).

BRENNAN CONAWAY

DEFINITION OF NEWSPEAK

Within the world of *Nineteen Eighty-Four*, Newspeak is 'the official language of Oceania', but it's still under construction at the Ministry of Truth and still being codified in ever-newer editions of the *Newspeak Dictionary*. 'In the year 1984 there was not as yet anyone who used Newspeak as his sole means of communication, either in speech or writing' (*CWGO* IX: 312), so the reader does not see this language within the story, despite characters making references to it, and a brief scene where O'Brien speakwrites a message in 'the hybrid jargon of the Ministries' (ibid: 176), which has Newspeak elements.

In *The Principles of Newspeak*, Orwell explains that the language has a severely limited lexicon full of government-built neologisms and an unyielding grammar structure. 'Newspeak was designed not to extend but to *diminish* the range of thought, and this purpose was indirectly assisted by cutting the choice of words down to a minimum' (ibid: 313, emphasis in the original). Orwell's concept of Newspeak is a brilliant satire about authority's attempts to redefine, reduce and restrict language use and language growth. 'Newspeak … vocabulary grew smaller instead of larger every year. Each reduction was a gain, since the smaller the area of choice, the smaller the temptation to take thought' (ibid: 322).

Newspeak is a malevolent application of the Sapir-Whorf hypothesis that language determines an individual's thoughts, that without the words to express it, a thought cannot be made. 'It was intended that … a heretical thought … should be literally unthinkable, at least so far as thought is dependent on words' (ibid: 312).

PROCESS FOR *YEAR84*

A Newspeak translation of *Nineteen Eighty-Four* was an old idea of mine, born from artistic impulse not linguistic curiosity, although that would come later. After reading the book for the first time at university in, yes, the year 1984, my first thought was something like: 'It'd be so cool to change this book into Newspeak!' I didn't articulate it, didn't know the terms *self-referential* or *ouroboros,* and didn't take any steps towards actually doing it. In my defence, this was the 'Beforetime': the internet was unknown, computers were in the university computer lab and books were on paper.

Fast-forward to 2020: *Nineteen Eighty-Four* was coming out of copyright and a PDF was floating around (Project Gutenberg of Australia, see https://ia802904.us.archive.org/6/items/NineteenEightyFour-Novel-GeorgeOrwell/orwell1984.pdf). I was in graduate school to aid a career change, and in a class about the wonderfully macabre-sounding subject of corpus linguistics I learned how to dissect a body of text to generate a list of individual words. No excuses this time. Some 35 years after that initial lightbulb moment, I set to work constructing the Newspeak language.

As an artist who usually creates physical objects, I viewed this as an art project, something closer to sculpture than literature. I wanted to make a book that looked and felt like a publication of the Records Department at the Ministry of Truth (*Minitrue* in Newspeak) where Winston worked. It would be poetic injustice to use Orwell's concepts about language and censorship to reword and censor his own writings. In *Nineteen Eighty-Four* and *The Principles of Newspeak,* I tried to read his mind and understand what he thought Newspeak would look like on the page, so I limited my research to the original text, as I consulted with Orwell, artist-to-artist.

I dived into the deep end. I re-read *The Principles* countless times, trying to isolate specific instructions about transforming Old- into Newspeak. Orwell's concepts about word-formation guidelines and grammar rules were intertwined, but for the purpose of this article, I will divide them into vocabulary and grammar sections. There were also contradictory commands, which I will discuss later, but in order to make a start, I decided the language-construction process would have to be dynamic and hands-on, dealing with individual words as they appeared in the text, and making decisions based on *The Principles*, my linguistics training and my instincts as an artist. The process was a combination of language creation, language censorship and content censorship.

VOCABULARY WITHIN *THE PRINCIPLES*

To start building a lexicon (or my personal edition of the *Newspeak Dictionary*) I had to find the words Orwell implicitly or explicitly regarded as Newspeak. From the narrative of *Nineteen Eighty-Four*, I gathered words such as *facecrime, speakwrite* and *ownlife* while in *The Principles* I found not only Newspeak words divided into A Vocabulary, B Vocabulary and C Vocabulary categories, but also rules to create other words and, more importantly, since this is Newspeak, rules to reduce the variety of words (or tokens) within the corpus.

The rules were basic and were supposed to be uniformly applied, but Orwell didn't always follow his own rules, which was OK because it freed me to make a few rules of my own. 'Between the verb and the noun form, *when they were of the same root*, there was never any variation' (ibid: 314), so the noun *thought* becomes the same as the verb *think*, as in *crimethink*. Orwell contradicts himself later in the same paragraph, when he says: 'Even where a noun and verb … were *not etymologically connected,* one or other of them

ARTICLE

was frequently suppressed' (ibid, emphasis added), so *cut* becomes an unword and *knife* is used as both noun and verb. (Orwell will contradict this entire rule again in the grammar section below.)

In the text of *Nineteen Eighty-Four*, Orwell shows the type of language the Oceania government encourages (*child hero, definitive edition*) with Winston making ironic comments about the manipulation of language. I treated those terms as something akin to Newspeak and used them unironically in *year84*.

The Principles explains the best-known aspects of Newspeak: 'any word ... could be negatived by adding the affix *un-*, or could be strengthened by the affix *plus-*, or, for still greater emphasis, *doubleplus-*' (ibid: 315) and it has examples of words retained from Oldspeak scattered throughout the text, such as *hit, run, tree, sugar, house, field, good, strong, big, black, soft, man, life*, and words that Orwell instructed me to purge: '*honour, justice, morality, internationalism, democracy, science* and *religion* had simply ceased to exist' (ibid: 318).

Orwell goes on to explain about 'words which had been deliberately constructed for political purposes. ... They consisted of two or more words, or portions of words, welded together' (ibid: 316). I used this rule for some occasional word-welding of my own (i.e., *memoryhole, flatface, trueheart*) but usually I disassembled these 'B Vocabulary' words and used the parts to reconstruct the Newspeak language. For example, *Newspeak* is a Newspeak word of course, therefore *new* and *speak* are Minitrue-approved morphemes. I used *speak* to replace *appeal, claim, comment, communicate, describe, discuss, explain, mention, pronounce, relate, say, speech, squeak, statement, talk, tell* and *utter*. *New*, in turn, should have become *unnew* by following Orwell's rule of adding the prefix *un-* to 'negative' a word, but both *Newspeak* and *Oldspeak* are Newspeak words, so I deduced that *old* was not yet an unword.

I found more pairs of opposites such as *new/old* which did not easily follow the *un-* rule, labelled them as prefixes and retained them. They included *top/bottom, in/out, up/down, high/low, push/pull* and *start/stop*. Orwell believed these 'prepositional affixes' (*prefixes* in Newspeak?) would do some heavy lifting when constructing the new language. 'Prepositional affixes ... bring about an enormous diminution of vocabulary' (ibid: 315). For additional guidance in affixing morphemes prepositionally, I read Winston's work orders 'in the abbreviated jargon – not actually Newspeak, but consisting largely of Newspeak words – which was used in the Ministry' (ibid: 40). Orwell recounts only four of these orders, but I believe that was enough to give readers the impression that *Nineteen Eighty-Four* contains a lot of Newspeak, as I discussed above. The fourth order shows prefixes in action and a glimpse of the language on the page:

'reporting bb dayorder doubleplusungood refs unperson rewrite fullwise upsub antefilling' (ibid: 41). I learned the feel and mood of Newspeak from this limited example.

Sometimes my disassembly of Newspeak words produced serendipity, which delighted both the artist and the linguist in me. According to *The Principles*, the Newspeak word for the Ministry of Love is *Miniluv* (ibid: 6), so I respelled *love* as *luv* throughout *year84* and found the homonym was only a homonym; it wasn't a synonym. If Julia writes: 'I luv you' in a note to Winston, her dangerous raw emotion appears tame. If Winston finally accepts that 'He luved Big Brother,' he feels only a pathetic replacement, a saccharine substitute, for true love. These proclamations of luv are good examples of Newspeak's subtle censorship.

I was surprised to learn that, in accordance with *The Principles*, I should censor Big Brother himself from the pages of *Nineteen Eighty-Four*. 'Abbreviating a name ... narrowed and subtly altered its meaning, by cutting out most of the associations that would otherwise cling to it' (ibid: 320). Minitrue wouldn't want Big Brother to be associated with the negative qualities of *big*, such as *excess*, nor would they want citizens to cling to the idea of family, implied by the word *brother*, so I looked for the Newspeak translation. Winston's abbreviated work order refers to 'bb' (ibid: 40), and he writes in his journal about the Two Minutes Hate when O'Brien catches his eye and Julia watches him carefully. At the end of that session, 'people broke into a deep, slow, rhythmical chant of 'B-B! ... B-B!' (ibid: 18). In *year84*, Big Brother never appears, only the initials BB.

GRAMMAR WITHIN *THE PRINCIPLES*

'The grammar of Newspeak had two outstanding peculiarities. The first of these was an almost complete interchangeability between different parts of speech. Any word in the language ... could be used either as verb, noun, adjective or adverb' (ibid: 314). This rule is a continuation of the noun/verb vocabulary rule discussed above, but extends the idea to include all types of words – a radical inclusivity. I applied this rule immediately, using *in* as a verb in the translation of the book's first paragraph. '... to prevent a swirl of dust from entering along with him' (ibid: 3) became 'to stop a spiral of dust from inning with him' in *year84* (Conaway 2023: 3).

After learning that any word, by dutifully following *The Principles*, can do any linguistic task, I was confused to read instructions for making Newspeak adjectives and adverbs. Hadn't Orwell just banished those Oldspeak labels? 'Adjectives were formed by adding the suffix *-ful* to the noun-verb, and adverbs by adding *-wise*' (ibid: 314). In *year84*, I followed these seemingly contradictory grammar rules. Sometimes I took words out of their Oldspeak roles and used them in Newspeak ways, but with adjectives and adverbs I usually added the prescribed suffixes. I did this because the translation was still understandable but looked plusNewspeakful.

Standardisation was Orwell's prime directive, as I constructed the language. 'The second distinguishing mark of Newspeak grammar was its regularity ... all verbs (in past tense) ... ended in *-ed*. ... All plurals were made by adding *-s* or *-es* ... comparison of adjectives was invariably made by adding -er, *-est* (*good, gooder, goodest*)' (ibid: 315-316). With the fanaticism of a convert, I extrapolated that rules about regularity and invariability should apply to the final *-y* of nouns like *beauty* when adding the required *-ful* for all adjectives. Thus, *beautyful*. Likewise, *un-* was the invariable prefix of negation; *unsane* and *unpossible* the Newspeak words. If it seems as if I were not strictly following *The Principles*, Orwell comes to my defence with an understated and humorous zinger about the Newspeak process: 'No etymological principle was followed here' (ibid: 314). *Principles* which follow no principle are the goodest of doublethink.

THE LANGUAGE-CONSTRUCTION PROCESS

With an understanding of Newspeak linguistics and an alignment with Orwell's artistry, I began the translation by running a word-count, which revealed *Nineteen Eighty-Four* was 104,000 words long. I then generated a corpus and calculated the number of individual words, or tokens. The goal was not only 'the destruction of words' (ibid: 54) through censorship, but also the 'reduction of vocabulary ... as an end in itself' (ibid: 313). I achieved the first goal primarily through four methods. First, I performed an appendectomy, removing *The Principles* from the Appendix. Second, I deleted the extended excerpts of Goldstein's book, which had no place within a Minitrue publication. Third, I censored all scenes of enhanced interrogation, so it appears that O'Brien is helping Winston, and exterminated the rats in Room 101. Fourth, I updated Orwell's Oldspeakful prose to give it 'a harsh sound and a certain willful ugliness' approximating 'a machine-gun spraying forth bullets' (ibid: 322). The end result was *year84*, with a word-count half that of the original: 52,000 words.

The second goal was to reduce the breadth of the book's vocabulary. The primary targets were the single-use, or single-token, words within the text. (I kept *unreproved* as the only single-token word because it seems like double-prefixed Newspeak.) Rather than a top-down approach, which would have required writing a complete Newspeak dictionary before even beginning the translation, I opted, instead, for a bottom-up methodology. I slowly reread *Nineteen Eighty-Four* and made decisions about individual words and phrases as I came to them. I used my laptop's find/replace function, eventually making more than 1,600 substitutions and emerging with a coherent and consistent form of Newspeak.

Related to the idea of reading Orwell's mind about Newspeak was my decision to limit the vocabulary to only those words that were already in the book (i.e., *speak*, *think*) and building a lexicon from there, although I added acronyms such as *AM, PM, POW, KIA* and abbreviations like *physed*, which seemed to fit the rules or intentions of Newspeak.

I changed British spelling to American because I interpret Oceania as an America Made Greater, with England reduced to an airstrip (although the first among airstrips), and because American English can be 'a gabbling style of speech, at once staccato and monotonous' (ibid: 321) which makes it a better fit for Newspeak. I reverted all numbers that had been spelled out to numerical figures, which I saw as a technocratic and pseudoscientific approach to linguistics, and, because Orwell's contradictory instructions allowed me some freedom, I translated any word that expressed an ordinal number (i.e., years, dates, ages) using my own Newspeakful rule: [{noun − space} + number = ordinal term]. The title *year84* obeys that rule.

My goal was to bring Newspeak out of *The Principles* and on to the page. I hoped readers would compare *year84* and *Nineteen Eighty-Four* side by side to see how I had changed the language, but there were dangers. 'Newspeak sentences, even when not containing newly-created words, would be barely intelligible to an English-speaker of our own day' (ibid: 313). I found myself threading the needle. I wanted to construct this language according to *The Principles*, but I didn't want to make it unreadable 'to an English speaker of our own day'. Luckily, Orwell offered me a way through the needle's eye. 'The version in use in 1984, and embodied in the Ninth and Tenth Editions of the Newspeak Dictionary, was a provisional one, and contained many superfluous words and archaic formations which were due to be suppressed later' (ibid: 312). The Newspeak I constructed for *year84* is an early version of the language, as would be found in *Newspeak Dictionary*, Ninth Edition, but it's not a direct translation from Oldspeak to New-. It's ideological.

'IDEOLOGICAL TRANSLATION' PROCESS

Beyond constructing the language, another directive added to my workload. *The Principles* instructed me to actively censor the narrative. 'No book written before approximately 1960 could be translated as a whole. Pre-revolutionary literature could only be subjected to ideological translation …' (ibid: 324). Syme is explicit about what 'ideological translation' means: 'not merely changed into something different, but actually changed into something contradictory of what they used to be' (ibid: 56). To make Orwell's novel contradict itself, I found three methods to be effective.

First, wholesale censorship of Goldstein's book and *The Principles* stripped the narrative of, well, a narrator. Goldstein is no longer present to give the reader context about the origins and attributes of the Oceania government, and Orwell himself is unable to explain the diabolical design of Newspeak. Second, I changed my mind. I wrote *year84* as a dutiful Party member, accepting as true and necessary whatever I was told about Oceania and Big Brother. Winston is a Minitrue censor, but he's never directed to censor anything. He's told to rectify 'slips, errors, misprints, and misquotations' (ibid: 43). I took this description of his duties at face value. By removing Winston's labours to transform Eurasia from enemy to ally, for example, I transformed his mundane job as a 'fact-checker' into a mundane job as a fact-checker. I did something similar to make O'Brien's torture machines painless, to paint Julia as a sex maniac and to portray the proles as jabbering animals. Third, I dehumanised Winston. This process began with using only his government name, 6079 Smith, continued with small text alterations to suggest he was a paedophile and lone-wolf rebel, and ended with his love for Big Brother as a sign of good mental health. *year84* became the story of an anti-social, middle-aged man who is seduced into the Brotherhood terrorist group, but is rescued by the benevolence and guidance of an inner Party member.

An ideological translation also required me to rewrite the absurdist slogans 'WAR IS PEACE', FREEDOM IS SLAVERY', 'IGNORANCE IS STRENGTH' (ibid: 18) that I doubleplus love. Since 1984, those slogans have been my linguistic barometer for the pressures of government doublespeak and corporate adspeak in my daily life. Again, Syme is clear: 'Even the slogans will change. How could you have a slogan like "freedom is slavery" when the concept of freedom has been abolished?' (ibid: 56). With these doublethinkful slogans, the Oceania government was propagandising its citizens to accept war, slavery and ignorance. What would these slogans look like when 'the concept of freedom (and peace and strength) has been abolished'? For *year84* I looked to ideas about the forever war, fun workplaces and herd mentality to rewrite the slogans as 'Forever at War, Joyful in Work, Strong in Party' (Conaway 2023: 5). The evil in these phrases was so banal that I thought I had inadvertently plagiarised them from somewhere, but no: I Googled and found no exact matches. They just sound like something you've heard before, which should be terrifying.

FINDINGS AND REVELATIONS ABOUT NEWSPEAK

Both Newspeak and the Party slogans are Orwell's warnings about the power of language and the language of the powerful. His conceptualisation of Newspeak is a brilliant commentary about the ways governments and organisations can lie to you without being untruthful, manipulate you without touching you and control you without your knowledge. I'm grateful to Orwell for this forewarning. I've already discussed some of the contradictions I discovered when applying *The Principles* to construct Newspeak, but I also had surprising revelations about how a language will adapt, overcome and survive, despite governmental or cultural efforts to censor and strangle it.

The Newspeak 'vocabulary … was extremely small, while their meanings were far more rigidly defined' (*CWGO* IX: 314). Orwell seems to be warning that an extremely small vocabulary will result in an extremely narrow range of thought, as according to the Sapir-Whorf hypothesis, but when I loaded a single word such as *speak* with the weight of expressing a dozen subtly different words (*discuss, explain, say*) I found the words were less rigidly defined, became more generalised, and I think that readers/listeners in the world of *Nineteen Eighty-Four* would need to consider carefully which of the myriad meanings was being conveyed with one multi-purpose word. Would this lead to an expanded range of thought, rather than a constriction? As Syme explains in the cafeteria: 'In the end the whole notion of goodness and badness will be covered by only six words – in reality, only one word' (ibid: 54). I think that one word is *good*, but if Winston tells Syme: 'The joycamps are ungood,' then Syme must ponder the meaning of *ungood* at length, put himself in Winston's shoes, think about what Winston himself means by that word, imagine what Winston may be feeling and become closer and more empathetic to Winston to understand the sentence. I think this process would increase both thoughts and feelings during mundane conversations, contrary to the plans of the Oceania government.

Orwell presents Newspeak as a linguistic abomination, 'the only language in the world whose vocabulary gets smaller every year' (ibid: 55), but I found that parts of Newspeak did not seem new and horrible to me. It felt familiar. I sometimes thought it was the language in *Nineteen Eighty-Four* which was strange and anachronistic. Maybe parts of Newspeak are Orwell's documentation (with exaggerations, of course) of linguistic changes he was witnessing in the late 1940s. 'For example, *speedful* meant "rapid" and *speedwise* meant "quickly"' (ibid: 314-315). I would probably just use one word, *fast*, as both adjective and adverb, and regard *rapid* as Oldspeakful. Related to

ARTICLE

BRENNAN CONAWAY

my comfort with Newspeak, was the shock in discovering that the find/replace function was *too* effective.

My translation method was to move through the book, word by word. I stopped at Oldspeak words, determined their Newspeak translation, used the find/replace function to transform all instances, or tokens, of that word in the rest of the book, and continued onwards to the next Old word. This process began immediately, with the fourth word of the novel. Here's that paragraph with annotations of the process:

> It was a bright (find/replace with *lightful*) cold day in April (*month04*, per rule about ordinals) and the clocks were striking (find/replace with *flashing*) thirteen (numerate as *13:00*). Winston Smith (find/replace with government name *6079 Smith*), his chin nuzzled into his breast (find/replace with *down*) in an effort (find/replace with *attempt*) to escape (find/replace with *avoid*) the vile (find/replace with *plusungood*) wind, slipped (find/replace with *goed*) quickly (find/replace with *speedwise*, per Orwell's explicit instructions) through (find/replace with *thru*, American spelling) the glass doors of Victory (find/replace with *Winful*) Mansions (find/replace with *House*), though (find/replace with *tho*, consistent with American spelling of *thru*) not quickly enough (*quickly* has already been found/replaced, find/replace *not enough* with prefix *under-* to yield *underspeedwise*) to prevent (find/replace with *stop*) a swirl (find/replace with *spiral*) of gritty (delete as unnecessary) dust from entering (find/replace with *inning*) along (find/delete) with him (Conaway 2023: 3).

The Newspeak translation in *year84*:

> It was a lightful cold day in month04, and the clocks were flashing 13:00. 6079 Smith, his chin down in an attempt to avoid the plusungood wind, goed speedwise thru the glass doors of Winful House, tho underspeedwise to stop a spiral of dust from inning with him (ibid).

From the above example, you can see the translation process transforming words ahead of my encountering them. After the first instance of *quickly*, for example, the find/replace function had automatically changed the second instance to *speedwise* later in the very same sentence. As I moved deeper into the book, much of the text had been translated in this way, but it was often grammatically and logically correct. This was deeply disturbing and brought to mind the infamous quote by William Burroughs that 'language is a virus' (2014). It's self-organising, self-replicating and robust. At times I had to check sentences in Orwell's novel to see how the automatised find/replace function had transformed them. In brief, the translation process worked, sometimes with viral efficiency.

CONCLUSION

After constructing the Newspeak language, translating *Nineteen Eighty-Four*, censoring Orwell's storyline, and publishing *year84*, the artist in me is amazed by the physical book that I hold in my hands. By design, it's an unappealing government publication. The cover has a matte finish that feels rubbery and stain-resistant. The graphic designer for the *year84* project, Rion Echigo, went against her skills and deep knowledge of fonts and layout and did everything intentionally wrong. The kerning is wonky, the cover design is an official form that's been partially filled out, erased and written over, as if a harried bureaucrat has done a rush job. For the cover, I wanted to move away from the red-white-and-black colour scheme that's the obvious choice for books about totalitarianism. Those colours were too dramatic for the workaday world of *Nineteen Eighty-Four*, where things were miserable but apolitical. Orwell warns about the commonplace within tyranny: 'It struck [Winston] that the truly characteristic thing about modern life was not its cruelty and insecurity, but simply its bareness, its dinginess, its listlessness. … Great areas of [life], even for a Party member, were neutral and non-political, a matter of slogging through dreary jobs, fighting for a place on the Tube, darning a worn-out sock, cadging a saccharine tablet, saving a cigarette end' (*CWGO* IX: 77) To convey the unremarkable omnipresence of the Party in the daily grind, Echigo chose a bland and horrible blue for the front and back covers. It's a colour you have seen before, but probably can't quite remember. I think it's a bit of design genius.

year84 is more than a sculptural object or an investigation into constructed languages. As an educator, I hope it will also be a companion volume to *Nineteen Eighty-Four*, offering students the chance to read Newspeak on the page, discuss issues about languages and censorship with their teachers, and discover the so-called 'Easter eggs' within the book. With language as a virus, the translation process created some amusing and startling synchronicities, which are waiting for readers to discover.

At the end of this *year84* project, I feel that I have got to know Orwell as an artist and as a linguistic conceptualist. I'm not sure how he would regard my use of Ministry of Truth directives to rewrite his novel, but I think he would appreciate someone using *The Principles* to construct Newspeak and bring it to life.

BRENNAN CONAWAY

REFERENCES

Burroughs, William (2014) *The Ticket that Exploded*, New York: Grove Press

Conaway, Brennan (2023) *year84*, Ministry of Truth

CWGO (1998) (*Complete Works of George Orwell*) *Vol. IX, Nineteen Eighty-Four*, Davison, Peter (ed.) London: Secker & Warburg

NOTE ON THE CONTRIBUTOR

Brennan Conaway is an artist and university lecturer in the Tokyo megalopolis. To produce *year84*, he used a newly-acquired knowledge of corpus linguistics to analyse the text of *Nineteen Eighty-Four* and construct the Newspeak language based on Orwell's original conception. He is currently working on an art project to explore urban coastlines and define the term *tidalpunk*.

That Bloody Book

The prisoner in your charge
steps aside to avoid a puddle
on his way to the gallows.

Light fades over Sea of the Hebrides,
Black Jagg roll-ups fug the room,
inhaled through infected lungs.

You sit to write, the first crimson specks
caught in a laundered handkerchief,
death counting each laboured breath.

You resist, as in those long winters,
wrapped in an old coat, recording
the poor and the dispossessed

in mud-bound trenches,
where seeds of betrayal germinate,
and a sniper's bullet finds your throat.

You resist, the wounded elephant
who won't die, until your agony is complete,
until *that bloody book* is written.

To warn the world
of what it is capable.

John Scarborough's poems have been published in *Orbis, Reach, Spelt, Black Bough, Acumen, Dawntreader, High Window, Ekphrastic Review* and Dreamcatcher. He is currently working on his collection, 'Alone in the Blue Hour'. His poem, 'To Siobahn', was shortlisted for the Reach Autumn Poetry Prize. John is a member of both Louth and Nunthorpe Poets. He lives in Louth with his partner, Sheri.

POEMS

Elephant

Beneath bright sun a rampage slowly wanes,
no longer thunderous, its musth declines,
but shadows dance and fear's tendril constrains
colony master's imperial sign.

He knows the truth: the storm has passed its crest,
no threat remains, just cooling, noisy might.
Tradition calls, its whisper brooks no rest
for holding power silken bonds grip tight.

He feels its weight, the gaze upon his back,
a burden born in ruling's shifting sand.
But duty calls, a twisted, stretching rack,
then rifle raised, pressures none can withstand.

A shot rings out, ringing moment of fear,
while empires teeter, built on shadows here.

George Ponders Dictatorship

Those battles vast where mud and death are lore
his pen writes truth that on the wireless bides
black ink, a mirror to enemy's core
reveals such metamorphosis war hides.

Within tight folds of conflict's cold embrace
faces grim with scars of battles fraught
yet questions hang in time and empty space,
when does a man become that monster fought?

His narratives of war a solemn hymn
inscribed by hands that tremble as they write
while shadows cast grow long and prospects dim
life's boundary blurs between relentless night.

On war's bloody stage where truth dies its death,
The answer fades veiled in sorrow's ebbing breath.

Short But Full

Colonial shadows cast long with might
for a Crown's fate, an elephant's demise,
injustice veiled in imperial light.

Parisian alleys and poor streets converge
where dim lanterns shine on poverty's curse
and talks of struggle make paths diverge.

Beneath Spanish sun-black shadows unfold
doublethink cues, for a smoke-ring dance.
Conflict's Sardana danced an homage told.

Airwaves crackling voice, subtle and bold
from city ruins where courage abounds.
Auntie's talk soothes through night's blitz throttlehold.

Ink's entanglement, rebellion's maze,
truths deep hidden under newspeak's paw,
numeric coded weaves prophetic haze.

In life, beholding love's intricate dance
below glim stars, connections expand
tragedies and unions, fate takes its chance.

From shared ideals to sorrows hard to hold,
in shadows, in light, personal tales emerge
of partnerships forged in stories told.

Then creeping illness breathes a weakening sigh,
tuberculosis stole its due coughing death,
time's cruel dance a body's slow goodbye.

In sanatorium's clean air, hope's deferred
legacy lingers in freedom's indelible breath,
through pages well written, truths are interred.

Steve Dalzell came to writing after a long career in the military, criminal intelligence and business as a way of unleashing a pent-up creative urge that had been bursting to escape for all of those long years. Steve writes in a wide variety of styles and genres and particularly enjoys writing short stories, flash fiction and scripts. He came to poetry as a result of attending a number of workshops and being more or less persuaded into writing a sonnet, at the point of a pen, by his peers and colleagues. He facilitates a weekly creative writing group and workshop and, being a strong advocate of the notion that writers write, he writes every day. His works have been published in a variety of magazines and anthologies and he self-publishes multiple books of flash fiction, short stories and poetry on Amazon.

BOOK REVIEWS

Julia

Sandra Newman

New York: Mariner, 2023 pp 385

ISBN: 9780063265332 (hbk)

The plight of women within power structures not designed by women is the focus of Newman's *Julia* (as it is in Anna Funder's *Wifedom*, reviewed in the last issue of *George Orwell Studies*). In George Orwell's *Nineteen Eighty-Four*, Julia is a mechanic in the Fiction Department of the Ministry of Truth who fixes the machines that produce the official narrative for Oceania, the totalitarian state in which she lives. At the outset, the novel situates itself within current discourses about the capabilities of artificial intelligence to replace humans in endeavours particular to humans, such as writing. Newman's retelling of the novel through the female character spotlights the thin and troubling representation of Julia in the original novel that depicts her as sexually compliant, intellectually agreeable and, ultimately, all too easily sacrificed by Winston when he is faced with the possibility of being tortured in Room 101 ('Do it to Julia! Not me! Julia! I don't care what you do to her. Tear her face off, strip her to the bones. Not me! Julia! Not me!' [Orwell 1977 [1949]: 286).

Newman's retelling is neither a cancellation of the original, nor an attempt to fix those elements a 2020s audience may find reprehensible, such as Winston's desire to rape and kill women, which is maintained. After their first attempt at sex, Winston says to Julia: 'I hated the sight of you. I wanted to rape you and then murder you afterward. Two weeks ago I thought seriously of smashing your head in with a cobblestone' (p. 109). Rather, Newman adds dimension and nuance to Julia's world by giving her a backstory that helps to account for her character's motivations and behaviours.

For example, we learn that Julia's sexual awakening during her teenage years is facilitated by a much older man, Gerber, who has come to stay where she lives – while readers may interpret the frequent visits Julia makes to Gerber's room in the night as the product of Gerber's successful grooming, Julia's excitement about sexual pleasure disrupts the notion of her victimhood in intriguing ways. For example, 'If she thought of hope or comfort, she thought of Gerber. The sexual pleasure, too, was a revelation; he might as well have taught her to levitate. It didn't matter that she had to close her eyes and pretend he was an airman' (p. 157). Newman's Julia is sexually assured and desirous of physical pleasure from a young age in a culture where women are generally treated like livestock. Further, because the narrative is focalised through Julia, readers are invited into her decision-making processes and memories and are better able to understand the limited options available to her. While she is careful about publicly presenting herself as a devotee of the Big Brother regime, the adult Julia finds many ways to subvert the systems for her own pleasure. All these components are commonplace in feminist dystopian fiction and Newman uses them to build a storyworld that centres on the impossible conditions in which the women find themselves.

Newman's novel – which was authorised by the Orwell Estate – invites some interesting critical inquiry into the way Julia is reimagined. What are we to do with a woman like this, who wants to use her sexuality for both pleasure and for the purposes of the state? Is Julia exhibiting feminist strength in the face of a brutally oppressive society? Or is the autonomy she seems to exhibit merely an illusion? Is it possible for Julia to have access to any knowledge that could truly empower her in a world of misinformation? These questions complicate the retelling in productive ways, making Newman's book ripe for the critical discourse central to feminist recovery and reconsiderations of canonical, male-authored texts of the mid-century.

Lastly, Newman's novel facilitates a useful bridge between then and now for those of us who teach modernism and mid-century literature. Winston's desire to rape and murder Julia and his willingness to sacrifice her in the original makes the text a difficult (or impossible) one to teach in today's classrooms. But the way the same sentiments are expressed in the retelling where backstory and motivations are explored may make more sense to contemporary readers and invite robust inquiry. In a political and social climate where female autonomy is in peril and authoritarian regimes are attempting to annihilate democracies, pairing Newman's counterfiction with Orwell's fiction may offer us a fresh way to engage students in vital conversations about systems of power, dominance and oppression and how to upend such systems from within. Perhaps Newman is upsetting the systems from within with this highly readable and thought-provoking work.

REFERENCE

Orwell, George (1977 [1949]) *Nineteen Eighty-Four*, New York: Signet Classics

Sarah E. Cornish,
University of Northern Colorado

Burma Sahib

Paul Theroux

London: Hamish Hamilton, 2024, pp 391

ISBN: 9780241633342 (hbk)

A Smoking-Room Story, Orwell's last novel, unfinished and indeed barely begun, starts with a 24-year-old Englishman sailing back from Burma to England in 1927, at the same age and in the same year as Eric Blair made the voyage. Paul Theroux's new novel, *Burma Sahib*, begins at the other end of Orwell's Burma story, on the steamer *Herefordshire* coming through the Suez Canal in November 1922, with a nervous and socially awkward Eric Blair, still a teenager, heading to Burma to take up his post in the Imperial Police. There is a kind of symmetry to this, and Theroux is on record as finding Orwell an inspiring precursor.

On board the *Herefordshire* are a number of Scots passengers. Theroux, alas, thinks Scots say things like 'puling togaither' and 'it's a right bug bowl' (15, 17). But he has quickly registered the young Blair's antipathy against the Scots, dating from St Cyprian's, and inserts several other biographical details – Jacintha, Blair's immersion in Kipling and Wells, his attempts at writing poetry, even the anecdote of the quartermaster who steals a pudding. Similar biographical facts are scattered through the fiction.

When the new recruits arrive in Rangoon they are received by the governor, Spencer Harcourt Butler, who treats them to a speech about the British mission in Burma: 'We are here to bring law and order to parts of barbary, and to maintain that order,' he tells them. (Barbary?) Democracy, he adds, is a thumping lie. 'Our mission is to conserve, not to destroy, their social organism. With a fertile country, with no pressure of population on subsistence, with few wants, why should the Burman strive or cry out? …. Political power is to be deposited in the hands of a natural aristocracy' (30).

And so on. But no such speech would have been delivered by an official to police probationers in 1922. Butler (who didn't become governor until 1923) was sent to Burma to implement the Montagu-Chelmsford reforms, which had already been introduced in India in response to political pressure from the Congress Party and others. Their purpose was precisely to introduce a measure of self-government – 'these dreadful Reforms', as Mrs Lackersteen calls them in *Burmese Days* (Orwell 1997 [1934]: 26) – and the governor of Burma would hardly denounce them to newly-arrived police recruits. Theroux doesn't show any awareness of this quite complex situation and the one-note reactionary imperialism of his portrayal of the country is not an accurate picture of the government of Burma in the 1920s, though there were certainly plenty of red-faced racists in those Kipling-haunted clubs.

As for the need to 'conserve … their social organism', it was a bit late for that. The British had already imposed on a largely feudal country a model of administration which they had developed for India itself, and this involved, according to a Burmese historian, 'nothing less than a complete dismantling of existing institutions of political authority and the undermining of many established structures of social organization' (Thant Myint-U 2001: 2-3). This is the unstable political environment in the background of *Burmese Days*, with the localisation of the reforms dramatised in the question of the admission of a local member to the European Club in Kyauktada, recommended by the deputy commissioner.

What is Theroux good at? Though he may not always be very nuanced in his version of the political scene, he is as ever expert in rendering a sense of place and its sensory environment. This is what Blair hears at the station, ready for the journey upcountry:

> Then a familiar sequence of sounds, the clang and grip of the coupling, the clunk-jerk of the bogie, the long moan of the whistle, and the grinding wheels – steel against steel, with the click of rail ends – as the train began to roll out of the station (37).

This passage is chosen more or less at random. Of course, Theroux is a railway man – he made his name with *The Great Railway Bazaar*, in 1975 – but his writing is full of this expert and exact observation of what things look, sound and smell like. The train departs for Mandalay, leaving behind the hot glare of the city:

> They had entered the jungle and its green shadows and its leaf-scented air, its sheltering trees, the glimpses of green fields and fences, a geometry of gigantic earthen trays of standing water, with rice shoots poking through, his first sight of paddy fields that he'd known only from an illustration in a schoolbook – and those pictures had not revealed the beauty of them he saw now. And bamboo – fountains of it in tight clumps, and some of it dense in thickets, birds nesting in the green striped canes (38).

'In all novels about the East,' Orwell wrote, 'the scenery is the real subject-matter' (Orwell 1997 [1937]: 101). It is a surprising statement, as in *Burmese Days*, apart from Flory's excursion into the jungle, there is not much scenery. Theroux, master travel writer, has scenery aplenty, and for the most part it is better observed than Orwell's.

The narrative is entirely focused through Blair's perceptions, punctuated by moments of introspection and poignant intimations of his awkwardness and loneliness. Theroux's young Blair is inarticulate and morose, as his real-life model probably was, but this tends to make the early chapters on Mandalay a bit dull. 'He could not see how he belonged among so much strangeness' (39). But in some ways Mandalay in 1922 is not at all strange. To a young man who has been to St Cyprian's and Eton, and served in the cadet corps at both, there is a depressing familiarity about the rituals and snobberies of the police training school.

Things look up after Blair meets H.R. Robinson, an ex-soldier who would become a Buddhist monk and opium addict, who initiates him into life in Mandalay beyond the training school. Something odd happens here. Robinson was a real person, and Blair did befriend him. But when Theroux's Robinson introduces Blair to the *pwe* dance in a Mandalay street (78), he gives Robinson several lines of dialogue copied verbatim from Flory in *Burmese Days*. This is a disconcerting moment, a sort of postmodern *mise en abyme*, in which the actual Robinson has become a Theroux character, here speaking the words of the fictional John Flory, which will be written more than ten years later by the novelist George Orwell, the name assumed by the actual Eric Blair, who is simultaneously a fictional character listening to Robinson in 1922 in Theroux's novel in 2024. Or perhaps Theroux is just being lazy. Some of the same dialogue reappears at another *pwe* scene, three hundred pages later. (It has to be said, incidentally, that Theroux has not benefited from recent research – see particularly https://www.darcymoore.net – some of it published in this journal, which among other discoveries has unearthed a fund of new material about Blair's experience in Burma.)

We follow Blair through his various postings, to Myaungmya and Twante in the Irrawaddy delta, then to Insein, then Moulmein, finally up-country to Katha, which will become the Kyauktada of *Burmese Days*. At each place he somehow blots his copybook in the eyes of his superiors. The British he lives among are pretty awful, inhabiting their colonial bubble, dressing for dinner and eating roast beef and Yorkshire pudding and spotted dick with custard, considering it something of a handicap to speak the local language, and forming no friendships with local people. 'You must always stand apart from the native or you will lose your ability to observe,' Blair is advised (157). He is warned of the danger of becoming 'a Kipling rascal' (157) – that is, of going native, like Kipling's character McIntosh Jellaludin, who somewhat resembles H.R.

Robinson – but the warning only reminds him of the Burmese woman who shares his bed. He soon realises that it was a mistake to come to Burma. Nonetheless, thinking of his Eton contemporaries now cocooned in their colleges at Oxford or Cambridge, he is grimly pleased that he has come to a place where actual risk, justice and order are a reality.

At one point Blair is ordered to take action against a subversive Buddhist priest and then against his acolytes, no more than children; they are all sent to jail. The situation develops which will be described in Orwell's 1936 essay, 'Shooting an elephant', with the officer tormented by the hostility of Burmese children, and feeling that his greatest satisfaction would be to stick a bayonet into a Buddhist priest's guts. These threadbare malcontents will reappear later in Insein jail, to trouble Blair's conscience.

Sometimes Theroux doesn't have much to go on. He imagines Blair's visit to his Limouzin relatives in Moulmein (this happened, but no account of it survives), their house with its atmosphere of decay and failure, and his discomfort at meeting his Eurasian cousin. 'They were down on their luck in a seedy netherworld, neither English nor Burmese, in a twilight of playacting that seemed hopeless yet everlasting' (186). It's a reminder, when we think of the infinitely sad Francis and Samuel in *Burmese Days*, that there were Eurasians in Blair's own family.

Blair's political instincts are, up to this point, largely undeveloped and unshared. With his visiting old Etonian friend Christopher Hollis for example, a loyalist to the imperial project, he speaks like a pukka sahib. Orwell later claimed he always loathed being involved in the dirty work of empire, though just when he developed this feeling remains moot – whether after leaving Burma or while he was there and, if the latter, at what stage of his five years' service. In this book Blair's anti-imperial feelings develop slowly and secretly, while to disguise his disloyalty he becomes more severe in his police work, which is plausible enough.

There are moments when Theroux teases his reader, sometimes cheekily, with glimpses of the George Orwell who will later emerge from this unpromising chrysalis. There is a chapter entitled 'A hanging'. Among minor characters we may notice a Comstock and a Bowling, names to be set aside for later use. There is a dog called Flo. Theroux's Blair considers the jail at Insein – a vast panoptical structure, which is still in use today – and imagines a whole society built on carceral surveillance, a thought experiment that will bear fruit in Airstrip One. And the writer-to-be is momentarily visible when Blair thinks there is a slim chance that his time in Burma may be redeemed in literature. 'There was hope and shape in a book, even the dream of one yet to be written' (203). This task will be

BOOK REVIEW

consigned to his secret, other self, 'the sneak, the rebel, the sensualist … the inner man Blair thought of as George' (234).

Judging the book as a novel and not as a version of Orwell biography, Theroux has creditably evoked life in this tropical backwater in a restless decade, and the psychology of a callow, unpopular young man making his way in the disciplined services of an outpost of empire five and a half thousand miles from home. Admirers of Orwell will find a satisfaction in the way a vacant space in our understanding of the author has been supplied with fictional material that may help us to imagine it, without making claims for the actuality of that material. Theroux's gift for conjuring sensory experience provides the texture that makes the story convincing.

In the last section, when Blair is posted to Katha, Theroux seems in a hurry to reach the end. Much of the plot of *Burmese Days* is bundled together in a sort of anagrammatical form – the Indian friend and his Burmese enemy, the visit of an English girl called Elizabeth, the timber business, the scandal about club membership, the despised Eurasians, the Burmese mistress, the terrible showdown in church. Then it's disgrace, dengue fever, medical leave, the boat home. It is 1927. Disembarking at Marseilles, Blair vanishes into the European crowd. The rest, in due course, is the history of George Orwell.

REFERENCES

Orwell, George (1997 [1934]) *Burmese Days, CWGO, Vol. II*, Davison, Peter (ed.) London: Secker & Warburg

Orwell, George (1997 [1937]) *The Road to Wigan Pier, CWGO, Vol. VI*, Davison, Peter (ed.) London: Secker & Warburg

Thant Myint-U (2001) *The Making of Modern Burma,* Cambridge: Cambridge University Press

Douglas Kerr is the author of *Orwell & Empire* (Oxford University Press, 2022) and *Wilfred Owen's Voices* (Oxford University Press, 1993), *George Orwell* (Northcote House Publishers, 2003), *Eastern Figures* (Hong Kong University Press, 2008) and *Conan Doyle: Writing, Profession and Practice* (Oxford University Press, 2013). He was Professor of English and Dean of Arts at Hong Kong University and is Honorary Research Fellow at Birkbeck College, London University.

AND FINALLY

George Orwell's struggles to find books come to mind when thinking about this year's court case in the USA (*Hachette vs Internet Archive*), in which the archive was found to be guilty of copyright infringement. The consequence has been that one goes to the archive and finds that after a cover and title page much of many works – even of deceased authors – can no longer be read.

Consider Orwell's struggles with one of his favourite novelists, George Gissing: 'There are several of his books that I have never read, because I have never been able to get hold of them, and these unfortunately include *Born in Exile*, which is said by some people to be his best book.' Cost, it seems, was not the problem, but distribution. Of P.G. Wodehouse, Orwell wrote 'that there are many books by Wodehouse – perhaps a quarter or a third of the total – which I have not read. It is not, indeed, easy to read the whole output of a popular writer who is normally published in cheap editions'.

Orwell was fortunate when preparing his essay on James Burnham: Hilaire Belloc's sister got in touch to thank Orwell for praising her brother's humour in 'Funny, but not vulgar'. Orwell had to take the opportunity to ask: 'It is possible that you might be able to lend me (I would promise to return it) a copy of "The Servile State," which I have also been trying to get hold of.' Wikipedia – of which New Pitcher approves – has a good article on the Belloc book, by the way, including Orwell's references.

Could we be reverting to times and searches as difficult as they were for Orwell? With university and public libraries selling not just duplicate but unique acquisitions that seems to be the threat.

And while also remembering the difficulties Orwell had in laying hands on a copy of Yevgeny Zamyatin's *We* (a dystopian novel which had some influence on *Nineteen Eighty-Four*) – one of the pleasures of this summer has been the appearance of *The Utopia of Us* (Luna Press, the Scottish independent publishers), an anthology of new stories celebrating Zamyatin's work, edited by Teika Marija Smits, published in the centenary of the original novel.

Of course, there is another way that older books are being kept available: facsimile reprints. Some are from especially reputable publishers such as Cambridge University Press, others from honest and useful smaller sellers. One or two (re-)publishers use names suggesting that they are making a business of it. The drawback is that it's impossible to guarantee that the edition looked for is the one available in facsimile. Take the book that Orwell used when he dramatised Darwin's voyage of the Beagle in 1946, *Chronological Tablets, Exhibiting every Remarkable Occurrence from the Creation of the World down to the Present Time* (1801). There are versions of it available but none of them are the edition and pagination that Orwell used.

***

While being brought round with sal volatile after seeing the prices online auction sellers now ask for first editions (more than £2,000 for an original set of the *Complete Works*, £1,500 for a copy of *Talking to India*, in August 2024) New Pitcher remembered that in his book of talks to India Orwell included not only the British contributions but also one from the nazis for comparison purposes. Meanwhile, students returning to a college in Florida discovered the contents of one of its libraries in a dumpster. Should that have shocked New Pitcher as well?

New Pitcher

George Orwell Studies

Subscription information
Each volume contains two issues, published half-yearly.

Annual Subscription (including postage)

Personal Subscription

UK	£45
Europe	£50
RoW	£55

Institutional Subscription

UK	£100
Europe	£115
RoW	£120

Single Issue copies can be purchased (subject to availability)

Enquiries regarding subscriptions and orders should be sent to:

> Journals Fulfilment Department
> Abramis Academic
> ASK House
> Northgate Avenue
> Bury St Edmunds
> Suffolk, IP32 6BB
> UK

Tel: +44(0)1284 717884
Email: info@abramis.co.uk

www.ingramcontent.com/pod-product-compliance
Lightning Source LLC
Chambersburg PA
CBHW080739300426
44114CB00019B/2626